T0163273

Perplexities of Identification

Perplexities of Identification

Anthropological Studies in Cultural Differentiation and the Use of Resources

Edited by Henk Driessen and Ton Otto

AARHUS UNIVERSITY PRESS

AARHUS UNIVERSITY PRESS
Langelandsgade 177
DK-8200 Aarhus N
Fax (+ 45) 8942 5380

73 Lime Walk
Headington, Oxford OX3 7AD
Fax (+ 44) 1865 750 079

Box 511
Oakville, CT 06779
Fax (+ 1) 860 945 9468

ANSI/NISO
Z39.48-1992

Preface

From 16-17 January 1998 anthropologists from several countries gathered at Plasmolen in the hinterland of Nijmegen, The Netherlands, for a conference on 'Multi-Tiered Identifications and Cultural Resources'. The contributors dealt with widely different yet similar ways in which identifications are at stake in the lives of peoples around the world. The aim was to advance the anthropological discussion of the concept and phenomenon of identification in relation to the use of resources. The conference papers offered a broad spectrum of ethnographic cases, ranging from the persistence of corporate identity among the nobles of Poland and identity management of Catholic converts in Irian Jaya to the rhetorics of indigeneity in Ladakh and the role of violence in identity formation in Palestine. A forceful plea was made for ethnographic fieldwork as a major strategy for studying identification as experience in socio-cultural context in order to counteract the one-sided focus in identity studies on discourse and representation. Many questions were raised, some answered and others rephrased. Nine thoroughly revised papers were selected for inclusion in the present volume. This book does not represent a definitive position on what identifications are or can be in relation to resources but rather explores various intersections of identification and power in specific ethnographic cases.

During the conference and in the course of planning and editing this book we have enjoyed the encouragement, advice and help of many persons and institutions. We would like to thank André Droogers, Willy Jansen, Ton Robben, Eric Brandt, Els Jacobs, Jean Kommers, and Peter Versteeg for their stimulating contributions to the conference; the Aarhus University Research Foundation, the Nijmegen Institute for Comparative Studies in Development and Cultural Change, and the Danish Research Council for the Humanities for their generous sponsorship; the Dutch Research School for Resource Studies for Development, and the Department of Ethnography and Social Anthropology at the University of Aarhus, Denmark, for offering institutional backing; Toke Bjerregaard for his diligent text processing, and Mary Lund and Tønnes Bekker-Nielsen of Aarhus University Press for their invaluable assistance in the editorial work.

Aarhus, March 2000   *Henk Driessen and Ton Otto*

Table of Contents

Chapter 1: Protean Perplexities: An Introduction
Ton Otto & Henk Driessen   9

Chapter 2: Relatives and Rivals: The Narcissism of
Minor Differences
Anton Blok   27

Chapter 3: The Two Deaths of Basem Rishmawi: Identity
Constructions and Reconstructions in a Muslim-Christian
Palestinian Community
Glenn Bowman   56

Chapter 4: A Case of Identities: Multiple Personality Disorder
Poul Pedersen   95

Chapter 5: Ritual and Conflicting Identifications: The Case
of a Female *Bricoleur*
Louise Thoonen   125

Chapter 6: Indigenous Struggles and the Discreet Charm
of the Bourgeoisie
Jonathan Friedman   141

Chapter 7: Dissimulations: Representing Ladakhi Identity
Martijn van Beek   164

Chapter 8: 'We Are One But Still Different':
Communality and Diversity in Aboriginal Australia
Ad Borsboom & Janneke Hulsker   189

Chapter 9: Cultural Resources of Elite Identity:
The Vicissitudes of the Polish Gentry
Longina Jakubowska   218

Chapter 10: Thinking Together What Falls Apart:
Some Reflections on the Concept of Identity
Hans Siebers   232

About the Authors   257

Name Index   260

Illustrations

Mudmen from Papua New Guinea   *8*

Social Practice and its Constitutive Components   *18*

Basem Rishmawi   *58*

Continuum of Identity Strategies in the Nation State   *151*

Ladakhi Buddhist anti-Muslim Protest   *178*

Aboriginal Protest Meeting in Sydney   *204*

Madonna Dressed Up as a Q'eqchi' in the
Midst of Agricultural Offerings   *244*

Mudmen from Papua New Guinea as featured in a two-page car advertisement. (*The Independent on Sunday*, 23/4/95).

CHAPTER 1

Protean Perplexities: An Introduction

Ton Otto and Henk Driessen

The multiplicity of identification

Readers of the British *Independent on Sunday* of 23 April 1995 may have paused for a while to take in a rather peculiar advertisement occupying two full pages. It shows a four-wheel-drive vehicle standing in rugged terrain and surrounded by four mud-covered men wearing a kind of grass skirt and holding spears, bows and arrows in their hands. Most prominently their heads are covered by heavy clay masks displaying bizarre facial features. The accompanying text reads, 'Mudmen from Papua New Guinea get their first glimpse of a Frontera, thanks to its powerful engine and anti-clog brakes'. Apparently the advertisers attempted to create an image of a remote, exotic and wild place to which only a Frontera can take you. The ad may appeal to a potential buyer who identifies with the sense of adventure, strength and masculinity evoked by the picture. This is not the only time that images of the Mudmen have been used to appeal to consumer identities. Throughout Europe, Australia and the USA, Mudmen have appeared in advertisements for cars, orange soda, perfume, pop and house music. Where does this evocative image for Western identifications with the wild and exotic come from?[1]

Tourists travelling to Papua New Guinea will no doubt be informed about the Mudmen through their travel guides, tourist brochures or newspaper advertisements, as the Mudmen are considered as one of the major tourist attractions of the New Guinea Highlands. In order to encounter this well-advertised phenomenon they have to travel to Asaro valley in the Eastern Highlands Province. Here inhabitants of Komunive village will put on their Mudmen gear and perform for the tourists against a fixed rate per person. The tourists, lured by their guides, expect to experience something of a

---

1. The description of the Mudmen is based on Otto and Verloop (1996).

primordial, unspoiled and warlike lifestyle, of course within the safety of an organised tour. They have been told that the Mudmen masks originated in intertribal warfare and were used to scare and chase the enemies with their ghostlike appearance. Images of primitivism, aggression, and tribal belief in spirits abound and titillate the tourist to ponder over their Western selves: they are inclined to believe — or make believe? — that they witness a primordial state of humankind that has been superseded by modernity elsewhere in the world.

For the Asaro people the Mudmen have quite a different meaning. Based on local practices of disguise and decoration they were originally created for the purpose of performing at the first Eastern Highlands Agricultural Show in 1957 as part of a tribal finery competition. The performance was very successful and in response to growing public and tourist interest the Mudmen masks and dance were further developed in line with consumer expectations. For the Asaro people the Mudmen are not only a salient mark of their local identity, known within and without the country, but also a relevant source of income to which they extend an exclusive copyright. The prestige of the big man Ruipo Okohoro, who was the main 'inventor' and instigator, is largely attached to the success of the Mudmen. In addition, individual performers derive recognition for their masks, which have a distinctive personal touch.

Because of their public success, the Mudmen have become an essential part of regional and national festivities and celebrations. Therefore they have come to represent the identities of larger groups than their tribal owners. For example, in the context of the National Independence celebrations on 16 September, the Mudmen are seen as referring to the rich cultural heritage of Papua New Guinea as a whole. Therefore they may also be considered as a symbol of national identity.

This vignette of the Mudmen shows how the same symbol or image may serve to evoke very different identities. Unlike the Greek God Proteus who was able to change his appearance according to circumstance, the Mudmen change their significance according to the context in which they appear. Remaining the same in appearance they mean different things to different actors. For the Asaro people the Mudmen primarily signify a local identity and copyrighted product. The villagers gain status as well as wealth from their identification with their artistic creation. For Papua New Guinea politicians the Mudmen are a welcome symbol for projecting notions of national unity and identity. For tourists the confrontation with the exotic Mudmen performance provides an enhancement of their Western selves as well as social distinction. Finally, global advertisers use the potential connotations of wildness and originality carried by the Mudmen image to stimulate consumer identifications with the products they want to sell.

Thus the example of the Mudmen teaches us that, however perplexing they may appear, all instances of identification involve three constitutive elements. In the first place there have to be self-reflexive human actors who in their presentation to others and in their categorisation of others, appeal to identities to make sense of their relationships. Second, the act of identification needs cultural constructions or symbols to be effectuated, in this case the image of the Mudmen. Finally, identifications involve always more than actors making cultural distinctions. The allocation of identities connects these actors with a social environment characterised by differential access to economic, political and symbolic resources. Therefore identities become focal points for strategic interaction, being invoked or disavowed according to perceived interests by the actors. In the case of the Mudmen, different groups of actors deploy this image as a cultural resource to attain various symbolic, political and economic objectives: individual self-enhancement and social distinction (tourists, consumers, and Asaro producers), social and political group formation (Asaro people and Papua New Guinea politicians), and finally economic gain (Asaro performers, tourist agents and advertisers).

The Mudmen story also illustrates another aspect of the perplexities of identification in the late twentieth century. It shows how a locally created image becomes appropriated by variously placed actors and starts floating around in different circuits of communication: regional competition, national politics, international tourism and transnational advertising. Partly these circuits operate independently but there is also mutual interaction and impact. For example it is likely that tourists' tastes and preferences have had an effect on the shape of the Mudmen masks (Otto and Verloop 1996: 359). In addition, international success has led to increased local competition and dispute about cultural ownership. The Mudmen are thus an interesting example of how the global and the local are connected in modern times with extended means of communication and the increased movement of people and goods.

A consequence of the global flow of cultural constructs is that life at a local level often appears more fragmented than in the (idealised) past. From the perspective of the individual actor it may appear that there is a perplexity of choices and identities to negotiate. This leads to another reading of the meaning of the mythical character of Proteus. Moving from one identity to the other in the fragmented parts of our lives — work, home, leisure, politics, etc. — is there a common and persisting substrate to ourselves? Or is the ideal of a well-integrated and fixed identity a cultural

construction of modern society, dictated by the needs of large-scale bureaucratic institutions? Contemporary thinkers such as Bauman (1995) and
Giddens (1991) try to come to terms with this puzzling problem of our time
(see especially Ch. 10).

Clearly, the notion of identity has received particular urgency and relevance. For the past two decades, questions about concepts and practices of
identification have circulated widely through departments, journals, books,
conferences, and courses, not only in cultural anthropology but also in
related disciplines. Moreover, mass media, politics and social movements
have raised similar issues. Globalising markets and media, the worldwide
flow of people, cultural artefacts, ideas and values, the ethnic revival and the
re-drawing of political frontiers, have all contributed to a cultural chain-
reaction of identity questions around the world and at all levels of socio-
political integration and differentiation. As a result, identity has become a
key term of public language and thought.

How do identities emerge, persist and change, and which power resources
are tapped in the course of this process? Such questions are of overarching
concern in academic and popular debates today. They are at the core of the
present volume forcing us to rethink an old and fundamental puzzle of the
social sciences, i.e. how power and meaning interact in the ways people
define and represent themselves and others.

There is now a burgeoning literature on 'identity' to such an extent that
scholars writing about this wide-scoped theme run the risk of overlooking
relevant literature (see Driessen 1999). Moreover, identity has become a
shibboleth, often used casually as part of an academic litany that presents it
as relational, mixed, shifting, constructed, negotiated, re-invented, and
conjunctural. The repetition of such qualifications has itself sometimes
become an academic rite of intensification. Our first task then must be
tracing the major lines in the genealogy of the identity notion and link it to
'resources', the other focal concept of this book.

A genealogy of concepts and debates

European notions of individualism have deeply influenced academic thinking
about identity. They are rooted in the profound subject-object dualism of the
Western intellectual tradition which takes for granted the existence of an 'I'
as a distinct individual, that is a discrete, unique, and bounded entity
separated from the outside world by the skin (see Peacock 1986: 11-15).[2]

This cultural heritage entered the first empirical definitions of identity in
psychological research. The concept of 'identification' was coined by Sig-

mund Freud in the early 1920s as 'the earliest expression of an emotional tie with another person' (see Buchanan 1968: 57-58). Freud was well aware of the multiple nature of identification and the self-other dynamics in identity formation. Erik Erikson further developed the Freudian legacy in the concepts of 'personal identity' ('a subjective sense of continuous existence and a coherent memory') and 'psychosocial identity' ('at once subjective and objective, individual and social') (see Erikson 1968: 61).[3] Erikson, who followed a life cycle approach, stressed the complementarity of an inner (or ego) synthesis and role integration in the person's group and was particularly interested in the phenomenon of 'identity crisis', i.e., 'a crucial time or an inescapable turning point for the better or for worse' (ibid.: 63). Social psychological theory in general, and Erikson's approach in particular, reveal a strong preoccupation with unity, closure, and durability of identity, both in 'its individual and collective aspects' (ibid.: 61). Lack of integration and stability was considered to be a state of illness. Several elements of Freudian theory, including his ideas about socialisation and identification, were elaborated in American anthropology during the 1930s and 1940s as part of the culture-and-personality approach.

Apart from the more individualistic psychodynamic approach, as exemplified by the work of Freud and Erikson, there is also a more sociologically oriented line of research into identity formation. This line owes much to the work of George Herbert Mead, who emphasised a social conception of the self, arguing that individuals experience themselves from the perspective of the collectivities to which they belong (see Brown 1985: 771). Identification became a central issue in symbolic interactionism, especially in the work of Erving Goffman.[4] According to this approach, people continuously observe themselves and others. In doing so, they are involved in an ongoing process of making conjectures about identity.

Until the 1970s, the vast majority of publications on 'identity' remained within the confines of social psychology and micro-sociology. Research in

---

2. To be sure, the problem with brief excursions into the history of 'Western' ideas is that they totalise complex notions and neglect counterpoints, for instance Nietzsche's idea of the subject's multiplicity and notions of self in peasant society. There has always been a current in Western intellectual thought that emphasised the primacy of collectivism which was elaborated in Durkheimian sociology.

3. Note that there are separate entries for the 'political' and 'psychosocial' dimensions of identification in the *Encyclopedia of the Social Sciences* which mirrors the dualism in Western thought.

4. Goffman (1959), (1963) and (1979) deserve special mention here.

both fields was rife with unreflected cultural preconceptions, including personal-social and private-public dichotomies and ideological notions of unity and integration. Cross-cultural research remained scarce, as most anthropologists preferred a culture concept in which identification was a dimension of minor importance. One of the exceptions is Edward H. Spicer's attempt to develop a comparative study of 'identity systems'. He argued that the 'essential feature of any identity system is an individual's belief in his personal affiliation with certain symbols, or, more accurately, with what certain symbols stand for. (...) The display and manipulation of the symbols calls forth sentiments and stimulates the affirmation of beliefs on the part of the individuals who participate in the collective identity system' (Spicer 1971: 795-96). Spicer's identity concept foregrounded the relationship between human beings and their cultural products and brought individual motivation into the field of analysis. Unfortunately, his programme for identity research remained largely unnoticed.

The pathbreaking idea to examine identity as cultural construction and process goes back to the anthropological studies of ethnicity and gender which began to appear in the late 1960s and mushroomed in the 1970s and 1980s. Prolonged controversies followed the seminal collection of papers published in 1969 under the editorship of Fredrik Barth.[5] At one extreme of the debate the 'primordialist' position argues that ethnicity is an innate dimension of human identity, a given, permanent and essential condition. At the other extreme the 'instrumentalist' position maintains that ethnicity is an artifact, constituted by individuals or groups to bring together a group of people for some common purpose.[6] Three decades of ethnic studies have led several scholars to abandon ethnicity as an over-used concept in favour of the catch-all term of identity which in the 1990s became an analytically specific concept 'even if its exact meaning rests on its broadness' (Banks 1996: 143). Sharon Macdonald, for instance, writing about 'identity complexes in Western Europe', holds that identities (national, ethnic, or gender) do not exist apart, above or beneath their socio-cultural representation in spite of the tendency of most actors to fix its 'real nature', its 'essence' (1993: 4-12). In 1995 a new journal, *Social Identities. Journal for the Study of Race, Nation and Culture*, was launched, again a move away from the limited concept of ethnicity.

A second catalyst for a broader use of the term identity has been the cross-

---

5. In particular Barth's (1969) introduction is frequently referred to or cited.
6. See Banks (1996: 39 ff.) for a summary of the debate.

cultural study of gender. Conflicting representations of women by women and men reveal the inherently political nature of identity, i.e. the power and right to define. Cross-cultural research highlights the perplexity and multi-tieredness of identifications and complicates the simple notion of identity as made up of gender, ethnicity, religion, age, sexuality, and kinship. Moreover, when the interaction between the predominantly white, middle-class, and Western researcher and the women studied is considered, the use of the identity concept is also questioned at an epistemological level. This made the editors of a volume on femininity sigh that the identity concept 'seems to have become splintered to the extent that we sometimes despair of ever being able to fit the pieces into any sort of whole. There are so many ways of looking at ourselves, and others, it can be difficult to know where to begin' (see Brügmann, Heebing, Long and Michielsens 1993: 7-8).[7] We recognise the dilemma of relativism that is inherent in constructivism as soon as the constructivist approach is applied to ethnographic research itself.

The idea that people construct the social universe through their perceptions and interpretations of it and through the actions based on their interpretations, is of course an old one. It has been central to symbolic interactionism in sociology and in anthropology's attempt to understand other cultures from 'a native's point of view'. This constructivism, however, remained within the bounds of ethnographic realism and its claim on a more or less adequate representation of a cultural reality, as long as it was not applied to ethnographic fieldwork and writing itself.[8]

The debate about representation in anthropology in the 1980s resulted in a shift away from monographs depicting cross-section people performing roles and being perceived as more or less passive vehicles of cultural identities towards active, self-conscious individuals managing multi-layered and fluid identities. The widespread revival of the life story is part of this

---

7. Also see the special issue on feminist anthropology, the transfer of knowledge, and representation, *Tijdschrift voor Genderstudies* 2(1) (1999).

8. Interesting examples of recent identity studies which remain within the conventions of ethnographic realism are: Bringa (1995); Bax (1997); and Karakasidou (1997). These studies show that identification is a social process and that identities are crafted in specific contexts. Tragic events in the Balkans also reveal that constructed identities have 'real' and drastic consequences for the people involved. Moreover, the controversy over the publication of Karakasidou's study (the author received a death threat from Greek nationalists, whereupon Cambridge University Press decided not to publish her manuscript in order to protect the Press's material interests in Greece) points out that anthropologists and publishers may willy-nilly get involved in the cultural battle of identity formation.

paradigm shift (see Driessen 1998). The representation debate also led to the recognition that anthropologists are themselves involved in the creation of social and cultural worlds rather then simply documenting them (see Driessen 1993).

The contributors to this volume are aware of these epistemological issues and try to avoid the naive realism of earlier ethnography as well as the paralysing relativism to which constructivism may lead. They view identities as constructions which they are seeking to understand and explain, rather than judge as 'true' or 'false'.[9] Their thrust is two-sided, cutting both against the model of 'plastic multiple identity' *and* against the notion of identity as a reified essence. The first model is flawed by the ideology of voluntaristic pluralism celebrated by multiculturalists. They embrace the postmodern view of identity as merely a shifting assemblage of images and categories marketed through the media. The second model, which views identity as a fixed essence of primordial authenticity, is rooted in Herderian romanticism and conservative ethno-nationalism. Models of identity have largely oscillated between a series of opposite poles, of which primordialism versus instrumentalism, essentialism versus constructivism are obvious examples. Other dichotomies include, among many others, individual-collectivity, self-group, unity-fragmentation, consistency-ambiguity, integration-division, permanency-change, and structure-agency.

In this volume, we try to avoid locking the analysis up in such conceptual dichotomies. Instead, we opt for an open approach to identity with a preference for the term 'identification'. This term highlights the active and processual dimension of attributing meaning to experienced similarities and differences between 'us' and 'them'. This meaning-making, or constructive dimension goes back to the work of Max Weber and to earlier attempts at conceptualisation by anthropologists.[10] It is important here to stress that identification necessarily entails 'disidentification', i.e. perceiving and experiencing others as different and alien, a process that may lead to denial and projection of negative tendencies.[11]

---

9. For a discussion of realism and constructivism in ethnography see Hammersley (1992).

10. See for a good presentation of a number of useful basic ideas: Jenkins (1996), who emphasises that identity is never 'just there' but must always be established; it is about meaning and can only be understood as process. Also see Drummond (1980) who defines identity 'as a set of compelling ideas about one's own and others' distinctiveness that provide a basis for acting and for interpreting others' actions.' One should add 'ideas about similarities' to this definition.

Resources, identification and social practice

The authors in this volume (some more than others), explore identifications in relation to *resources*, which is the second focal term linking this volume to another founding father of modern social theory, Karl Marx, and his work on power and class formation. Although Marx never employed the term 'identity' (he used the related terms 'ideas' and 'ideology' instead), his reflections on the distinction between *Klasse-an-sich* and *Klasse-für-sich* are still relevant for the investigation of the internal-external dialectics in identification processes. Even more important is his analysis of the power dimension in this dialectic. Eric Wolf, one of the most influential anthropologists of the second half of the twentieth century, who carried on part of the Marxian legacy, phrased the interplay of meaning and power as follows: 'The ability to bestow meaning, to 'name' things, acts, ideas, is a source of power. Control of communication allows the managers of ideology to lay down the categories through which reality is to be perceived. Conversely, this entails the ability to deny the existence of alternative categories, to assign them to the realm of disorder and chaos, render them socially and symbolically invisible' (Wolf 1982: 388; also see his last work 1999). The ability to categorise and identify is indeed an important power resource, an integral aspect of all relations among people.

The term resource has been developed as a scientific concept within the discipline of economics. In the sense of 'natural resources' it refers to the sources of natural wealth of a country that can be made into economic gain. By extension the term also refers to other forms of economic supply, as in the case of human resources. The latter concept not only designates the labour of human beings but also their knowledge and skills, which enhance the quality and productivity of their labour. In the past three decades the term resource has become increasingly popular within anthropology and the social sciences, together with other terms derived from economics such as 'capital', 'rational actor' and 'maximisation'. Resource and capital are often used to refer to non-material realities but simultaneously keep a strong connotation of material-likeness. For example in the work of Pierre Bourdieu symbolic capital derives its relevance partly from the fact that it may be converted into economic or monetary capital.[12]

11. See de Swaan (1997). Whereas many anthropologists tend to avoid the psychological origins of the identity concept, sociologist de Swaan conserves the Freudian legacy of the (dis-)identification term.
12. See for example Bourdieu (1990: 112-21) and Bourdieu and Wacquant (1992: 118-19).

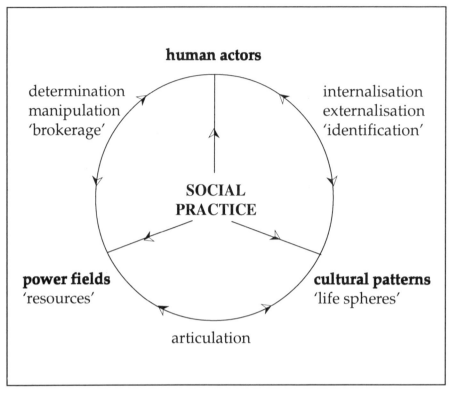

Fig. 1. Social Practice and its Constitutive Components

A common way to emphasise the materiality of social or cultural resources is to connect the term with the concept of power. We talk about power resources or sources of power as in the quotation from Wolf above. Of course this phrasing only shifts the question of definition to another term but its main purpose is to refer to an aspect of social reality which has an impact on social practice and which has a certain autonomy in relation to the human actor. In order to explain how we want to use the concept of resources in relation to actors and identifications we will refer to a diagram of social practice that has been developed by one of us in another context (Fig. 1; see Otto 1997).

The diagram serves to emphasise that social practice consists of three constitutive components or analytical dimensions: power resources (structured as 'fields' in a Bourdieuan sense), human actors and cultural patterns. The three components always work at the same time, they are an integral part of social practice. It is in our research practice that we may distinguish the different aspects as analytical perspectives on social life. The diagram is not intended as a theory of social practice but rather as a heuristic device to generate relevant questions about connections between the different dimensions.

If we talk about power resources we direct the analytical focus to the relative effect of human actions on other human actions. Norbert Elias (1971) makes a useful distinction between four kinds of power resources, namely means of subsistence, organisation, orientation and violence. Control over the available means of violence is an important source of power in any social configuration. The same applies to control over production and distribution of goods and the management of social organisations. We should add communication and biological reproduction as important power fields. Orientation is a special case as it refers directly to the use of culture as a resource — in the form of ideology, religion or worldview. To the extent that culture can be manipulated and controlled, it is indeed, as Wolf asserts, a formidable source of social power. Identities are cultural constructs which may be used as a resource. The following chapters will show how identities as crucial means of cultural orientation are linked with economic gain, group formation and the use of violence.

Just as we have argued in relation to the concept of identity, the term resource needs to be linked with the concept of culture in order to make it suitable for intercultural, comparative research. The different kinds of power resources that have been identified above reflect the position of the researcher, a so-called 'etic' perspective. If we approach social practice from the analytical perspective of 'cultural patterns' (see Fig. 1), we want to understand how these power resources are represented in the cultural worlds we study. It is well-known that Western scientific categories, such as economic production, political organisation and ideology, only partly correspond with indigenous, 'emic' categories. For example political organisation is often expressed in terms of kinship in tribally organised societies. Therefore we have to investigate the particular 'articulation' of power resources and cultural spheres in the cases under study. This is expressed by the circle-segment connecting these terms in the diagram. We use cultural spheres, that is the plural, intentionally because we believe that the notion of fully integrated cultural worlds belongs in the anthropological wastebasket. As Louise Thoonen (Ch. 5) shows, remote societies in Irian Jaya are also characterised by cultural diversity (cf. Otto and Borsboom 1997). Fragmentation is not only a feature of modernity, although the scale and intensity of fragmentation appear to have multiplied in the global era.

The third component of social practice as represented in Figure 1 is the human actor. It is a commonsense assumption that there can be no social practice without interacting human individuals, but we again have to take account of the cultural dimension. What is considered as a human actor may vary substantially in different cultural worlds.[13] For example the spirits of the recently deceased are seen as powerful human agents in many New Guinean societies. Ethnographers use different terms to refer to different aspects of the human actor, but there is no consensus in this area (cf. Cohen 1994: 2). We find Harris' (1989) conceptual distinctions useful in this context. She defines the 'individual' as a single member of human kind, the 'self' as referring to the experience of being an individual, and the human 'person' as the public conception of a human being as an agent, 'the author of action purposively directed toward a goal' (ibid.: 602).

It will be clear that constructs of the 'person' will vary culturally and that the experience of 'self' will also be largely informed by cultural context and available cultural models. Nevertheless it is important to stress that there is an aspect of creativity and reflexivity to human agency that appears irreducible and universally present (cf. Cohen 1994, Sökefeld 1999, Otto 1997). Human actors cannot be reduced to their cultural environment, on which they depend in order to interact meaningfully with others. There is space for individual variation and the idiosyncrasies of individual life histories. Persons and selves are constituted in a dialectical process between internalisation and externalisation in which human actors absorb their cultural environment while simultaneously impacting thereupon. In the process of identification actors draw on the available cultural repertoires to define their relationships with relevant others. Therefore identification can be said to be at the heart of the cultural, communicative dimension of social practice. To the extent that human actors consciously interpret and manipulate the cultural worlds they inhabit with the intent to tap power resources, they can be said to act as cultural brokers. Examples of such brokerage are discussed in a number of the following chapters (especially Chs. 3, 5, 6, 9).

The chapters

Identification can sometimes be a matter of life and death. Chapters 2 and 3 explicitly discuss the relationship between violence and identity. Anton Blok shows with a range of ethnographic examples that violence is often

---

13. See for example Geertz's (1984) well-known comparison of personhood in Java, Bali and Morocco.

used to maintain cultural difference between groups that are very much alike. Especially if a group feels that its specific identity is under threat because another group has become too similar, this may create an explosive situation leading to the use of extreme violence as recent happenings in Rwanda and the former Yugoslavia illustrate. Blok takes theoretical inspiration from Freud's notion of the 'narcissism of minor differences' and from Bourdieu's thesis that social identity lies in difference and that difference is asserted against what is closest. Blok argues strongly that the disappearance of cultural difference poses a threat to group identity and that violence should be considered as an important resource for re-establishing cultural distinction. This is an important contribution to the theme of identification and resource use, even though the reversed thesis, i.e., that greater cultural difference leads to greater stability and less violent conflict, is argued less convincingly.

Glenn Bowman offers a fascinating case study of the dynamics of identification in social practice. He shows how a changing context of violence (and the threat of violence) induced actors to variously engage different cultural repertoires in dealing with the implications of a brutal murder. Different collective identities were evoked as well as disavowed in alternative narrations of the events. The case demonstrates how external circumstances — geopolitical processes in Israel, the Middle East, and the 'New World Order' — interact with internal Palestinian processes of de-differentiation and re-differentiation. In this complex power struggle, Israeli violence was constitutive of an encompassing, communal, and almost corporate Palestinian identity. Violence bred martyrs, fuelled a common identity of Palestinians as a persecuted people, and de-emphasised internal differences. As a result of the recent peace settlement, sectarian identifications began to re-appear in the emergent Palestinian nation while the larger political context was relegated to the background or even completely elided.

Chapters 4 and 5 deal with identification at the level of the individual actor. Poul Pedersen presents the case of Multiple Personality Disorder, which he treats as a cultural construct or fiction that is very real at the same time. The possibility of harbouring multiple personalities in one body is a relatively recent historical phenomenon. The history of MPD shows that once a new kind of identity becomes available as a cultural construct, it may rapidly spread due to interested actions of various types of actors: psychiatrists, potential patients, journalists and other authors. Pedersen analyses the role of the media in the development of MPD as well as its gendered and sexual background: 90% of the patients are women and the common explanation for the disease is sexual abuse in early childhood. Interestingly,

MPD also forces us to rethink common Western notions about individual identity as integrated and simple. Empowered by the possibilities of the Internet a sub-culture is emerging which defends MPD as a 'normal' and rich form of being rather than a disorder that needs treatment. The case of MPD thus illustrates how a new identity may be used by different actors as a resource to attain various kinds of objectives: self-enhancement, social recognition and emancipation (so-called 'multiples'), status, career development and economic gain (psychiatrists, lawyers, journalists).

In Chapter 5, Louise Thoonen presents the life history of an influential female leader in an Irian Jaya society. During her eventful life Maria Baru became exposed to the different cultural worlds of ancestral tradition and Catholicism. While these worlds existed next to and separate from each other for a long time, certain events induced Maria Baru to work on their integration. The case beautifully illustrates how two distinct cultural spheres with different ways of creating identities may be accommodated in the life of one influential person who then acts as a cultural broker for a larger group of followers. Elements derived from two ritual complexes and belief systems were successfully forged in the creation of a new identity. Thoonen discusses tensions between self and personhood and shows that rituals are important means for decentering existing identities and establishing new ones.

Chapters 6, 7, and 8 cluster around the issue of constituting indigeneity as a cultural resource in the struggle for land and other state resources. Jonathan Friedman argues that the failure of modernism and the dislocations caused by globalisation create new identities of rootedness. The construction of indigeneity is not only a struggle for recognition of difference, but also about the way difference must be construed and integrated into daily life. Global changes thus create the cultural basis for new identities as well as new arenas for the struggle about the redistribution of resources connected with global flows of capital. A new supra-national elite is emerging, cosmopolitan in outlook but at the same time rooted in local identities. Described as tribal capitalists, members of this new class exploit identities of indigeneity to tap resources provided by national and international organisations.

Martijn van Beek adopts a sophisticated constructivist stance dealing with representations of identity in Ladakh. Locating identification in between the real and the really made up, he considers identities as necessary fictions in the context of contestation over access to and allocation of resources. Whereas identification is ambiguous and fluid in social practice, bureaucratic procedures require the temporary elision of the problematic and contested nature of 'fixed' identities. People know very well that they disagree about what a certain identity refers to but the politics of resource competition make it necessary to 'forget' such disagreements, at least temporarily. Therefore, van Beek argues, identification always implies the dissimulation of differences. Anthropologists have to be careful to avoid the identity 'fetishism' and reification that is inherent in the practices of state bureaucracies and development organisations and to keep an open eye for the indeterminacies of identification in social practice.

In Chapter 8, Borsboom and Hulsker present processes of identification in two different types of Australian Aboriginal communities: a rural one in Arnhem Land and an urban one in Sydney. The Arnhem Land Aborigines draw on their rich cosmological system of the Dreaming to express both unity and diversity on the various occasions of social interaction. The same cultural system thus provides the means for an overarching identification and the possibility for asserting sectarian identities in connection with claims to local resources. Urban Aborigines refer to a history of colonisation and oppression to construct both unifying and differential identities. According to political context and the kind of resources that are at stake they may articulate their identity as indigenes, as regional groups or as Aboriginal nations (tribes). United under the common identity of Aboriginality, both urban and rural Aborigines mutually invoke their respective historically and cosmologically constructed identities to strengthen their position within the context of the Australian state.

In Chapter 9, Longina Jakubowska offers another fascinating case of how a sustained group identity can function as an important cultural resource in a changing political context. Like the nobility in other European countries, the Polish gentry's power base was their ownership of the land and the means of production in a rural society. They differed, however, in their relative large size (ten percent of the total population) and in their egalitarian ethos among themselves as a group. In their self-understanding they constituted a special 'race' as well as the Polish nation. Jakubowska follows their history through several shifts of political regime (pre-communism, Stalinism, post-Stalinist state socialism and post-communism) during which the gentry became stripped of their economic assets as well as their legal privileges. Nevertheless the group has survived and even flourished by exploiting various aspects of their common cultural heritage and identity: their (international) networks, their education and fine manners, their language skills and history, and their belief in their own inherited superiority. The case illustrates that a strong sense of group identity may help a group to convert elements of their shared cultural capital into economic resources and thus secure their survival as a group.

The concluding chapter by Hans Siebers takes up the important discussion between Anthony Giddens and Zygmunt Bauman about problems of identity construction in the late modern era. Whereas Bauman emphasises cultural fragmentation and a performative attitude towards identity, Giddens wants to uphold the viability of modern identities through the construction of self-narratives. Siebers argues that both authors tend to conflate reflexivity with rationality. Drawing on insights from cognitive anthropology and psychology he makes a strong case for another mode of reflexivity which he calls associative. He illustrates this concept with an etnographic example from the Q'eqchi' Indians of Guatemala among whom the associative mode of reflexivity appears to dominate. Siebers argues that associative reflexivity allows the Indians to articulate continuity and change and to interrelate the different cultural repertoires and fragments of their lives in a selective and meaningful way. In western societies the dominance of rational reflexivity, which is connected with the rise of modern bureaucratic organisations, makes such associative connections problematic. To consider the multiplicity of identities as a reflexive and philosophical problem is, therefore, a product and a feature of modernity.

Siebers suggests that we need to keep an open eye for the working of associative reflexivity in the present age and that, as researchers, we have to break down the conventional division between the study of individual experience and collective representation. His chapter makes a strong argument for the integrated study of the three components of social practice: actors, cultural representations and power resources. Through identifications actors invoke cultural repertoires and tap resources at the same time. Through self-narration, performance and associative reflexivity they create a Protean perplexity of identifications, which the authors of this volume try to unravel. In so doing they demonstrate that identities form the very stuff of which our cultural worlds are made.

Bibliography

Banks, M. 1996. *Ethnicity: Anthropological Constructions*. London: Routledge.

Barth, F. (ed.), 1969. *Ethnic Groups and Boundaries: The Social Organisation of Culture Difference*. London: George Allen and Unwin.

Bauman, Z. 1995. *Life in Fragments: Essays in Postmodern Morality*. Oxford: Blackwell.

Bax, M. 1997. 'Mass Graves, Stagnating Identification, and Violence'. In: *Anthropological Quarterly* 70(1), 11-19.

Bourdieu, P. 1990. *The Logic of Practice*. Stanford: Stanford University Press.

Bourdieu, P. and L. Wacquant 1992. *An Invitation to Reflexive Sociology*. Oxford: Polity Press.

Bringa, T. 1995. *Being Muslim the Bosnian Way. Identity and Community in a Central Bosnian Village*. Princeton, N.J.: Princeton University Press.

Brown, R. 1985. 'Social Identity'. In: A. Kuper and J. Kuper (eds.), *The Social Science Encyclopedia*. London: Routledge & Kegan Paul, 771.

Brügmann, M., S. Heebing, D. Long and M. Michielsens (eds.), 1993. *Who's Afraid of Femininity? Questions of Identity*. Amsterdam and Atlanta: Rodopi.

Buchanan, W. 1968. 'Identification, Political'. In: D.L. Sills (ed.), *International Encyclopedia of the Social Sciences* 7. New York: The Macmillan Company & Free Press, 57-60.

Cohen, A. 1994. *Self Consciousness: An Alternative Anthropology of Identity*. London and New York: Routledge.

Driessen, H. (ed.), 1993. *The Politics of Ethnographic Reading and Writing. Confrontations of Western and Indigenous Views*. Saarbrücken and Fort Lauderdale: Verlag Breitenbach Publishers.

Driessen, H. 1998. 'Introduction: Trends, Genres and Cases in Self-Revelation'. In: *Focaal. Tijdschrift voor Antropologie* 32, 7-14.

Driessen, H. 1999. 'Comment on Martin Sökefeld "Debating Self, Identity, and Culture in Anthropology"'. In: *Current Anthropology* 40(4), 431-32.

Drummond, L. 1980. 'The Cultural Continuum: A Theory of Intersystems'. In: *Man* 15(5), 352-74.

Elias, N. 1971. *Was ist Soziologie?*. München: Juventa Verlag.

Erikson, E.H. 1968. 'Identity, Psychosocial'. In: Sills (ed.), *International Encyclopedia of the Social Sciences* 7. New York: Macmillan & Free Press, 61-65.

Geertz, C. 1984. '"From the Native's Point of View": On the Nature of Anthropological Understanding'. In: R. Shweder and R. Levine (eds.), *Culture Theory: Essays on Mind, Self, and Emotion*, Cambridge: Cambridge University Press, 123-36.

Giddens, A. 1991. *Modernity and Self-identity: Self and Society in the Late Modern Age*. Cambridge/Oxford: Polity Press.

Goffman, E. 1959. *The Presentation of Self in Everyday Life*. Garden City, N.Y.: Doubleday.

Goffman, E. 1963. *Stigma: Notes on the Management of Spoiled Identity*. Englewood Cliffs, N.J.: Prentice Hall.

Goffman, E. 1979. *Gender Advertisements*. London: Macmillan.

Hammersley, M. 1992. *What's Wrong With Ethnography? Methodological Explorations*. London and New York: Routledge.

Harris, G.G. 1989. 'Concepts of Individual, Self, and Person in Description and Analysis'. In: *American Anthropologist* 91, 599-612.

Jenkins, R. 1996. *Social Identity*. London: Routledge.

Karakasidou, A.N. 1997. *Fields of Wheat, Hills of Blood. Passages to Nationhood in Greek Macedonia 1870-1990*. Chicago: The University of Chicago Press.

Macdonald, S. 1993. 'Identity Complexes in Western Europe: Social Anthropological Perspectives'. In: S. Macdonald (ed.), *Inside European Identities. Ethnography in Western Europe*. Oxford: Berg, 1-27.

Otto, T. and R. Verloop 1996. 'The Asaro Mudemen: Local Property, Public Culture'. In: *The Contemporary Pacific* 8(2), 349-86.

Otto, T. 1997. 'Social Practice and the Ethnographic Circle: Rethinking the "Ethnographer's Magic" in a Late Modern World'. In: E. Roesdahl, H. Thrane and T. Otto, *Tre Tiltædelsesforlæsninger på Moesgaard*. Aarhus: Faculty of Arts, University of Aarhus, 53-96.

Otto, T. and A. Borsboom 1997. 'Epilogue: Cultural Dynamics of Religious Change'. In: T. Otto and A. Borsboom (eds.), *Cultural Dynamics of Religious Change in Oceania*. Leiden: KITLV Press, 103-12.

Peacock, J. 1986. *The Anthropological Lens. Harsh Light, Soft Focus*. Cambridge: Cambridge University Press.

Sökefeld, M. 1999. 'Debating Self, Identity and Culture in Anthropology'. In: *Current Anthropology* 40(4), 417-31.

Spicer, E.H. 1971. 'Persistent Cultural Systems'. In: *Science*, 795-800.

de Swaan, A. 1997. 'Widening Circles of Disidentification. On the Psycho- and Sociogenesis of the Hatred of Distant Strangers: Reflections on Rwanda'. In: *Theory, Culture & Society* 14(2), 105-22.

Wolf, E.R. 1982. *Europe and the People Without History*. Berkeley: University of California Press.

Wolf, E.R. 1999. *Envisioning Power. Ideologies of Dominance and Crisis*. Berkeley: University of California Press.

CHAPTER 2

Relatives and Rivals:
The Narcissism of Minor Differences[1]

Anton Blok

It is not the differences but the loss of them that gives rise to violence and chaos (Girard 1979: 51).

Nella stessa faccia, l'occhio destro odiava il sinistro
(In the same face, the right eye hated the left, *Sicilian saying*).

Introduction

We often attribute conflict between individuals or groups to growing contrasts between them. The larger the (economic, social, cultural) differences, the greater the chance of violent confrontations. But an outline of a general theory of power and violence cannot ignore the fact that the fiercest struggles often take place between individuals, groups, and communities that differ very little — or between which the differences have greatly diminished. Civil wars are usually described as more merciless than other wars and the fiercest struggle is often between siblings. Recall the archetypes Cain and Abel, the biblical brothers one of whom was a shepherd and kept flocks, while the other tilled the soil. Hence the metaphorical use of the term 'fratricide' to describe a life and death struggle between groups or communities that are very similar, that are neighbours and maintain close ties.

1. An earlier version appeared in the *European Journal of Social Theory* (1998, 1: 33-56). For suggestions and comments on earlier drafts I am most grateful to Rod Aya, Peter Burke, Carlo Ginzburg, Johan Heilbron, and Longina Jakubowska. I also wish to acknowledge the inspiration of Johan Goudsblom with whom I discussed the narcissism of minor differences on various occasions over the past few years and whose remarks encouraged me to write this essay. I owe a special debt to Rod Aya for his sensitive editing.

Subtle distinctions rather than great differences between individuals and groups occasion many conflicts and ruthless struggles. Why should it be minor differences that move people to exclude others, to discriminate against them, to stigmatise them and subject them to extreme forms of violence? And to what extent have scholars recognised the role of subtle distinctions in explosive figurations?

Freud's contribution

One may begin with Freud (not with Marx, for he believed that the class struggle could only develop when the differences between entrepreneurs and workers, between capital and labour had increased: when all the means of production had come into the hands of the entrepreneurs). We start with Freud because he was probably the first to recognise the importance of small differences for understanding conflicts.[2] In at least four places in his work he discusses 'the narcissism of minor differences'. What does he mean by this phrase and what does he do with it?

The first time Freud discusses the narcissism of minor differences is in his essay 'The Taboo of Virginity' (1991a [1917]). He refers to a study by Crawley, who argues that people are separated from one another by a 'taboo of personal isolation', and that it is precisely the minor differences between people who are otherwise alike that form the basis of feelings of strangeness and hostility between them (1991a: 272). Freud writes:

It would be tempting to pursue this idea and to derive from this 'narcissism of minor differences' the hostility which in every human relation we see fighting successfully against feelings of fellowship and overpowering the commandment that all men should love one another (1991a: 272).

Some years later, Freud brings the subject up again. In 'Group Psychology and the Analysis of the Ego' (1991b [1921]) he first refers to Schopenhauer's parable of the freezing porcupines who crowded together to profit from one another's warmth, but soon felt each other's quills and had to separate again. Freud then extends the comparison to the rivalry between neigbouring towns — known as *campanilismo* (from *campanile*, churchbell): local or regional

---

2. Hobbes and Tocqueville have pointed at the close relationship between equality, similarity, and conflict. For a more recent exposé, see Dumont (1980: 13-20, 262-66), who draws heavily on Tocqueville.

patriotism, a form of solidarity that develops in reaction against and contempt for a village or town in the neighbourhood:

Of two neighbouring towns each is the other's most jealous rival; every little canton
looks down upon the others with contempt. Closely related races keep one another
at arm's length; the South German cannot endure the North German, the
Englishman casts every kind of aspersion upon the Scot, the Spaniard despises the
Portuguese (1991b: 130-31).

But Freud fails to recognise the importance of his discovery and even
manages to reduce the heuristic value of the narcissism of minor differences
by declaring immediately afterwards that we should no longer be surprised
that 'greater differences should lead to an almost insuperable repugnance,
such as the Gallic people feel for the German, the Aryan for the Semite, and
the white races for the coloured' (1991b: 130-31). Did Freud misunderstand
the quintessence of his own discovery?

The third time Freud focuses attention on the narcissism of minor
differences is in his famous essay 'Civilization and Its Discontents' (1991c
[1930]). It adds little to what he already said about the subject and cites the
same examples. Freud introduces the passage with an understatement. It is
not easy for people to give up the satisfaction of their inclination to
aggression: 'Sie fühlen sich nicht wohl dabei'. Referring to the earlier texts
in which he discusses the narcissism of minor differences, Freud continues
as follows:

I once discussed the phenomenon that it is precisely communities with adjoining
territories, and related to each other in other ways as well, who are engaged in
constant feuds and in ridiculing each other — like the Spaniards and Portuguese,
for instance, the North Germans and South Germans, the English and Scots, and
so on. I gave this phenomenon the name of 'the narcissism of minor differences',
a name which does not do much to explain it. We can now see that it is a
convenient and relatively harmless satisfaction of the inclination to aggression, by
means of which cohesion between the members of the community is made easier
(1991c: 304-5).

Freud thus did not see much in his find. Little remained of the temptation
he initially felt to pursue the idea. The narcissism of minor differences was
for him a name that did not explain very much. The idea referred to a
harmless satisfaction of aggressive inclinations that could promote the
solidarity of the members of a community.

At the end of his life, in his last essay, 'Moses and Monotheism' (1990

[1939]), in which he tries to explain antisemitism, Freud comes back to the issue. He argues that the hatred of the Jews is primarily related to the circumstance that they live for the most part as minorities among other peoples:

For the communal feeling of groups requires, in order to complete it, hostility towards some extraneous minority, and the numerical weakness of this excluded minority encourages its suppression.

There are, however, two other characteristics of the Jews which are quite unforgivable. First is the fact that in some respects they are different from their 'host' nations. They are not fundamentally different, for they are not Asiatics of a foreign race, as their enemies maintain, but composed for the most part of remnants of the Mediterranean people and heirs of the Mediterranean civilisation. But they are none the less different, often in an indefinable way different, especially from the Nordic peoples, and the intolerance of groups is often, strangely enough, exhibited more strongly against small differences than against fundamental ones (1990: 335).

The narcissism of minor differences continued to intrigue Freud, but his reservations and the expression 'strangely enough' suggest that he did not know what to do with it. This may be the reason why he hardly pursued the matter further. Yet considering the numerous conflicts that apparently go back to minimal differences between the warring parties that want to destroy one another, it should be clear that the notion of the narcissism of minor differences deserves further attention and elaboration. What will be explored in particular is how culture informs and shapes violent confrontations.

Coming too close

Freud's discovery links up with what other scholars have said about the importance of minor differences. First, Simmel's essay on discretion in *Soziologie* (1983 [1908]) mentions the 'ideal sphere' that lies around every human being:

Although differing in size in various directions and differing according to the person with whom one entertains relations, this sphere cannot be penetrated, unless the personality value of the individual is thereby destroyed. A sphere of this sort is placed around man by his 'honour'. Language very poignantly designates an insult to one's honour as 'coming too close': the radius of this sphere marks, as it were, the distance whose trespassing by another person insults one's honour (Simmel 1983: 265; 1950: 321).

The expression 'coming too close' has both a literal and a figurative meaning here: approach too close and thereby also threaten, offend, dishonour.[3] It is also mentioned by Crawley (Freud's source) and we will see how important propinquity is for understanding the narcissism of minor differences. Hence also Freud's reference to Schopenhauer's allegory of the freezing porcupines.

In their essay on primitive forms of classification (1963 [1903]), Durkheim and Mauss argue that social differentiation constitutes the model for the classification of nature: animals, plants, celestial bodies, the seasons — all parts of the natural world are differentiated in terms of their relationship to the main social groups:

It is because human groups fit into another — the sub-clan into the clan, the clan into the moiety, the moiety into the tribe — that groups of things are ordered in the same way.... And if the totality of things is conceived as a single system, this is because society itself is seen in the same way (1963: 83).

Lévi-Strauss further develops this idea in his studies of totemic classifications and shows how tribal groups such as clans and moieties, which share many features and are closely interconnected (in particular through intermarriage), articulate their differences by associating themselves with differences they find in the natural world:

the differences between animals which man can extract from nature and transfer to culture are adopted as emblems by groups of men in order to do away with their own resemblances. [Men] have to assume the symbolic characteristics by which they distinguish different animals (and which furnish them with a natural model of differentiation) to create differences among themselves (1966: 107-8; cf. 1969: 155-64; 1966: 115-17).

The importance of minor differences between groups has also been recognised by other anthropologists. Leach, for example, notes that 'The more similar the general pattern of two communities, the more critical will be the significance which is attached to minor points of reversal' (1976: 64). In an ethnographic analysis of a Cambridge college we find the following observation (of a famous historian who for obvious reasons prefers to use a pseudonym):

It may be doubted whether any member of a Cambridge college would admit that

---

3. About personal territoria and territorial violations, see Goffman (1971: 28-61).

his or her institution was typical — *campanilismo* is almost as strong in these bodies as it was in medieval Italian city-states, and one is encouraged, indeed expected, to see one's own institution as unique, a tendency which is strengthened by differences in local customs and titles. The head of most Cambridge colleges is called 'The Master', but King's has a Provost, Queens' a President, Newnham a Principal. There is a kind of narcissism in each college as in the University... (Dell 1987: 74).

In this essay, however, we will be mainly concerned with the role of minor differences in less peaceful confrontations.

The ethnographic literature on warfare in tribal societies suggests that violent confrontations usually take place in close circles, that is, within the limits of the tribe, between neighbours, friends or relatives — in short, between people who share many social and cultural features. As the Mae Enga in the western highlands of Papua New Guinea phrase it: 'We marry the people we fight'. Their ethnographer emphasises that war among these mountain people is most frequent between neighbours and fraternal clans (Meggitt 1977: 28-29, 42). Exchange and war can be understood as two sides of the same coin. A recent synopsis of tribal warfare confirms this pattern and mentions propinquity as a major cause: people interact most intensely with their nearest neigbours, 'whether those interactions are commercial, nuptial, or hostile' (Keeley 1996: 122-23). Even in more complex societies, the feud is part of a network of reciprocity and offers groups the occasion to distinguish themselves within a common framework (Black-Michaud 1975: 208). The writer Milovan Djilas, a native of Montenegro, makes a similar point in *Land without Justice* (1958) when he reflects on the blood feuds that affected his own family:

Though the life of my family is not completely typical of my homeland, Montenegro, it is typical in one respect: the men of several generations have died at the hands of Montenegrins, men of the same faith and name. My father's grandfather, my own two grandfathers, my father, and my uncle were killed, as though a dread curse lay upon them. My father and his brother and my brothers were killed even though all of them yearned to die peacefully in their beds beside their wives. Generation after generation, and the bloody chain was not broken. The inherited fear and hatred of feuding clans was mightier than fear and hatred of the enemy the Turks (1958: 8).[4]

---

4. Quoted in Boehm (1984: 60-61).

On the character of intertribal wars, Evans-Pritchard's observations on the Nuer in the southern Sudan are highly relevant. The Nuer feel closer to the Dinka than to other groups of strangers. At the same time, the Nuer show greater hostility toward the Dinka than toward other strangers. War between these two peoples amounts to more than just conflicts of interest. We are primarily concerned with a structural relationship because their animosity is deeply influenced by the extent of cultural differentiation between the Nuer and their neighbours:

The nearer people are to the Nuer in mode of livelihood, language, and customs, the more intimately the Nuer regard them, the more easily they enter into relations of hostility with them, and the more easily they fuse with them... The cultural cleavage is least between Nuer and Dinka; it widens between Nuer and Shilluk-speaking peoples.... Nuer make war against a people who have a culture like their own rather than among themselves or against peoples with cultures very different from their own (1940: 130-31).

Similar structural relations, which provide a common framework of co-operation and distinction marked by the use of violence, are also evident in modern societies. Violent encounters between supporters of football clubs in Western Europe provide an example. Rather than clashes of interest, we again see the articulation of minor differences between groups who share many features (age, gender, class, education, work, language, apparel, cultural interests, and 'identity'). Moreover, these groups are part of other dualistic formations, including clubs, bars, neighbourhoods, and cities. Fighting and aggressive behaviour have become part of 'going to the match'. As happened in dueling among the *jeunesse dorée* in Western Europe until the late nineteenth century, arrangements are made for a time and place of violent encounters *extra muros*, outside of the built-up area:

On occasions, rival groups communicate an intention to meet at a particular location before or after the match. Such locations are chosen because the hooligan fans believe that this will enable them to avoid the attention of the police and give them a chance to establish, without outside interference or fear of arrest, which is the 'superior' crew (Dunning et al. 1986: 168-71).

Next we come to Bourdieu, who illuminates two new aspects of minor differences between groups in *Distinction* (1984 [1979]) — without, however, referring to Freud. In his book (translated into German with the apt title *Die feinen Unterschiede*), Bourdieu emphasises the importance of minor differences for the formation and maintenance of identity and the threat to identity that comes from what is closest. Hence the importance of minor differences — the *narcissism* of minor differences — precisely when we are dealing with groups that are very close and similar. Writes Bourdieu: 'Social identity lies in difference, and difference is asserted against what is closest, which represents the greatest threat' (1984: 479).

Bourdieu's book on cultural distinctions in twentieth-century France has obviously been influenced by the work of Elias on court society and the civilising process. From these books we learn how in the course of the civilising process more refined and differentiated codes of behaviour (originally designed at court to domesticate the nobility) enabled the same French aristocracy in the course of the seventeenth and eighteenth centuries to distinguish itself from the upwardly mobile bourgeoisie. In this context, too, fine distinctions were at issue, important details, 'feinen Unterschiede', 'minor differences', which played a crucial role in the establishment and maintenance of identity, social distance, and power. As Elias summarises his view of civilising processes and emphasises that certain cultural differences do not merely reflect power differences but also help to shape and maintain them:

Relatively stricter morals are only one form of socially induced self-restraints among many others. Better manners are another. They all enhance the chances of a superior group to assert and to maintain their power and superiority. In an appropriate configuration civilising differentials can be an important factor in the making and perpetuation of power differentials, although in extreme cases it may weaken 'old' powerful groups to be more civilised and may contribute to their downfall (1965: 152-53).

Most significant for our purposes is Girard's important study *La Violence et le sacré* (1972). On the basis of literary, historical, and ethnographic material Girard argues that the loss of differences between groups is the main source of extreme violence:

A single principle is at work in primitive religion and classical tragedy alike, a principle implicit but fundamental. Order, peace, and fecundity depend on cultural distinctions; it is not these distinctions but the loss of them that gives birth to fierce rivalries and set members of the same family or social group at one another's throats. Modern society aspires to equality among men and tends instinctively to regard all differences, even those unrelated to the economic or social status of men, as obstacles in the path of human happiness (Girard 1979: 49).

To illustrate his theory about 'differences', Girard discusses the role of twins and other sets of brothers. In some tribal societies, twins inspire a particular fear. It is not uncommon that one or both of them are killed. Where differences are lacking, violence threatens. Girard points out the aspect of ritual pollution: when faced with biological twins, a common reaction of tribal communities is to avoid contagion. Therefore, the infants are 'exposed', that is, abandoned (1979: 56-58).

Girard ties up the theme of twins with that of brothers who are enemies. He refers to Kluckhohn (1960: 52), who argues that the most common conflict in myths is the struggle between brothers — a struggle that usually ends in fratricide. They are not always twins, they can be ordinary brothers who are very much alike and have been born shortly after one another. Even when the brothers are not twins, the difference between them is much less than between all other grades of kin relations. In many cases they occupy the same position with respect to other kinsmen, both close and distant relatives. Brothers have more rights, obligations, and functions in common than is the case with other members of the family. In a way, twins are 'reinforced' brothers from whom the last objective difference, that of age, has been taken away: it is often impossible to distinguish them. We are inclined, Girard continues, to consider the fraternal bond as a model of an affective relationship ('brotherly' as synonym for affectionate and loyal). But the mythological, historical, and literary examples that come to mind tell a different story: Cain and Abel, Jacob and Esau, Romulus and Remus. But it is not only in myths, writes Girard, that brothers are 'simultaneously drawn together and driven apart by something they both ardently desire and which they will not or cannot share — a throne, a woman or, in more general terms, a paternal heritage' (1979: 61-64).[5] This point can be taken one step

5. The theme of fratricide is not only mythical. The history of the early nineteenth-century Zulu Kingdom, for example, includes several cases of fratricide among despots. The terrorist regime of Shaka came to an end in 1828 through a conspiracy between his brothers Dingane and Mhlangana. Later, Dingane killed Mhlangana and succeeded Shaka as King of the Zulus. Dingane died in 1840 after his brother Mpande turned against him in a revolt (Walter 1969: 174-75, 209-11). According to a recent survey, about 10 percent of homicides in agrarian societies involve fratricide (Daley and Wilson 1988: 25, quoted in Sulloway 1996: 437). But brothers do not always fight and kill each other. In tribal societies, matrilocality entails internal peacefulness, while patrilocal societies often include 'fraternal interest groups', which are responsible for a high degree of open aggression (Thoden van Velzen and Van Wetering 1960; cf. Koch 1974: 166-71). The loyalty between brothers and other agnatic kinsmen is also important among Sicilian *mafiosi*, in particular in the struggle between 'families' (Blok 1988; 1996). Yet close kinsmen can easily end up as antagonists, as happened in the so-called

further. As Sulloway convincingly argues in his detailed and masterful study of birth order, sibling rivalry and sibling relations can be best understood in terms of survival strategies; siblings compete with one another for parental attention and investment: that is why siblings seek to be different (1996: 55-118 and *passim*).

How can the narcissism of minor differences — the idea that identity lies in difference, and difference is asserted, reinforced, and defended against what is closest and represents the greatest threat — clarify contemporary cases of extremely violent confrontations?

The Burakumin

The first example concerns the position of the Burakumin in Japan.[6] Formerly called Eta, the Burakumin do not differ in their appearance from other Japanese. They were and still are discriminated against and considered as second-class citizens because of their profession (butchering and leather work) and, therefore, lived in separate quarters. Their official emancipation in 1871 gave the Eta the same legal status and rights as other Japanese, but did not change the negative attitude toward them and their descendants. The state could not protect the civil rights of the Burakumin. In fact, these 'new ordinary people' lost the privileges they had enjoyed under the old feudal regime (the economic monopolies including slaughtering, butchering, skinning, tanning, and leatherwork) without receiving any compensation. Local farmers persecuted the Burakumin for fear of being reduced to the status of these former outcasts: they believed that government policy aimed to turn them into Burakumin. This fear of losing their identity is evident from a number of incidents in which mobs of angry farmers used extreme violence against Burakumin. In one major incident at the end of May 1873, the army had to intervene and arrested 400 people:

second *mafia* war in the early 1980s that ended in victory for the Corleonesi who double-crossed many closely related opponents (Stajano 1986: 16-37; Stille 1995: 99-120 and *passim*). In those days, as one newspaper puts it, in the same family one brother feared the other and sons were afraid of what their father had in store for them. These cases illustrate the popular saying, 'Nella stessa faccia, l'occhio destra odiava il sinistro': 'In the same face the right eye hated the left one' (*La Repubblica*, 7 June 1997, p. 2). Other expressions, like 'Fratelli, coltelli', 'Cugini, assassini', 'Genitori, traditori', and 'Per gli amici mi guarda Iddio', likewise suggest familiarity with the other side of affection and friendship.

6. This sketch is based on De Vos and Wagatsuma (1972: 33-67, esp. 34-38).

According to official figures, 10 houses of government officials, 47 homes of village heads, 25 homes of policemen, 15 school buildings, and more than 300 Buraku homes were wrecked or burned. Eighteen Burakumin were reported dead and 11 badly injured. It was estimated that about 26,000 farmers joined the riot (De Vos and Wagatsuma 1972: 37).

The American South

The mechanism of the narcissism of minor differences also played a crucial role in the American South after the abolition of slavery in 1865. Equality of ex-slaves before the law resulted (again unintentionally) in fierce discrimination and the use of extreme violence against them. The secret societies and the lynchings are post-civil war phenomena — that is, after slavery had been abolished — and reached their climax in the decades around 1900. Persecution came, in particular, from poor and lower middle-class whites, who predominated in the secret societies, mobs, and posses. They feared being put on par with the former slaves, and derived their identity and self-esteem from their social distance from the black population. In *Caste and Class in a Southern Town* (1988 [1937]), Dollard points out the importance of upward social mobility of blacks since the Civil War, their acquisition of middle-class status:

The Ku Klux Klan and other more powerful secret orders were folk movements for the intimidation of Negroes and for the re-establishment of the social distance that formerly existed between whites and Negroes. Although the work of such orders differed in different regions, this function was invariable (1988: 58).

Visiting Atlanta in the 1980s, Naipaul discussed the still tangible results of the 1912 Forsyth County lynching with a local lawyer, who observed that:

to understand, it was necessary to remember that 120 years or so ago there had been slavery. For poor white people race was their identity. Someone well off could walk away from that issue, could find another cause for self-esteem; but it wasn't that easy for the man with little money or education; without race he would lose his idea of who he was (1989: 29).[7]

Thus the theory of minor differences finds confirmation in figurations charac-

---

7. For a recent anthropological interpretation of lynching in the American South, see Brundage (1993). See also his notes on the Forsyth County case (1993: 43, 315, nt 87). Cf. Dumont (1980: 262-64, 425 nt 26).

terised by great differences. The one is the counterpart of the other. Where
social distance is greater, where differences in power and cultural differences
are more pronounced, the chance of conflict, struggle, and extreme violence
diminish accordingly (cf. Walter 1969: 15-16). Rather than overt forms of
violence, we encounter subtle forms of passive resistance, recorded in 'hidden transcripts', as Scott has carefully documented in two important studies
(1985; 1990). Of course, popular movements against established powerholders
are not lacking in ethnographic and historical accounts, but they prove
successful only if they can form coalitions with the rivals of their opponents.[8]

Violence and the code of honour

Social distance and identity go hand in hand. Of the court nobility in France
and Germany under the ancien regime, we learn that membership in the
'gute Gesellschaft' was closely linked to 'honour'. To be expelled, writes
Elias, meant loss of honour, the loss of a constituent part of a person's
personal identity. In fact, a nobleman put his life at stake often enough —
either as challenger or as the one challenged. He preferred to risk his life as
a member of the 'gute Gesellschaft' for this meant to be elevated above the
mass around him. Without this membership life had no meaning for him, as
long as the power of his privileged class remained intact (Elias 1969a: 145-
46). In his study of *satisfaktionsfähige* networks in nineteenth-century
Germany, in which an upper-class Prussian could not withdraw from a duel,
even if it would certainly end with his death, Elias describes the force of this
aristocratic code of honour — to demand and give satisfaction — as follows:
'To give up and go away would not only have meant losing his position, but
also losing everything which gave his life meaning and fulfillment' (1996: 70).

The duel is an example of stylised and refined violence between equals
one of whom has encroached on the 'ideal sphere' of another, who consequently gets the chance to vindicate his honour by putting his life at risk.[9]
As a miniature, the duel shows how culture and cultural differences —
between individuals, groups and national states — can be a matter of life
and death.[10] Simmel understood that the ultimate vindication of honour lies
in physical violence:

8. See, for example, Wolf's study of peasant revolts (1969) and Aya's reflections (1990:
   106-22).
9. For recent studies on the development of the duel in Germany, see Frevert (1995) and
   McAleer (1994).
10. Culture can be a matter of life and death. I owe this formulation to Rod Aya.

As one can consider it as the specific accomplishment of religion that it made people to turn their own salvation into an obligation — so can one mark it, mutatis mutandis, as the accomplishment of honour that it made man turn his social obligation into his individual salvation. That is why with respect to honour the aspects of right and obligation are interwoven and transitional: to keep one's honour is so much an obligation and duty, that one can derive from it the right to the most terrible sacrifices — not only self-imposed, but also sacrifices imposed on others (1983: 405, author's translation).

The Balkans

The Civil War in former Yugoslavia, where Croats, Serbs, and Muslims fought each other in turn, provides us with another situation in which minor differences exacerbated the struggle between the warring parties. In the words of one author:

Although long divided by history and religion, the South Slavs were both ethnically and linguistically one of the most homogeneous peoples in Europe. On the other hand, Tito never overcame the narcissism of minor difference which drove Croats and Serbs to harp on their essentially small divisions...[11]

In her observations on the disintegration of Yugoslavia and the revival of genocide, Bette Denich emphasises the exaggeration of 'minor distinctions' between Croatian and Serbian variants of the literary language:

The linguistic revisions provided an identity marker for 'good Croats', who were also expected to shed regional attachments in favour of Croatian culture both unitary and non-Serbian. Regional identities were eliminated: Dalmatia was renamed 'southern Croatia'. As a further infringement upon Serbian status, the Latin alphabet was designated as the sole alphabet throughout Croatia, limiting recognition of the Cyrillic alphabet to communities with Serbian majorities. The new government took control of the media, turning television and newspapers into articulators of the linguistic innovations and other cultural constructions of the new Croatian state (1994: 379).

11. Richard West, *Tito and the Rise and Fall of Yugoslavia* (1994), quoted by Michael Ignatieff (1995: 17). See also Ignatieff's statement in an earlier review (1993: 3), 'Freud once argued that the smaller the difference between two people the larger it looms in their imaginations. This effect, which he called the narcissism of minor difference, is especially visible in the Balkans'. Ignatieff returned to this theme in greater detail in his book *The Warrior's Honor* (1998: 34-71).

The issue of minor differences between ethnic groups in former Yugoslavia is also raised by another Balkan expert. Eugene A. Hammel distinguishes three primary elements of ethnic identification: kinship, language, and religion. But these principles are not neatly related and do not result in clearly demarcated ethnic groups. Ethnic identity is a matter of labels: Serb, Croat, Muslim — especially in the context of civil war. Language is a tricky criterion. Obviously there are sharp distinctions between the Slavic speakers and Albanians, Hungarians, Turks, Greeks and others. But local people are often bilingual and linguistic distinctions among the Slavic speakers are gradual:

Only minute attention to dialect makes ethnic identification possible. This dialect continuum has been segmented by internationally imposed political boundaries and the centralising efforts of core states, and the intellectuals of such states have sometimes been busy erecting linguistic boundaries to serve nationalist interests (Hammel 1993: 7).

What this amounts to is that the three dimensions of ethnicity — kinship, language, and religion — cross-cut. Religion cannot define ethnicity across the board of the major language divisions (e.g., no Catholic Croat claims common ethnicity with a Catholic Hungarian). In some cases, however, religion divides language communities into endogamous subsets, some of which formed identifiable ethnic groups, like Catholic and Muslim Albanians. On the other hand, 'Catholic and Orthodox Slavs do not recognise common ethnicity, and no Croat peasants claim co-ethnicity with Serb peasants, and neither of these with Muslim Slavs, even when they speak the same dialect' (Hammel 1993: 7). Moreover:

Croats, Serbs, and Muslims Slavs in Bosnia speak dialects that are only narrowly distinguishable. The dialect of the Bosnian Serbs is closer to that of most of the Croats of the region than it is to the Serbian of the core of Serbia. Similarly, the dialect of most Bosnian Croats is closer to that of the Serbs of the region than it is to that of the Croats of northern Dalmatia or the core of Croatia. The symbol that they use to differentiate themselves is religion, but religion fails in that task outside the region (for example with the Catholic Serbs of Dubrovnik) (1993: 7-8).

Hammel points to recent homogenising attempts of states to achieve a congruence of political borders and cultural qualities that were allowed under the communist regime. As an example, he mentions how Tudjman stripped the *krajina* Serbs of the cultural distinctiveness and privileges they enjoyed under Tito. These efforts to limit symbolic expression had the same effect as under Maria Theresa and Joseph II, namely, armed rebellion (Hammel 1993: 8).

Once more, we see the working of the narcissism of minor differences: the erosion and loss of distinctions and differences result in violence. We also see the importance of concomitant circumstances: the absence of a stable, impersonal central power that is willing and able to protect minorities and their rights.

The view of the British war correspondent Glenny in *The Fall of Yugoslavia* is very close to the position taken in this paper. Glenny notes that from the beginning of the conflict in Croatia one particular question has intrigued people in both Yugoslavia and abroad: 'What causes this depth of hatred which has provoked atrocities and slaughter on such a wide scale over such a short period of time?' (1992: 168). It became obvious that the struggle in this area during the Second World War did not end with the establishment of the communist regime under Tito. The conflict inside Yugoslavia between 1941 and 1945 'assumed such bloody proportions that, were it ever to revive, it was always likely to be merciless' (1992: 168). 'Even for people like myself,' writes Glenny, 'who have observed both the war itself and the political intrigue which led to it, the nature of the violence remains incomprehensible'. The conflict has complex historical and political causes; but the hatred has different origins. He notes that the wars of the Yugoslav succession have been nationalist in character:

They are not ethnic conflicts, as the media would often have it, as most of those doing the killing are of the same ethnos. Indeed what is striking about Bosnia-Hercegovina, in particular, is just how closely related are the Serbs, the Croats, and the Moslems (Glenny 1992: 168).

Another Bosnia watcher, David Rohde, who traced the misfortunes of Srebrenica, corroborates this point of view:

Bosnia's Muslims, Serbs, and Croats are racially identical. All three groups are white Eastern European Slavs. 'Yugoslavia' means 'land of the South Slavs'. All three groups speak Serbo-Croatian with a Bosnian accent. The difference between Bosnia's Muslims, Serbs and Croats is their religious faith. The only way a Serb, Croat or Muslim can distinguish one another is by their first or last name (Rohde 1997: xi).

Although religion has played a decisive role in dividing these people, it is not a confessional conflict. Writes Glenny:

For centuries, these people have been asked to choose between competing empires and ideologies, which have invariably been defined by religion. On occasions, great earthquakes have erupted along this powerful historical fault line. It is then that the Bosnians have been enlisted in the service of this or that great power. The Bosnian Serbs, Croats and Moslems have been adorned with many different cultural uniforms over the centuries by which they identify one another as the enemy when conflict breaks out. Despite this, underneath the dress they can see themselves reflected — it is the awful recognition that these primitive beasts (sic) on the other side of the barricade are their brothers which has led to the violence assuming such ghastly proportions in Bosnia. The only way that fighters can deal with this realisation is to exterminate the opposite community. How else does one explain the tradition of facial mutilation in this region? How else can we account for the high incidence of women and children being killed in cold blood? The Orthodox, the Catholics or the Moslems can only claim victory when the heretics have been wiped out or expelled from their homes (1992: 168-69).

The reflections of Glenny and Ignatieff come close to an explanation for the extreme violence in Bosnia and lead us back to the thoughts of Girard about the 'monstrous double' and, associated with it, his theory of ritual pollution and mimetic violence: the vicious circle of mutual violence that results from the erosion of differences. As the anthropological literature on symbolic classifications suggests, anomalies (if recognised) can invite either ritualisation or suppression and eradication.

Rwanda

The narcissism of minor differences also governs the relations between Tutsi and Hutu in Rwanda. Since their first civil war in 1959 we have been aware of 'fratricide' between groups whose differences have, in the course of the twentieth century, been dramatically diminished through the agency of the former colonial power. Both groups developed from initial feudal patron-client relationships toward factions with their own élites: the Tutsi with support from the Belgian colonial government which administered the area through indirect rule; the Hutu first with support from the Mission, which favoured the formerly subaltern group and sent its children to school, and later, in the 1950's, with full support from the Belgian authorities who encouraged ethnic equality and independence.[12] The diminishing of dif-

---

12. This outline is based on Prunier (1995). For a view of the relationship between Tutsi
    and Hutu around 1900, see the reconstruction by Maquet (1961: 129-72 and *passim*).

ferences — economic, social, cultural — reinforced by the increase of mixed marriages led to confusion about the ethnic identity of Tutsi and Hutu even among anthropologists.

Differences between Tusti and Hutu have in certain regards been far from extreme. Prunier describes Tusti and Hutu as 'the notorious rival twins of Rwanda'. They live side by side, 'on the same hilly slopes, in neighbouring hamlets — for better or for worse, for intermarriage or for massacre' (1995: 3). Although often called the tribes of Rwanda, they do not form separate tribes nor do they have separate homelands. Tutsi and Hutu speak the same Bantu language, have the same religion, followed the same cultural practices (patrilineal kinship, polygyny), have lived side by side with each other, and have often intermarried. But at the time of first contact with European explorers they were neither similar nor equal. The Tutsi were originally cattle-herders and patrons of the Hutu; the latter were originally peasants who cultivated the land. Each group had its own dominant somatic type. The Hutu, who formed more than 80 percent of the population, had a standard Bantu physical type and looked like the populations in neighbouring countries. The Tutsi were rather different: extremely tall and thin, and showed more angular facial features (Prunier 1995: 5).[13]

Between 1945 and 1959, Tutsi and Hutu became more similar, not only intellectually and as elites, but also in terms of property and wealth. By 1959 the average financial position of Tutsi and Hutu had generally become more equal. Well-to-do Hutu and poor Tutsi cancelled each other out on the economic average:

... under the banner of 'democratic majority rule' on one side and 'immediate independence' on the other, it was a fight between two competing élites, the newly developed Hutu counter-élite produced by the church and the older neo-traditionalist Tutsi élite which the colonial authorities had promoted since the 1920s (Prunier 1995: 50).

The loss of differences was also visible in their physical appearance. To understand this general loss of distinctions between both groups, we should look at the pattern of intermarriage. Frequent intermarriage between Tutsi

13. For a detailed account of these different racial types, see the photographic essay by Maquet (1957).

and Hutu, writes Prunier, had produced many Hutu-looking Tutsi and Tutsi-looking Hutu (1995: 249).[14]

In the 1950s Maquet sketched a profile of Rwandese society as it probably existed around 1900. He observes that marriages between Hutu and Tutsi were not prohibited. In fact, according to his Hutu informants these marriages happened frequently. His Tutsi interlocutors, however, argued that such marriages were rare, but admitted that Tutsi often had Hutu concubines (Maquet 1961: 65-66). From this discrepancy Maquet infers that:

For a Tutsi to take a Hutu as wife in primary marriage entailed a loss of prestige. It was resorted to mainly because of poverty. Bride-wealth was lower in these inter-caste unions (not in the sense that the standard bride-wealth among Hutu was much lower) and a Hutu girl worked harder than a Tutsi... A prosperous Hutu could marry a Tutsi girl, but then the bride-wealth was often greater than for a Hutu girl. It happened also that a Tutsi cattle-lord would grant a daughter to one of his Hutu clients (1961: 66).

Later in his book Maquet comes back to these marriages which were much sought after by socially upward Hutu:

A Tutsi who did not own any cattle was still a Tutsi but a very poor one, dangerously slipping down in the social stratification, whereas a Hutu who possessed cattle was very near the aristocractic group and not infrequently could marry a Tutsi girl (1961: 120).

Prunier also believes that the clientele system, through which a Tutsi patron transferred cattle to his Hutu client (a sign of wealth, power, and prestige), offered the chance of upward social mobility:

14. In his description of the genocide in the spring of 1994, Prunier notes that distinguishing Hutu and Tutsi in the countryside was not a problem because the identity of the villagers was generally known. It was different in the towns: 'It was not the same thing in the towns and even more in Kigali where people did not know each other. There the *Interahamwe* manning the roadblocks asked people for their identity cards. To be identified on one's card as a Tutsi or to pretend to have lost one's papers meant certain death. Yet to have a Hutu ethnic card was not automatically a ticket to safety. And people were often accused of having a false card, especially if they were tall and with a straight nose and thin lips. Frequent intermarriage had produced many Hutu-looking Tutsi and Tutsi-looking Hutu. In the towns and along the highways, Hutu who looked like Tutsi were often killed, their denials and proffered cards with the "right" ethnic mention being seen as a typical Tutsi deception' (1995: 249).

Once endowed with cattle, the Hutu lineage would become de-hutuised, i.e., tutsified. Similarly a very poor Tutsi who lost all his cattle and had to cultivate the land would in due course become hutuised. Marriage would tend to reinforce either trend, the children of the successful Hutu marrying into a Tutsi lineage and the children of the impoverished Tutsi marrying into a Hutu family (1995: 13-14n.).

Gravel, who did ethnographic research in Eastern Rwanda in the early 1960s, also mentions the blurring of distinctions between Tutsi and Hutu:

Although the social system tends to keep the poor Tutsi out of poverty, either by helping them out or by making them Hutu, there are many Tutsi of low rank and low status in every community. On the other hand, there are rich Hutu, who by dint of power and large family lineages, could oppose, or at least hold their own against, the encroachments and exploitations of the established Tutsi authority. In the past, such lineages, whose position could not be destroyed, were absorbed, and, although the newly rich generation was still regarded as Hutu, its sons could be 'Tutsi-ised' and its grandsons would be considered as Tutsi (1968: 23).

It would be incorrect to argue on the basis of this increasing mixture and overlapping of Tutsi and Hutu that the categories 'Tutsi' and 'Hutu' are not indigenous concepts, but categories 'invented' by the former (Belgian) colonial authorities and imposed on the Rwandese population. Observes Prunier:

Just as the 'different race hypothesis' has caused much crankish writing during the past hundred years, some modern authors have gone to great length in the other direction to try to refute this theory and to prove that Tutsi and Hutu belonged to the same basic racial stock. ...Sober critics pointed out that this 'anti-racist' interpretation ended up being exceedingly racist... (1995: 16-17n.).

It is obvious that one cannot reduce the struggle between Tutsi and Hutu to a narcissism of minor differences. Other important conditions cannot be disregarded, most notably the rapid growth of population,[15] the ecological situation, the superior numbers of Hutu and their domination of the state, and the threat of the Tutsi army from abroad. But it is difficult, on the one hand, to ignore the relationship between the gradual dissolution of hierar-

---

15. See population figures in Prunier (1995: 4), who comments on the rapid growth in population (from 1.5 million in 1934 to approximately 7 million in 1989): 'Grim as it may seem, the genocidal violence of the spring of 1994 can be partly attributed to that population density' (1995: 4).

chical interdependencies and the differences connected with them, and, on the other hand, the extreme violence used by Hutu against Tutsi. It is quite possible that for the originally subordinate Hutu the longtime dominant Tutsi in a process of 'mimetic desire' had assumed the features of a 'monstruous double' — a figure that looms large in Girard's theory of violence. Gravel, who carried out fieldwork in eastern Rwanda, describes the rise of a Hutu politician shortly after the first civil war in Rwanda (November 1959) and the establishment of a pro-Hutu Belgian administration. Before terrorising Tutsi in his community, this man had tried in vain to pass for a Tutsi of the royal lineage. Later he had tried in another community, likewise without result, to marry the daughter of a local Tutsi leader (Gravel 1968: 191 ff.).

Violence and the loss of differences

These examples, which can easily be supplemented with others, show how the imminent loss of differences precedes the use of extreme violence. Antisemitism in Germany intensified with the growing assimilation of Jews. As the antisemitic German scholar Carl Schmitt, who collaborated with the Nazis (and who stood trial in Nuremberg), puts it in his postwar notebook *Glossarium*, 'The real enemy is the assimilated Jew'.[16] Antisemitism in Poland and the Ukraine in the nineteenth and twentieth centuries shows the same pattern: the pogroms came after the emancipation of the peasants and the Jews. Before, the latter had a separate, somewhat privileged position as mediators between gentry and servile peasants. Sometimes the violence of exploited peasants found expression in a *jacquerie* against representatives of this middle class of Jewish managers of large estates and, as happened in the peasant revolt in Moldavia in 1907, acquired an antisemitic character.[17]

The narcissism of minor differences may also throw light on the so-called 'Troubles', the struggle between Protestants and Catholics in Northern Ireland.[18] O'Brien writes :

16. Quoted in Mark Lilla (1997: 39). Cf. Kris (1975: 467-68).
17. On the development of this uprising, which became the most important peasant revolt in the history of Eastern Europe and which was suppressed by the army (with much bloodshed), see the summary by Chirot (1976: 150-55) and the detailed study by Eidelberg (1974).
18. An indication of this can be found in an analysis of the first disturbances: 'The problem is one of the working class. There have been no riots in the prosperous areas of Belmont or the Malone Road in Belfast. Here the well-to-do middle classes are protected by their own mobility. They know that they have the resources to get up and

The Catholics of Northern Ireland are physically indistiguishable from the Protestants; they speak one common language with the Protestants, and generally no other language; they live in the same sorts of houses and watch the same television shows. A stranger could walk through any working-class area of Belfast without having any idea of whether he was in Protestant or Catholic territory — until he notices the slogans on walls, testifying to the abiding politico-sectarian mutual hostility of the two look-alike communities (1986: 442-43).[19]

Another example for further research is the struggle in South Africa between members of Buthelesi's Inkhata Freedom Party (with the support of over six million Zulus in Natal) and members of Nelson Mandela's African National Congress. Between September 1989 (after the abolition of *apartheid* and the inauguration of De Klerk) and January 1993 alone, this undeclared civil war claimed the lives of close to 10,000 people.[20]

Like many conflicts between archenemies, the struggle between Jews and Palestinian Muslims in Israel may be easily reduced to the issue of contested territories or 'competition over resources'. But in this case, too, political economy alone cannot explain their intense mutual hatred. For a better understanding it is worthwhile to explore what Jews and Muslims have in common (always anathema to warring parties, who narcissistically prefer to emphasise and exaggerate differences). Jews and Muslims are not only both 'Peoples of the Book', sharing many religious and cosmological views. There are also striking parallels in language (semitic origins), physical appearance, ecological regimes (pastoral origins), food taboos, patriarchal structures of kinship and marriage, male circumcision, and preoccupation with pollution.[21]

go if necessary — and more of them are now contemplating it — to a calmer part of the province, to the Republic, or across to England. But for the poverty-stricken ghettoes of the Shankill and Falls areas of Belfast, or the Bogside and Fountain districts of Londonderry, no such option is open. With a generally low level of industrial wages, high unemployment and an acute shortage of low-cost housing, the people trapped by their economic circumstances in these slums are ready victims of gut emotion whenever they feel a threat to what little stability they can cling to. It is those who have least to lose in material terms who most need to hug what they do have' (Jackson 1972: 5).

19. Akenson (1988) also aptly illustrates my argument, but came too late to my attention to be used here.

20. Source: State of the Nation Report, South African Institute of Race Relations, January 1993. Quoted in *New York Rerview of Books* (13 February 1993, 24 ff.). On the fierce fighting within the Zulu faction itself — a case of fratricide within fratricide — see Meredith (1997: 419-33).

Another case of extreme violence worth exploring in terms of the narcissism of minor differences is the struggle between Tamils and Sinhalese in Sri Lanka since the 1950s. The Sinhalese constitute more than 70 percent of the total population of about 14 million people. But there are also regions where the Tamils are predominant. Although there are important differences in language and religion, Tambiah describes the civil war between these two groups as 'fratricide':

Although the major identity components of the Sinhalese are their Sinhalese language and their Buddhist religion, and of the Tamils the Tamil language and their Hindu religion, both these populations share many parallel features of traditional caste, kinship, popular religious cults, customs, and so on. But they have come to be divided by their mythic charters and tendentious historical misunderstandings of their past (1986: 5).

In various areas where both groups once knew peaceful coexistence, Tamils were forced to give up their language and religion. Tambiah detects an 'overdetermination' in the anti-Tamil attitude among certain segments of the Sinhalese population:

In these two cases, of coastal peoples north of Colombo and interior peoples of the Eastern Provinces who have shifted from a relaxed symbiosis to an imposed Sinhalese identity, we see one reason for the 'overdetermination' in the anti-Tamil attitudes of certain segments of the Sinhalese population (1986: 100-1).

The 'overdetermined' enmity towards Tamils is also present in the southwestern coastal plain of Sri Lanka. According to Tambiah this is likewise related to the disappearance of important cultural differences. In the fervent religious nationalism of Sinhalese Buddhists, which entails the rejection of Tamils as foreign 'others', one can see an attempt to reinforce Sinhalese identity and to stress differences, both imaginary and real, like physical differences and ethnic origin (Tambiah 1986: 100-1, 183-84).

21. Huntington, who makes much of differences between civilisations, especially along their fault lines and in the realm of religion which he describes as 'possibly the most profound difference that can exist between people'(1996: 254), recognises that the long-standing and violent conflict between Islam and Christianity 'also stemmed from their similarities' (1996: 210-11). But it is precisely along these fault lines and borders, where conflicts are particularly bloody, that one may expect to find transcultural similarities that result from proximity and what Dumont in his essay on the relationship between Muslims and Hindus calls 'cultural osmosis' (1980: 206).

These examples do not remotely exhaust the cases of extreme violence between people who are (or have become) actually very close and similar.[22] But this preliminary survey gives some idea of the connection between extreme violence and threatened identity following the loss of differences between groups. The narcissism of minor differences manifests itself in the emphasis on and the exaggeration of subtle distinctions vis-à-vis others with whom there are many similarities. We are concerned with forms of symbolic action par excellence in which social, cultural, moral, mental, and cognitive elements are closely interwoven. The theoretical purport of the narcissism of minor differences suggests that identity — who you are, what you represent or stand for, whence you derive self-esteem — is based on subtle distinctions that are emphasised, defended, and reinforced against what is closest because that is what poses the greatest threat. This leads us back to Simmel, who argues that to preserve honour people are prepared to make and demand 'terrible sacrifices'.

22. From this point of view, the events in Bali in December 1965 deserve further investigation. In less than two weeks, about 80,000 people were killed ('largely by one another') in the aftermath of the unsuccessful coup in Jakarta on 1 October. See Geertz (1973: 452) for a marginal note and Robinson (1995: 273-313) for a detailed report on the post-coup massacre in Bali. The mass killings between Muslims, Hindus, and Sikhs in the Punjab shortly after India and Pakistan became independent in 1947 ('the twins born from the same egg', as one author puts it) are another example of violence following the imminent erosion of minor differences — minor differences that were previously respected under British rule, but now lost their self-evidence under the impact of the ideology of social equality. On the western side of the new border, Muslims killed Hindus and Sikhs, on the eastern border, Hindus and Sikhs massacred Muslims (*NRC Handelsblad*, 9 August 1997). Violent confrontations between Muslims and Hindus have long been an issue in India itself. To account for them, scholars often follow native views and emphasise the differences between the warring parties and neglect their similarities. In a review of the French edition of Dumont's book, Yalman writes: 'The problem however is not merely that the ultimate principles of Hinduism and Islam differ. In the Indian context, on the contrary, *the real issue is the extraordinary cultural similarities between Hindus and Muslims.* The general ideology may express the polarisation but does not, in Dumont's definition, take care of the nuances, particularly on the Muslim side' (1969: 128-29, italics added). The narcissism of minor differences can also help us understand why in modern urban settings many victims of violent crimes are killed by friends, relatives or acquaintances. A recent survey of 1,156 women, who died from crimes between 1990 and 1994 in New York City, mentions that almost half of the victims whose relationship with their killer could be traced were killed by their present or former partner (*International Herald Tribune*, 1 April 1997). We are dealing here with structural relationships characterised by the diminution of hierarchical and cultural differences between men and women that coincide with a growing mutual involvement.

In a suburb of an English town in the Midlands, investigated in the 1950s, two adjoining working-class neighbourhoods were at odds with each other: the better organised families who lived there the longest, excluded and stigmatised the newcomers who could not defend themselves because of their low degree of social cohesion (Elias and Scotson 1965). The established working-class families felt threatened by the newcomers and feared to be put on the same level as their colleagues who tolerated in their midst a small minority of deviant families. The people in the nearby middle-class neighbourhood (where some working-class families also lived) formed a reference group for the established working-class families, but were not bothered by the presence of the newcomers. For them there was no need to be concerned since the social distance was great enough for them not to feel threatened.

The English example demonstrates, on a small scale, that stigmatisation accompanies minor rather than great differences and that social distance, more control and a stable balance of power protect people against both contamination and fear of contamination.[23] *Les extrêmes se touchent*, also literally. In his book on seventeenth- and eighteenth-century court-life etiquette, Elias describes how ladies of the nobility could undress and bathe unceremoniously in the presence of their servants — a form of intimacy also found in other stratified societies, which qualifies Simmel's observations on discretion.[24]

The English example also shows that the narcissism of minor differences does not automatically result in violence. As pointed out before, other factors help determine the colour and tone of relationships between rival groups. Next to demographic and ecological conditions, especially the political context — the role of the state — is critical. To what extent is there a relatively stable, effective and impersonal monopoly over the means of violence? In all cases where a loss of differences resulted in extreme violence we find unstable states: the minorities, their rights, their social and cultural

---

23. Compare Dumont's comparative view, which he summarises in a number of aphorisms in a paragraph on American racism with the title 'From hierarchy to discrimination'. For instance, 'Make distinction illegitimate, and you get discrimination' and 'Segregation has replaced etiquette as a mode of social distance' (Dumont 1980: 262ff.).

24. Elias (1969a: 77 nt). In his essay on the 'nonperson', Goffman quotes a passage from Mrs Trollope's *Domestic Manners of the Americans* (1832) about the intimate association between masters and slaves: 'I once saw a lady, who, when seated at a table between a male and a female, was induced by her modesty to intrude on the chair of her female neighbor to avoid the indelicacy of touching the elbow of *a man*. I once saw this very young lady lacing her stays with the most perfect composure before a Negro footman' (1959: 151-52).

identity remain unprotected. In some cases the state and the army more or less openly side with one of the warring parties, as in Sri Lanka, Bali, Rwanda, and former Yugoslavia.

Conclusion

I have argued that the loss of differences — especially cultural differences — represents a threat and can lead to explosive situations. Hence the importance of the contributions of Girard — and those of Freud, Simmel, Elias, and others — to an outline of a general theory of power and violence. It is to the merit of Bourdieu that he has re-opened the discussion on the narcissism of minor differences with an apt phrase. Social identity lies in difference, and difference is established, reinforced, and defended against what is closest — and what is closest (in several senses of the word) represents the greatest threat.

We started with Freud and it is fitting also to conclude with him because he was well acquainted with the problem of the 'monstruous double' — also from his own experience. Freud and Arthur Schnitzler lived in the same city, were both medical doctors, belonged to the same generation, and, moreover, were kindred spirits. For years, Freud had been aware of a strong similarity between his views and those of Schnitzler, but it took him a long time before he decided to contact the famous playwright. In a letter to Schnitzler written in May 1922, he explains why:

I have avoided you because of a sort of *Doppelgängerscheu* (fear of double)... Your determinism like your scepticism..., your being gripped by the truths of the unconscious, by the instinctual nature of man, your subversion of cultural-conventional certainties, the clinging of your thoughts on the polarity of loving and dying — all these things touched me with an uncanny familiarity.

Freud then continues in a more detached tone: 'I thus gained the impression that, through intuition — but really in consequence of fine introspection — you know all that I discovered about other people through toilsome work'.[25]

These reflections by Freud do not suggest that he suspected a close relationship between his *Doppelgängerscheu* and the narcissism of minor differences; but he did recognise the critical importance that people attribute to subtle distinctions in their everyday lives.

25. Letter from Freud to Schnitzler, 14 May 1922. Quoted in Scheible (1978: 119, 121).

Bibliography

Akenson, D.H. 1988. *Small Differences. Irish Catholics and Irish Protestants, 1815-1922. An Interpretational Perspective*. Kingston and Montreal: McGill-Queen's University Press.

Aya, R. 1990. *Rethinking Revolutions and Collective Violence. Studies on Concept, Theory, and Method*. Amsterdam: Het Spinhuis.

Black-Michaud, J. 1975. *Cohesive Force. Feud in the Mediterranean and the Middle East*. Oxford: Blackwell.

Blok, A. 1988. *The Mafia of a Sicilian Village, 1860-1960. A Study of Violent Peasant Entrepreneurs*. Cambridge: Polity Press.

Blok, A. 1996. Mafia and the Symbolism of Blood. Paper presented at the conference 'Risky Transactions, Kinship, and Ethnicity', organised by the Max-Planck-Gesellschaft at the Werner Reimer Stiftung. Bad Homburg, September 1996, 23-35.

Boehm, C. 1984. *Blood Revenge. The Enactment and Management of Conflict in Montenegro and other Tribal Societies*. Philadelphia: University of Pennsylvania Press.

Bourdieu, P. 1984 (1979). *Distinction: A Social Critique of the Judgement of Taste*. London: Routledge.

Brundage, W.F. 1993. *Lynching in the New South. Georgia and Virginia*. Urbana: University of Illinois Press.

Chirot, D. 1976. *Social Change in a Peripheral Society. The Creation of a Balkan Colony*. New York: Academic Press.

Daley, M. and M. Wilson 1988. *Homicide*. New York: Aldine.

Dell, W. 1987. 'St Dominics: An Ethnographic Note on a Cambridge College'. In: *Actes de la Recherche en Sciences Sociales* 70, 74-90.

Denich, B. 1994. 'Dismembering Yugoslavia: Nationalist Ideologies and the Symbolic Revival of Genocide'. In: *American Ethnologist* 21, 367-90.

De Vos, G. and H. Wagatsuma 1972. *Japan's Invisible Race. Caste in Culture and Personality*, Revised Edition. Berkeley: University of California Press.

Djilas, M. 1958. *Land without Justice*. New York: Harcourt Brace.

Dollard, J. 1988 (1937). *Caste and Class in a Southern Town*. Madison: University of Wisconsin Press.

Dumont, L. 1980. *Homo Hierarchicus. The Caste System and Its Implications*, Complete Revised Edition. Chicago: University of Chicago Press.

Dunning, E. *et al.* 1986. '"Casuals", "Terrace Crews", and "Fighting Firms": Towards a Sociological Explanation of Football Hooligan Behaviour'. In: David Riches (ed.), *The Anthropology of Violence*. Oxford: Basil Blackwell, 164-83.

Durkheim, E. and M. Mauss 1963 (1903). *Primitive Classification*. Chicago: University of Chicago Press.

Eidelberg, P.G. 1974. *The Great Rumanian Peasant Revolt of 1907. Origins of a Modern Jacquerie*. Leiden: Brill.

Elias, N. and J.L. Scotson 1965. *The Established and the Outsiders*. London: Frank Cass.

Elias, N. 1969a. *Die höfische Gesellschaft*. Berlin: Luchterhand.

Elias, N. 1969b (1939). *Über den Prozess der Zivilisation*. München and Bern: Francke Verlag, 2 vols.

Elias, N. 1996. 'Duelling and Membership in the Imperial Ruling Class: Demanding and Giving Satisfaction'. In: Michael Schröter (ed.), *The Germans. Power Struggles and the Development of Habitus in the Nineteenth and Twentieth Centuries*. Cambridge: Polity Press, 44-119.

Evans-Pritchard, E.P. 1940. *The Nuer*. Oxford: Oxford University Press.

Freud, S. 1990 (1939). 'Moses and Monotheism'. The Penguin Freud Library. Albert Dickson (ed.). Translated from the German and edited by James Strachey. In: *The Origins of Religion*, vol. 13. Harmondsworth: Penguin Books, 237-386.

Freud, S. 1991a (1917). 'The Taboo of Virginity'. The Penguin Freud Library. A. Richards (ed.). Translated from the German and edited by J. Strachey. In: *On Sexuality*, vol. 7. Harmondsworth: Penguin Books, 261-83.

Freud, S. 1991b (1921). 'Group Psychology and the Analysis of the Ego'. The Penguin Freud Library. A. Dickson (ed.). Translated from the German and edited by James Strachey. In: *Civilization, Society and Religion*, vol. 12. Harmondsworth: Penguin Books, 91-178.

Freud, S. 1991c (1930). 'Civilization and its Discontents'. The Penguin Freud Library. A. Dickson (ed.). Translated from the German and edited by J. Strachey. In: *Civilization, Society and Religion*, vol. 12. Harmondsworth: Penguin Books, 243-340.

Frevert, U. 1995. *Ehrenmänner. Das Duell in der bürgerlichen Gesellschaft*. München: Deutscher Taschenbücher Verlag.

Geertz, C. 1973. 'Deep Play: Notes on the Balinese Cockfight'. In: *The Interpretation of Cultures*. New York: Basic Books, 412-53.

Girard, R. 1979. *Violence and the Sacred*. Baltimore: Johns Hopkins University Press.

Glenny, M. 1992. *The Fall of Yugoslavia. The Third Balkan War*. Harmondsworth: Penguin Books.

Goffman, E. 1959. *The Presentation of Self in Everyday Life*. New York: Anchor Books.

Goffman, E. 1971. 'Territories of the Self'. In: *Relations in Public*. New York: Harper & Row, 28-61.

Gravel, P.B. 1968. *Remera. A Community in Eastern Ruanda*. The Hague and Paris: Mouton.

Hammel, E.A. 1993. 'Demography and the Origins of the Yugoslav Civil War'. In: *Anthropology Today* 9(1), 4-9.

Huntington, S.P. 1996. *The Clash of Civilizations and the Remaking of World Order*. New York: Simon & Schuster.

Ignatieff, M. 1993. 'The Balkan Tragedy'. In: *New York Review of Books*, 13 May.

Ignatieff, M. 1995. 'The Politics of Self-Destruction'. In: *New York Review of Books*, 2 November.

Ignatieff, M. 1998. *The Warrior's Honor. Ethnic War and the Modern Conscience*. London: Chatto and Windus.

Jackson, H. 1972. *The Two Irelands: The Double Minority — A Study of Intergroup Tensions*. Report no. 2, New Edition. London: Minority Rights Group.

Keeley, L.H. 1996. *War Before Civilization. The Myth of the Peaceful Savage*. New York and Oxford: Oxford University Press.

Kluckhohn, C. 1968. 'Recurrent Themes in Myth and Mythmaking'. In: H.A. Murray (ed.), *Myth and Mythmaking*. Boston: Beacon Press, 46-60.

Koch, K.-F. 1974. *War and Peace in Jalémó. The Management of Conflict in Highland New Guinea*. Cambridge, Mass.: Harvard University Press.

Kris, E. 1975. *Selected Papers of Ernst Kris*. New Haven: Yale University Press.

Leach, E.R. 1976. *Culture and Communication*. Cambridge: Cambridge University Press.

Lévi-Strauss, C. 1966 (1962). *The Savage Mind*. Chicago: University of Chicago Press.

Lévi-Strauss, C. 1969 (1962). *Totemism*. Harmondsworth: Penguin Books, 9-63.

Lilla, M. 1997. 'The Enemy of Liberalism'. In: *New York Review of Books*, 15 May, 39.

McAleer, K. 1994. *Dueling. The Cult of Honour in Fin-de-siècle Germany*. Princeton: Princeton University Press.

Maquet, J.J. 1957. *Ruanda. Essai photographique sur une société africaine en transition*. Avec la collaboration de Denyse Hierneux-L'Hoest. Bruxelles: Elsevier.

Maquet, J.J. 1961. *The Premise of Inequality in Rwanda. A Study of Political Relations in a Central African Kingdom*. Oxford: Oxford University Press.

Meggitt, M. 1977. *Blood is Their Argument. Warfare Among the Mae Enga Tribesmen of the New Guinea Highlands*. Palo Alto: Mayfield.

Meredith, M. 1997. *Nelson Mandela. A Biography*. London: Hamish Hamilton.

Naipaul, V.S. 1989. *A Turn in the South*. Harmondsworth: Penguin Books.

O'Brien, C.C. 1986. *The Siege. The Saga of Israel and Zionism*. London: Nicolson & Weidenfeld.

Prunier, G. 1995. *The Rwanda Crisis, 1959-1994. History of a Genocide*. London: Hurst.

Robinson, G. 1995. *The Dark Side of Paradise. Political Violence in Bali*. Ithaca, N.Y.: Cornell University Press.

Rohde, D. 1997. *Endgame. The Betrayal and Fall of Srebrenica: Europe's Worst Massacre Since World War II*. New York: Farrar, Strauss and Giroux.

Scheible, H. 1978. *Arthur Schnitzler*. Hamburg: Rowohlt.

Scott, J.C. 1985. *Weapons of the Weak. Everyday Forms of Peasant Resistance*. New Haven, Conn.: Yale University Press.

Scott, J.C. 1990. *Domination and the Arts of Resistance. Hidden Transcripts*. New Haven, Conn.: Yale University Press.

Simmel, G. 1950. *The Sociology of Georg Simmel*. Translation, K.H. Wolff. New York: The Free Press.

Simmel, G. 1983 (1908). *Soziologie*. Berlin: Duncker & Humblot.

Stajano, C. (ed.), 1986. *Mafia. L'atto d'accusa dei giudici di Palermo*. Rome: Editori Riuniti.

Stille, A. 1995. *Excellent Cadavers. The Mafia and the Death of the First Italian Republic*. London: Jonathan Cape.

Sulloway, F.J. 1996. *Born to Rebel. Birth Order, Family Dynamics, and Creative Lives*. New York: Vintage Books.

Tambiah, S.J. 1986. *Sri Lanka: Ethnic Fratricide and the Dismantling of Democracy*. Chicago: University of Chicago Press.

Thoden van Velzen, H.U.E. and W. van Wetering 1960. 'Residence, Power and Intrasocietal Aggression'. In: *International Archives of Ethnography* 49, 169-200.

Walter, E.V. 1969. *Terror and Resistance. A Study of Political Violence With Case Studies of Some Primitive African Communities*. New York: Oxford University Press.

Wolf, E.R. 1969. *Peasant Wars of the Twentieth Century*. New York: Harper & Row.

Yalman, N. 1969. 'De Tocqueville in India: An Essay on the Caste System'. In: *Man* (N.S.) 4, 123-31.

CHAPTER 3

The Two Deaths of Basem Rishmawi: Identity Constructions and Reconstructions in a Muslim-Christian Palestinian Community[1]

Glenn Bowman

The sheer brutality of the events remains. On the wet and windy evening of 23 March, 1981, sometime between 8 and 9 p.m., Basem Rishmawi left the home of his fiancée in the West Bank town of Beit Sahour to walk the short distance to his own family's house. He never arrived. Five days later his family received a late night call from the Bethlehem offices of the Israeli military police in which a Shin Bet officer announced that Basem's body had been found on the 25th in the vicinity of the town dump lying in a valley between the Mar Elyas monastery and the outskirts of the town. According to the officer a military investigation had revealed that Rishmawi had been killed while preparing explosives which had prematurely exploded. He announced that the body would be returned to the family that night, and that only a small number of people would be allowed to attend the funeral in the Greek Orthodox church before the body's interment. Some soldiers who came to the church before the arrival of the body allowed only around a dozen people — immediate family members and a priest — into the church, and it was these people who were able briefly to examine the body when it was delivered at approximately 1.30 a.m. on the 29th. It was immediately clear that there was something wrong with the officer's story; the body had been dismembered by an explosion, but there seemed to be no connection between the damage caused by the force of the explosion and the

1. This paper is based on fieldwork carried out over the past ten years, funded for the most part by the Wenner Gren Foundation for Anthropological Research (a short field trip to Beit Sahour in January 1990 was paid for by the Middle East Research Information Project). In an earlier article — 'Nationalizing the Sacred: shrines and shifting identities in the Israeli-occupied Territories' (Bowman 1993) — I have discussed *intifada*-period responses to Basem Rishmawi's killing.

other wounds evident on the body, such as heavy bruising on the face, multiple penetration wounds, and deep gouging — seemingly caused by brutally tight binding on the wrists of arms which had been torn off by the explosion and then gathered together with the other remains. As the mourners whispered to each other their suspicion that a bomb had been set off inside or next to the body after death, armed soldiers watched over the brief funeral service and the subsequent entombment in the family plot.

First death: intimations of *intifada*

I first encountered Basem's name and image in January of 1990 after members of one of the town's numerous *intifada* 'committees' had smuggled me into the town by bypassing the roadblocks which the military authorities had erected to enforce the siege imposed upon the community by the Israeli government in response to Beit Sahour's protracted maintenance of a tax strike.[2] The cramps in my legs, caused by spending part of the trip curled on the floor of the car, loosened as I sipped bitter-sweet coffee in the house of the aunt and uncle of one of my guides after the tense trip between Bethlehem and Beit Sahour. Hung in a place of honour on the wall of the room in which guests were entertained was the picture of a solemn-looking young man. When I asked about it, I was told the story of Basem's killing, and it was made clear to me that although no one knew whether he had been killed by Jewish settlers or by the Israeli military he was an arbitrarily-chosen victim of Israeli oppression of Palestinians: 'it could have happened to anybody, and by chance the victim was Basem' (8.1.90).[3]

Although in the nearly nine years since his murder a number of other Beit Sahouris had been killed by soldiers, it was clear that Basem occupied an emblematic position in the social imaginary of this militant town. I would come across his picture again and again in the following days as I interviewed people whose houses and shops had been stripped by tax collectors accompanied by military squads, whose husbands, fathers, sons or daughters

---

2. See Hunter (1991: 121-28) on the *intifada* tax revolt strategy in general and Robinson (1997: 66-93) for Beit Sahour's role in it.

3. Because the issues raised in the Rishmawi killing have not, by the time of writing (24 March 1999), been resolved, I have decided not to mention informants by name other than when their identities are already commonly known by the townspeople. Insofar as sequentiality is highly significant in this paper's tracking of discursive developments in the story of Basem's death, I follow each direct quotation with a parenthetical dating of when it was stated.

Basem Rishmawi, 25 March 1981
(from Martyr's Calendar)

had disappeared into Israeli prisons or were avoiding arrest by constantly moving from house to house, and whose revolutionary ardour was fanned by the attempts of the government to break the will of a town which Jerusalem Palestinians lauded at the time as being 'tougher than Gaza' (6.1.90). During that week of tense skirmishing with Israeli 'tax collecting' squads, informants continuously stressed to me that all Beit Sahourans, and by extension all Palestinians, were rendered equivalent by the activities of an occupying force which — in its attacks on a Palestinian presence — refused to distinguish between Muslim or Christian, male or female, young or old, rich or poor. One man — a Christian shopkeeper — said to me, 'there is no difference; we are under the same conditions, the same oppression, the same hopes, the same policy... the occupation does not differentiate between Muslim and Christian' (8.1.90), while later in the week a Muslim school-teacher told me 'we have never felt a difference, we live together as the same people; we feel there is another one who is enemy to us both' (11.1.90).

Basem — who, despite being described as no more than a young man in love, had evidently been kidnapped, tortured to death, and then torn to pieces by his Israeli captors so that his remains could bear the brand 'terrorist' — stood in this situation as a sort of Palestinian everyman. He had already suffered the martyrdom that was, in the eyes of Palestinians under occupation, the inheritance which every one of them could expect to receive as long as the logic of the Zionist occupation of Palestine held sway. When, on 18 July 1988, Edmond Ghanem was killed by a soldier who dropped a building block on him from a guard post on the top of a three story building, people saw the event as yet another assertion of that exterminatory logic, and strengthened their resolve to protect themselves by uniting to fight the common enemy. The 1993 calendar published by the Arab Orthodox Club[4] of Beit Sahour presents — beneath an image of the town prominently showing the Catholic and Orthodox churches as well as the mosque — a series of photographs of seventeen Beit Sahouris who had in common not their religious affiliation but the fact that they, Muslim and Christian alike, had been martyred by the forces of the occupation.

In some ways the idiom of martyrdom can be seen to have become the language of community in those days of the early *intifada*. In my notebook I record two comments collected during my short stay in Beit Sahour. In the first a man, when telling me of the killings in Gaza which sparked off the

4. The Arab Orthodox Club is the chief site of men's social gathering in Beit Sahour, and all members of the community (whether they be Christian, Muslim or atheist) are welcomed. Its name is redolent not with religious affiliation but with the revolt of Orthodox Christians against the power of the Greek Orthodox Church in the early 20th century. Increased awareness of discrimination against local Orthodox Christians by the exclusively Greek Brotherhood of the Holy Sepulchre had led to the lay creation of the Arab Orthodox Movement, an organization dedicated to wresting control of the church and its substantial properties from a 'foreign' priesthood. Although this movement was supported by the Russian Orthodox church before the revolution and by the British Authorities during the Mandate period, it was subsumed — after the Israeli occupation — into more generalised Palestinian nationalism.

clashes which had evolved into the *intifada*,[5] commented that he — like all his neighbours — responded to the news of Palestinian deaths by thinking 'why am I not this man?' (8.1.90). The response is one of identification; as the man subsequently elaborated, he knew Israeli soldiers killed Palestinians simply because they were Palestinians and since he was a Palestinian it had just been a matter of contingency that he had not been in the car that was crushed. In the eyes of the occupying forces, there was nothing about him which made him any different from those they chose to kill — he was, after all, just another 'Arab' to the soldiers — and therefore there was nothing to prevent them from choosing to kill him the next day. It was this potential 'fate' that gave rise to his, and his neighbours' resolve to overthrow an occupation which offered that future to all Palestinians: 'We see that one day it is one person, and the next day another. The following day it may be us, so we say *"Hellas"* [enough] and begin to work to stop it'.[6] The undifferentiating gaze of the soldier (or the settler) created a defensive 'Palestinian' community out of a multi-sectarian community which, without that antagonism, might have been riven by allegiances to family, localised identities, and conflicts of class.

The second comment evidences the presence of a prestige economy which demonstrates the constitutive relation of acts of persecution or martyrdom to activist Palestinian identity. On my third day in the town I was the guest in the modern apartment of a couple who kept a small electrical goods shop. As I stood in the midst of scattered clothing, bedding, and broken furniture (the flat had that morning been stripped of everything of value in the course of a visit from a group of soldiers directed by a man calling himself a tax collector) the woman, while comforting her young children, told me that 'the people who have not had their things confiscated by the tax men are envious of those who have; it's like building a new house' (10.1.90). Here, in the midst of a town which had extensively developed small industry over the

5. On 8 December 1987, at an Israeli checkpoint in Gaza, an Israeli tank transport vehicle swerved across the road and flattened a car full of Palestinian workers waiting to be cleared to cross into Israel in order to go to their jobs in Tel Aviv; four residents of the Jabaliya refugee camp were killed in the incident which subsequently proved to have been the response of the transport vehicle's driver to the knifing of an Israeli tax collector in Gaza city the previous day.

6. I discuss this congeries of antagonism, identification and identity at greater length and with critical reference to Benedict Anderson's theory of the genesis of imagined community in 'A Country of Words: Conceiving the Palestinian Nation from the Position of Exile' (Bowman 1994: 140-47 and 161-62).

past twenty years,[7] a potlatch-like counter-economy was developing wherein status accrued to those who 'gave freely' (and aggressively) to the enemy (Mauss 1969: 31-45). The 'new houses' constructed in the burgeoning economy of martyrdom were very different than those which had been erected during the pre-*intifada* years when Beit Sahouri innovation and industriousness had enabled its inhabitants to 'piggy-back' on Israeli economic expansion and thus to build up their capital and properties; in this counter economy Beit Sahourans played a vanguard role by refusing to pay taxes to the occupying government and by systematically disengaging from the Israeli economy. They prided themselves in throwing back at the Israelis the wealth which had come to be considered no more than payment for accepting occupation. A recently-plundered pharmacist told me that 'if the bedouin can live in tents, so can we. We have our agriculture and it is very good. The *Jerusalem Post* called us the "Japan of the Palestine/Israel" but we can lose all that and go back to the fields' (12.1.90).[8]

That 'rebuilding' extended, at least through the first three years of the *intifada*, through all aspects of Beit Sahouri life. Landscape, history, sectarianism, and social organisation were reworked in the popular discourses which circulated through and constituted the self-professed revolutionary community of that period. Parts of the town which had previously been designated by topographic features or by the name of the family which predominated in that area were renamed so as to resonate with the mytho-

---

7. Much of this involved the finishing of clothing for the Israeli market, consequently raising the town's standard of living considerably above that of other West Bank communities.

8. The story with its assertion of the ease with which Beit Sahour could return to its 'agricultural roots', is somewhat idealised. Beit Sahourans claim that, unlike the other non-urban communities in the area (Khadr and Beit Jala are cited), they had never had much land; from the town's beginnings it had rented land from the Bethlehemites and needed, therefore, to work out ways of making money to buy land if it was to develop. Initially this was done through stone cutting — Sahouri men went north (to the area around Nablus) to practise this craft and make money to bring back — and later the Latin church supported residents in developing an artisanal crafts industry focussed on mother of pearl cutting for the tourist trade. As a result of such entrepreneurial developments Beit Sahour was largely independent of agriculture by 1967 and well prepared to take advantage of Israel's drive to increase commodity circulation (and market dependence) in the Territories (see Mansour 1988 and others essays in Abed 1988 on occupation economics). Beit Sahour attempted, during the *intifada*, to become agriculturally self-sustaining so that it would not need to purchase food from the Israelis (see Frankel 1994: 42-66, Hunter 1991: 144-45 and 211-12, Schiff and Ya'ari 1990: 247-48 and Robinson 1997: 74-76).

graphy of Palestinian resistance. The town's highest sector (previously known as the *ras* or 'head') was renamed 'Shqeef Castle' so as to recall a famed Palestinian victory, while other sectors of the town became 'Tell al-Za'ter' and 'Shateela' to evoke militant refugee camps in the Lebanon.[9] A new emphasis predominated in narrating the history of the town whereby stories were accentuated of coordinated resistance by towns-people to earlier oppressions. Various people recounted to me stories about Beit Sahour's resistance to the Ottoman draft during the First World War,[10] about Muslims and Christians marching together to Nebi Musa in opposition to the British Mandate, of an Orthodox priest who cachéed arms to be used in fighting the British during the 1936-39 revolt, of Baathist, Nasserite and finally Communist demonstrations against the Jordanian occupation, and of the long history of Beit Sahouran support for the Popular and Democratic Fronts during the period of Israeli hegemony. In these the 'we' of an historic and enduring community was reified and affirmed, and the repeated return to emphasising resistance to Israeli rule stressed that it was in this particular struggle that the community realised the quiddity of its identity: 'since 1936 we have been in struggle with Israel — in 1948 and 1967. We will struggle until the last man. Even if the young men are gone the old men will fight on' (9.1.90). Underplayed or simply excluded in these identity narratives were historic clashes with local Bedouin communities (the *ta'amra*), disputes over land ownership, class, feuding between family groups, and the divisive responses of local Christians and Muslims to the differentiating policies of the various colonising powers which had dominated the town. Beit Sahourans — at least in the presence of a foreign anthropologist[11] — vied to relate stories of the

9. Shqeef is Beaufort Castle in South Lebanon. It was held by *Fateh* from 1970 until 1982, and gave rise to stories of heroism and impregnability, especially because it held out in the small Israeli invasion of 1978. I am grateful to Rosemary Sayigh for this information. Tell al-Za'ter had heroically resisted a several month siege by Maronite militia in early 1976.

10. One told me that 'people here were under people who claimed to be Muslims but who oppressed the Muslims too. They had to ask themselves 'what are we? Is this a religious war or not? Is this an occupation?' (11.1.90).

11. Although I note the proviso here that this particular discourse might have been produced solely for the ears of the outsider, I do not believe this to be the case. Internal solidarity, which was extremely strong despite the oppressive challenges posed to it during this period, depended on the verisimilitude of assertions of communal solidarity. Furthermore a text in Arabic — *The White Revolution in the Disobedient City* — published in 1990 by Izzat Dragma, a Beit Sahouri, also validates and circulates the elements I note above.

past which extrapolated from the present onto history the same spirit of intercommunal solidarity against oppression which they saw as uniting the town in the contemporary period.

At the heart of these stories was an awareness of the necessity to under-play or elide the significance of the fact that the population of Beit Sahour could be classified in terms of sectarian affiliations which elsewhere served to divide rather than unite communities. The Beit Sahouri population in 1984 was, according to a census carried out by a Franciscan priest, made up of 8,900 persons of whom 17% were Sunni Muslim, 67% were Greek Orthodox, 8% were Roman Catholic, 6% were Greek Catholic, and 2% were Lutheran (Pena 1984).[12] Repeatedly Muslims and Christians alike relayed to me varia-tions on the following statements, the first made by the Muslim school-teacher cited above and the second by a Christian member of the medical committee which had smuggled me into town (itself made up two Greek Orthodox, one Roman Catholic and one Muslim):

We do not remember we are from different religions unless somebody from outside reminds us... We [Muslims] carry *arak* [a local anis-flavoured hard alchohol] and seeds to weddings; we bring to them what makes them happy. We are not fanatic; we do not have such sensitivities. We are trying to keep living in the same way, not being influenced by the occupation mentality. They [the Israelis] are trying to break apart a culture we have built over centuries (11.1.90). It is you, outside, who try to make a difference between the Christians and the Muslims. We are a people, we all go to each other's feasts, we visit with each other, we live the same life. We are one people (8.1.90).

That intercommunality was evident in public manifestations of solidarity such as the martyrs' calendar mentioned above, the joint Christian-Muslim scout marches on Christmas Day through the town's streets from the Catholic church, past the mosque and to the Orthodox church, and the

12. The Christians and Muslims I spoke to in Beit Sahour in 1990 quoted much higher figures for the Muslim population — between 25% and 30% — but just as Pena's interest in Christian communities and his dependence on local parish priests for his information may have caused him to underestimate the number of Muslims in Beit Sahour, so Beit Sahourans' pride in having overcome the opportunities for fragmen-tation thrown up by religious differences may have led them to inflate Muslim numbers. The overall accuracy of Pena's figures is suggested by the December 1997 census which shows the total population of Beit Sahour to be 11,250 of which 7,972 were over twelve years of age and 620 over 65 (Palestinian Central Bureau of Statistics 1999: 50 and 55).

decision of the committees organising the 'Day of Prayer for Peace' on 5 November 1989 to invite Sheikh Said al-Din al Alami, Mufti of Jerusalem and head of the Islamic Council, to announce from the pulpit of Beit Sahour's Orthodox Church a *fatwa* against the purchase of the confiscated Beit Sahouran goods which Israeli tax officials were putting up for auction in Tel Aviv. It was also memorialised in the Municipality's decision to refuse to allow any of the Holy Land's churches to claim and build a shrine over the site of recent apparitions of the Virgin Mary in a cistern under the town market, but to erect instead a non-denominational municipal shrine there (the only one I know of in all of Israel/Palestine). The building the Municipality erected over the cistern was evocative of a *makam* (a building with a dombed chamber characterising a Muslim holy place) rather than a church, and I was told by one of the workers in the surrounding market that 'it is not a church; it is a wall to protect it [the well of Marian]' (11.1.90). The shrine's caretaker, employed by the Municipality, stressed that the site was communal rather than sectarian: 'we are Muslim and Christian here, there are two Christian groups. The Municipality builds for all the people and the people all own and use the well' (12.1.90).[13]

Glenn Robinson describes the radical reworkings of the socio-political terrain which accompanied these *intifada*-period refigurations of the social imaginary in the chapter he dedicates to Beit Sahour in *Building a Palestinian State: An Incomplete Revolution* (Robinson 1997: 66-93). Here he details the ascent of a new elite, basing its authority on its members' education and their engagement in political activism, which largely supplanted the dominance of the previous elite. That group had instead legitimated its control by the patriarchal positioning of its members within the *hamula* (clan) structure and bolstered it in pre-*intifada* times by mediating between the occupation authorities and the local populations.[14] Robinson describes the manner in which the membership of the *intifada* committees, which functioned as *de facto* 'Soviets' during the period of Beit Sahour's revolt, was elected by the residents of their respective neighbourhoods (there were thirty five com-

13. I have discussed this shrine at some length in Bowman 1993, comparing and contrasting it with more traditional church-run holy places in the vicinity.
14. See, for an up-to-date, unsurpassed, study of the techniques the Israeli government used to control Palestinian populations under its jurisdiction (in this case pertaining to the 'Israeli Arab' population within the borders - behind the 'Green Line' - of the pre-1967 state), Ian Lustick's *Arabs in the Jewish State* (Lustick 1980). Abner Cohen's *Arab Border Villages in Israel* (Cohen 1965) examines the workings of the *hamula* system in a manner fiercely criticised for ideological bias by Talal Asad (Asad 1975).

mittees representing an equal number of neighbourhoods) rather than appointed by clan elders to represent clan interests in town affairs (Robinson 1997: 68). This territorial locus of selection served to raise as political issues common concerns pertaining to living in the contemporary situation — health care, security, provision of water, electricity and food, income for the families of people killed, injured or imprisoned, etc. — rather than inter-familial problems or communitarian disputes.[15] The *Sulha*[16] committee was a parallel municipal authority established in 1989 to coordinate the activities of the neighbourhood committees and deal with issues pertaining to the entire town. It was directed by an executive committee elected by representatives of the twenty-two major political, cultural and social organisations in town and concerned itself with issues pertinent to the entirety of the town — raising money to support the needy, settling disputes, and coordinating responses to *intifada* situations (Robinson 1997: 80-81).

Thus, in what Robinson refers to as a 'revolution' (albeit 'incomplete'), the Beit Sahouri community restructured not only its imaging of itself as a community but also the social and political structures through which it decided and expressed its collective will. Although dying before the shifting configuration of occupier and occupied allowed him to participate in this reworking of Beit Sahouran identity, and despite being both a Greek Orthodox Christian and a member of the al-Qazaha *hamula*, Basem Rishmawi functioned throughout the years of *intifada* for all Beit Sahouris as an icon of their collective identity as Palestinians under Israeli occupation, regardless of religion and familial affiliation. Basem's martyrdom was a particularly gruesome and spectacular instance of what Palestinians in Beit Sahour and throughout the West Bank and Gaza had learned (under Likkud's Sharon and then through the tutelage of Yitzak Rabin's 'iron fist policy' which

---

15. As Beit Sahour's population increased substantially in the course of the 20th century, its population spilled out of the old part of the town - where *hamula* residence had been the norm - and into the surrounding hills and valleys where in large part neighbourhoods were made up of members of two or more families. Thus a territorial system of representation, in lieu of the traditional system where issues of family concern were debated in family forums before being forwarded through a family representative for handling by the Municipal council (which was constituted of the representatives of the eight major families, six of which were Christian and two Muslim), ensured that the topics considered and treated were for the most part posed in the idiom of community rather than that of family (14.3.1999).

16. *Sulha* refers to negotiated settlements between two parties in dispute, and refers to the committees' important role in settling inter-group conflicts without involving occupiers' law.

entailed breaking the bones and bulldozing the houses of stone throwers) was the fate they too could expect under Israeli occupation.[17] Before photographic images of Basem (with his sad, yet severe, gaze) — in framed pictures hanging on the walls of reception rooms, on torn posters illegally plastered on the street walls of Beit Sahour and Bethlehem, or in the martyr's calendar distributed by the Beit Sahour Arab Orthodox Club — people in Beit Sahour and its environs struggled to find ways of celebrating the Palestinian identity which Basem personified, but without necessarily following his path to a terrible death in the midst of a smoking dump on a back road.

Second death: the dissolution of community

Basem's name began to circulate again two years after the Oslo Agreements had brought the *intifada* to a close.[18] There was a substantial period between the signing of the peace accord in Washington and the handing to the Palestine National Authority of control over Bethlehem and Beit Sahour (so-called 'A Category' areas which were put under full Palestinian jurisdiction), but in the summer of 1995, soon after the Israeli withdrawal, a Beit Sahouri, Faez Qumsiyyeh, was arrested by Palestinian security for questioning about non-political criminal activities. During his imprisonment Faez confessed to having been involved, along with his cousin Sammer Qumsiyyeh and a Muslim man from a neighbourhood between Beit Sahour and Bethlehem, in the abduction, torture and murder of Basem Rishmawi. He reiterated this admission in front of two members of the Palestinian Legislative Council and then his parents, who some say he asked to arrange reconciliation with Basem's family.

For the second time events related to the death of Basem Rishmawi engaged all of Beit Sahour; one woman, an affinal relative, told me that 'it was like he had been killed again, and all the Rishmawis and much of the

17. In mid-November 1981 the family homes of five Beit Sahouri youths arrested for throwing molotov cocktails at military vehicles were bulldozed. Ariel Sharon, then Minister of Defense, responded to Israeli as well as Palestinian criticism by saying that 'Beit Sahur was always a centre of terrorist activity... and in general I would suggest not to regard the Christian Arabs as less extremist in their attitude towards Israel than others' (interview, 9 December 1981, cited in Aronson 1990: 260).

18. The *intifada* ran from 9 December 1987 until 13 September 1993 when Declarations of Principles (the Oslo Agreements) were signed by Rabin and Arafat following U.S.-brokered secret negotiations which took place in Oslo, Norway.

rest of the town went into mourning' (19.12.97). This time, however, the context within which those events were revealed was not, as before, that of a burgeoning nationalist mobilisation leading to *intifada* but instead that of a 'winding down' of commitment and solidarity in the wake of a partial amelioration of occupation. Since the heady days of the tax strike, Beit Sahour's fervour had been substantially diminished not so much by any change in Israeli policy towards the town but rather by the failure of the Palestine Liberation Organization to provide the verbal and financial support necessary to bulwark commitment in the face of fiercely punitive measures. As Robinson points out:

the PLO in Tunis failed to support Bayt Sahur's campaign, as it feared the political consequences of such grassroots initiatives... Tunis's — and particularly Yasir Arafat's — disregard for Bayt Sahur's campaign of civil disobedience was strongly felt by members of the new elite in Bayt Sahur [who]...were nearly unanimous in their view that Tunis not only failed to support Bayt Sahur's efforts but actually tried to thwart them by privately urging others to pay their taxes and by more closely aligning itself with members of the old elite (Robinson 1997: 88 and 89).

The refusal of the 'outside' to support the strike provided the conditions under which communal solidarity began to unravel as those who had already lost considerable property grew increasingly aggrieved by others who, fearful of finding themselves in similar penury, began covertly to pay their taxes.

Furthermore, after the arrests in March 1990 of the last members of the underground grassroot committees of the United National Leadership of the Uprising, which had coordinated internal *intifada* strategy, the *intifada* was directed through internal cadres from outside by the leadership of the various external factions which operated semi-autonomously under the umbrella of the PLO (*Fateh*, Democratic Front for the Liberation of Palestine, Popular Front for the Liberation of Palestine, Palestine People's Party). From that point on political activity in Beit Sahour, as elsewhere in the Territories, was coordinated and carried out by competing political factions which were paid for their activism and remunerated for their losses by the outside organisations. Many saw this as a retrograde move which took the revolution away from the people and gave it to the politicians: 'the *intifada* was made by those on the street and broken as soon as they began "throwing stones for money"'(29.7.94). Robinson's analysis of the reasons for the subsequent disbanding of the *Sulha* coordinating committee foregrounds not only an argument between two families rendered irresolvable by the fact that one family was aligned with *Fateh* while the other was with the PFLP, but also incidents in which personal or business interests proved more compelling than continued adherence to the community's policy of resisting the occupation.

These tendencies towards fragmentation were aggravated by the peace settlement. This, although it failed to ameliorate day to day deprivations,[19] removed Israeli soldiers from the streets of the town and hid the operations of the Israeli security apparatus behind the proxy Palestinian 'Preventative Security Force'.[20] The consequent near-disappearance of a previously omnipresent Israeli presence deprived the community of the everyday evidence of 'another one who is enemy to us both'. With the loss of focus which that antagonist had provided, the sense of collective solidarity with which Beit Sahour had faced that enemy began to dissipate. That sense of solidarity had already been substantially undermined by forces influencing the community from outside which made it more and more difficult to see one's neighbour as 'the same as' one's self. Political factionalism as well as strategies allowing differential access to support and greater or lesser protection from loss eroded the sense of 'equivalence' which Laclau and Mouffe point out is a fundamental element of popular mobilisation (Laclau and Mouffe 1985: 63).

In the earlier period of Beit Sahouran solidarity, differential aspects of identity — based on religion, class position, *hamula* affiliation, party membership, and even to some degree age and gender — had been *subsumed* within an enveloping political and public identity. Thus a contingent political identity appears essential, while more ingrained and enduring identities become supplemental.

The following scenario of an appropriate response to the presence of soldiers was sketched for me by a militant who was also a devout Muslim. It displays the way differentiating identity is articulated only to be dissolved in organising the imagined act of opposition: 'If I want to throw a stone I will not call to my neighbour to say "become a Muslim and then we will throw stones together". We forget our religion, we forget our political

---

19. The Oslo Agreements effectively institutionalised the closure of the Occupied Territories. This closure, which barred access to Jerusalem to all but the very few who could attain permits from the military authorities, etiolated trade links between West Bank businesses and forced un- or alternative employment on many workers who after 1967 had become dependent on work in Israel. Since then *per capita* income on the West Bank has dropped by 23% (personal communication with Graham Usher).

20. The PNA is now generally referred to by Palestinian and Israeli intellectuals and activists alike as a 'sub-contractor' government.

groups' (12.1.90). With a different emphasis the following quote, drawn from an interview with a Roman Catholic deeply involved in committee organisation, demonstrates that the elements of identity which make for difference remain salient, but are — in cases where communal solidarity is hegemonic — limited as to the contexts in which they are voiced: 'my relation with my God is in my heart and my house; it does not concern the public. In the street I am Aissa' (10.1.90).[21]

Outstanding in such cases, however, is the presence of a perceived antagonist which, in its hostile alterity, dissolves the differences between those to whom it offers the same threat. The space of communality is not created by the routines of everyday life which structure and manifest systems of difference and orchestrate relations between the variant vertical and horizontal role positionings of age, class, gender, education, appearance, religion, etc., but the presence of an antagonism perceived as threatening all within its purview with either physical extermination or the wholesale extirpation of their differentiated, subsumed identities. The overarching political identity becomes a powerful expression of self and community because it explicitly counters — as an antithesis — the threat to all existing identities posed by the antagonism. An antagonism is not a relationship of subordination since, as unpleasant as being under another's dominion might be, subordination remains a structured relationship within a system which establishes identities. Antagonism is about death — either literal (which is why martyrdom plays such an important metaphoric role in mobilising Palestinian identity) or social (the destruction of the familial and/or communal context supporting identity). An antagonism comes from 'outside' a system of social and cultural meanings and renders the system inoperative by nullifying its capacity to create and maintain identities.[22] Someone who

21. Both quotations embed the trajectory of the discursive shift I observed developing in Jerusalem's Old City between 1983 and 1985 as Palestinians were forced by increasing hostile attention from soldiers, settlers and tax collectors to recognise that their communality as 'Palestinians' was more salient than the differences religious affiliation opened between them. People who in the early months of my fieldwork called themselves 'Palestinian Christians' or 'Palestinian Muslims' began pointedly reversing the order of the substantive and the adjectival in talking to me and to other foreigners - 'I am not a Palestinian Christian; I am a Christian Palestinian' (14.2.95 and *passim*) or 'I am a Palestinian first, then a Muslim' (Bowman 1986: 5).

22. '[W]ith this "exterior" we are not reintroducing the category of the extra-discursive. The exterior is constituted by other discourses. It is the discursive nature of this exterior which creates the conditions of vulnerability of every discourse, as nothing finally protects it against the deformation and destabilization of its system of differences by

defeats her partner in chess, whether by playing straight or by cheating, overcomes the other player according to a rule-governed process (those rules can still function after the defeat to enable the defeated player to claim the other's victory is void because she cheated). If, however, someone stands up and throws the chessboard to the floor, scattering pieces all over, they can be accused of being a poor loser, but by that time the site of interaction is no longer that of the game. The game, and the positions it distributed and mediated, is overturned and whatever new identities emerge will be generated by new rules organising a new situation. Laclau and Mouffe, perhaps more simply, write that 'it is because a peasant *cannot be* a peasant that an antagonism exists with the landowner who is expelling him from his land' (Laclau and Mouffe 1985: 125).

Palestinian-Israeli relations were by definition antagonistic because of the axiom underlying the main currents of Zionism, clearly expressed in Golda Meir's famed assertion that Palestine was 'a land without a people for a people without a land'. In the system mobilised by those terms, it is impossible to have a 'Palestinian' identity. The discourse created a relation of subordination between Israeli and 'Arab' within the Israeli system, but that system was antagonistic to — and antagonised by — any assertion of collective 'peoplehood' by the Palestinians.[23] Thus, as long as Palestinians were not 'Palestinians' (i.e., a people) but 'Arabs' — a subordinate and stateless group with no inherent link to the specific territory the Israelis were claiming as their own, they could be tolerated as labourers within a Zionist state. However, as they increasingly began to assert their rights to maintain their hold on the land they were perceived as antagonistic to the state-building project and were subjected to various forms of violence, ranging from expropriation and expulsion through to assassination and — with the 1982 Israeli invasion of Lebanon to destroy the PLO — extermination.[24] A

---

other discursive articulations which act from outside it' (Laclau and Mouffe 1985: 146. n. 20)

23. This positioning is demonstrated by Rabbi Aviner of the Gush Emunim settlers' movement who writes 'the sons of Ismael among us have a right to live on the land, but, needless to say, this is true only on condition that they accept the Kingdom of Israel, agree that political sovereignty belongs to the People of Israel, and are prepared to be loyal and obedient citizens of the state. As Maimonides says: "They must not raise a head in Israel, but be submissive under hand"' (quoted in Karpin and Friedman 1999: 42).

24. See *Land and Power* (Shapira 1992) on the ideological redefinition of the Zionist project in the face of resistance, and the Israeli revisionist historians (Morris 1987; Morris 1990; Pappe 1992) on its translation into practice in the foundation and consolidation of the

mutual antagonism between the two peoples thus came into play which served to strengthen and focus nationalist identities amongst Israeli and Palestinian populations. 'Israelis', be they secular or *haredim*, *Ashkenazi* or *Sephardi*, 'white' or 'black', were consolidated as a unitary people against the threat posed by 'Arabs' while, as I've outlined above, Palestinians were forged into a cohesive national and nationalist bloc by the collective threat they perceived as coming from the Israeli other. I have examined elsewhere the historical evolution of an explicitly Palestinian identity in which strong collective identities are set up 'defensively' in response to what is perceived as a threat to a community whose borders are precisely defined by that threat (Bowman forthcoming).

In Beit Sahour a local example of that wider process had been visible in the period leading up to and through the first years of the *intifada*. However, by the time Faez Qumsiyyeh confessed to the killing of Basem Rishmawi, the consensus of the townspeople on Israel's antagonism had been eroded not only by factionalisation within the community but as well by the sense of many that the establishment of the PNA was the first move in an inexorable progression towards Palestinian statehood. That perception of the Authority transformed the Israeli state from a force which had the disallowance of a Palestinian state and people as its *modus vivendi* to another player in the arena of international politics which, rather than being antagonistic to the Palestinians, was in fact engaged in mutually beneficial contractual relations with the entity which represented them. 'Palestinian' — when no longer the marker of a domain at risk but instead the collective label of those gathered within the embrace of a territorially defined state — loses its defensive salience, and new articulations of identity, spawned by new perceptions of antagonism operating *within* the Palestinian community, rather than *against* that community as a whole, begin to emerge. In such a context the 'second death' of Basem Rishmawi would be understood, and acted upon, in ways which differed very substantially from those which followed his 'first death'.

The most significant difference between the knowledge which circulated as a result of what I've called Basem's 'first death' and that which followed his 'second' is that while the perpetrators of the 'first' were known to be national 'others' — either soldiers or settlers — those who killed Basem the 'second' time were acknowledged as Beit Sahouris. The devastating implications of that knowledge stands out strongly in the response of one

state. Lustick (1980) is excellent on the attempts to stifle Palestinian consciousness during the early years of the Israeli state.

informant to my query as to whether some member of the victim's extended family might in turn kill one of the killers: 'no one in Beit Sahour kills others in Beit Sahour' (16.4.98).[25] The fact that the second killing showed precisely that Beit Sahouris could kill Beit Sahouris not only invalidated that adage but threatened as well to dissolve the collectivity that was Beit Sahour.

The description of Basem's killing which circulated rapidly through the community was particularly ugly. A car had pulled up next to Basem, apparently to offer him a ride as protection from the poor weather. As he got in he was quickly overcome and bound with wire by the three men inside — Faez Qumsiyyeh, Faez's cousin Sammer, and an unnamed man, a Muslim — who then drove him into the valley within which his body was later found where they tortured him. The torture was, according to those who spoke of it, not motivated by any desire for knowledge but by a combination of sheer sadistic pleasure and the fact that Sammer Qumsiyyeh felt that Basem had once slighted him. Basem was beaten and his face, arms and body were burned with cigarettes. He was then non-mortally stabbed in his stomach, arms and legs, and was finally chained — conscious — to the rear bumper of the car and dragged along the road. Finally, after between three and four hours of abuse, he was fatally stabbed. The disposal of the body in the rubbish dump was not merely practical; it was an intentional gesture of degradation and shaming (19.12.97 and other locations).

It is difficult to tell where the details laid out in the above story originated; it seems unlikely that Faez — except under extreme duress — would have divulged such information in a confession. The source most commonly attributed for them was a file alleged to have been left behind by Israeli security when they turned the Police Station in Bethlehem over to their Palestinian successors. The file, clearly labelled 'Basem Rishmawi', indicated that the three men, under instructions from Bishara Qumsiyyeh — Sammer's father — had kidnapped and executed Basem because of Basem's association with *Fateh*. The file is alleged to have supplied details of the torture and the killing, and is as well supposed to have recorded the Shin Bet's recovery of the body and the way the body was subsequently mutilated with an explosive device to make it appear as though Basem had been killed preparing a bomb.[26]

25. I was told in 1994, before the 'second death', that 'no Christian or Muslim has ever been killed by another here' (21.7.94).
26. Persons I interviewed who were involved in 'official' negotiations between the Qumsiyyeh and Rishmawi families, and can therefore be assumed to have access to the most authoritative details, denied the vivid details of this version, attributing them (and

Whether or not the file existed or simply serves as a means of providing the circulating stories with verisimilitude, there was no question of Bishara Qumsiyyeh's involvement in the case. Bishara Qumsiyyeh had been leader of the Bethlehem region 'Village League'[27] throughout the 1980s, and under his direction an Israeli-armed 'militia' made up of thugs and criminals had imposed a reign of terror on Beit Sahour as well as on neighbouring sites of nationalist sentiment such as Bethlehem University. Although — prior to the time when the narrative of Basem's second death began to circulate — it had been believed that League members had never killed Palestinians, the League was well known for collaboration and for acts of intimidation such as the breaking up and spraying with machine gun fire of the premises of the Arab Orthodox Club in the late 1980s. One of the great victories of the *intifada* had been Beit Sahour's defeat of the Village League's power over the community; a number of people proudly told me the story of the community forcing Bishara Qumsiyyeh, in March 1988, to stand at the pulpit of the Orthodox Church, in front of a capacity crowd, to confess his previous collaboration with the military government and to renounce all further association (various dates in January 1990). From that point on he was considered neutralised and had, until the time of the 'second death', remained isolated from the community behind the walls of the large, pill-box protected, house from which he had previously ruled.

Basem Rishmawi's murder had fitted the Village League agenda perfectly. Although friends had earlier hinted to me of a panicked dispersal into exile of a local *Fateh* cell after Basem's death (16.12.97), it was not until this year that I was told straightforwardly that Basem had, six months before his

the file) to unverifiable gossip. Tellingly, when I asked people who attributed the story to the found file why Israeli Security would have left behind such a self-condemning report they answered with variations on one man's succinct answer - 'to tear us apart' (17.4.98).

27. Formally the *Harakat al-Rawabet al-Filistiniyya* or 'Movement of Palestinian Leagues', the Village Leagues were set up in 1981 after the new Likud government appointed the orientalist Menahim Milson head of the new Civil Administration of the West Bank. The Village Leagues were patronage structures, put in place by the Civil Administration, which simultaneously functioned to mediate between the military government and local communities (providing services which the latter considered most vital, such as family reunion permits, travel permits, driving licenses, jobs in the civil service, building permits, abrogations of house demolition orders, intercessions on behalf of jailed relatives, and reductions in prison sentences) and to organise and run proxy military units dedicated to the destruction of the PLO and the intimidation and closure of institutions providing civil alternatives to Israeli structures of governance (Tamari 1983, see also Aronson 1990: 248-53).

murder, broken with the Palestine People's Party (Communist) to join *Fateh* (telephone interview: 14.1.99).[28] It was furthermore believed that he had received military training in guerilla camps in Syria during a subsequent supposed family visit to Jordan (14.1.99, 13.3.99).[29] It is not immediately clear, therefore, why Beit Sahouris did not simply assess the killing as an expression of past Israeli-Palestinian antagonism. It was certainly known that the Village Leagues had worked as extra-legal extensions of Israeli rule, and the role of the military in returning the body evidenced its involvement in the murder. Despite these clear indicators that Basem had been executed fourteen years earlier by agents carrying out an explicit Israeli policy of eliminating PLO operatives in the Occupied Territories, the town took the killing as very much an intra-communal concern.

The town had, in effect, been given no choice. The Palestinian officials who had overseen Faez's confession refused to try Faez and his accomplices for collaboration and murder, and instead instructed the Rishmawi and Qumsiyyeh families to settle the case between them by *Atwah*, or tribal law (16.12.97). Although it is likely unprovable, many Beit Sahouris believe the Palestinian judiciary was prevented by unpublished agreements behind the Oslo Accords from prosecuting former collaborators whom Israel felt were important enough to be put under its protection (13.12.97). Bishara Qumsiyyeh had been named in the confession and would inevitably have been implicated in any trial of Faez and his accomplices had such a trial been allowed to proceed.[30] Since the Rishmawi and Qumsiyyeh families knew of Faez's confession, informants assumed that the Palestinian Security Force knew the only way quickly to quiet the case and its dangerous ramifications was to hand it over to them, through the medium of tribal law, for extra-judicial settlement. The police wanted the case closed quickly, and they intervened at several points during the subsequent negotiations to insist that rapid progress be made towards an amenable settlement (16.12.97). At one point, when they feared the Rishmawis were intent on preventing a settlement, they arrested Basem's brother and another Rishmawi and beat

---

28. There remains substantive variation in the accounts; one man, who claims he was Basem's best friend, says Basem joined the DFLP rather than *Fateh* (13.3.99).

29. It is unlikely that this would have been known to anyone other than fellow cell mates (and Israeli military intelligence) prior to the establishment and consolidation of the PNA which rendered the knowledge safe for surviving cell members.

30. One informant told me that no formal record of Faez's confession was kept and that his and Sammer's arrests were legitimated by charges distinct from anything relating to Basem's murder (11.3.99).

them badly in order to let the family know they would not tolerate further extension of the case (telephone interview, 14.1.99; fieldnotes, 15.3.99).

The problem posed to the town of Beit Sahour by the case being handed over to tribal law, rather than being pursued under 'general law', is that the categories involved in the former are collective whereas the latter deals with individuals. *Atwah*, or tribal law,[31] is designed to negotiate the payment of blood money in cases of inter-group rivalries so as to effect a reconciliation between two groups forced into hostilities by the actions of individual members. However Emrys Peters, articulating the logic of blood money negotiations among the Cyrenaica *badu*, shows that homicide 'within' corporate groups initiates processes leading to the groups' dissolution:

[c]orporate identity is conceptualised as 'one bone' or 'one body'. An offence against one of its members is held to be an offense against all; if one of its members is killed 'we all lose blood'. Blood money, when received, is shared by all save for a special portion reserved for the 'owner of the blood', the nearest agnate of the victim. In opposite circumstances, all adult males accept the responsibility of con-tributing an equal share to the blood money... Homicide within the *'amara dam* [the corporate group referred to above] brings about an impasse in relationships. A blood money payment is out of the question since the acceptance of blood money by one part of a tertiary section from another of its parts is tantamount to a statement of split (Peters 1990: 61, see also 107).[32]

Before and during the *intifada* a conception of communal identity had evolved within the town which was not far from the corporate identity of 'one bone, one body' Peters describes, and in 1995 people were not yet ready to discard openly that view of communal solidarity. Beit Sahour, despite the changes effected since the early days of the tax strike, still saw itself in terms

31. The details of procedure and terminology in tribal law pertaining to murder are laid out comprehensively in Aref el-Aref's *Bedouin Love, Law and Legend* (El-Aref 1944: 86-115) which is based on his work among the Beersheba *badu* in the 1930s. Hilma Granqvist gives a wonderfully detailed description of traditional dealings with matters of unnatural deaths in the 1920s in the village of Artas, which borders on Beit Sahour (Granqvist 1965: 110-132). The implications of the feud amongst segmentary North African Bedouin is examined in 'Aspects of the Feud' (Peters 1990: 59-83) while both Cohen (Cohen 1965: 139-145) and, more recently, Ginat (Ginat 1987) describe and analyse blood disputes in Israel/Palestine. The classic study of Mediterranean feuding is, of course, *Cohesive Force* (Black-Michaud 1975).

32. Beit Sahouris claim to be descended for the most part from Bedouin stock, and, while not fully analogous to those of the pastoral nomadists studied by Peters, Beit Sahouri concepts of kin relation and blood money are quite similar (see below).

very much like those of the 'amara dam Peters discusses, and the Basem
Rishmawi case was to prove radically threatening to that image of community. To handle the case in the manner that the PNA authorities
demanded was to risk tearing Beit Sahour's social fabric in two.

Relations within Beit Sahour — particularly amongst the Christian families
— were very tightly imbricated, and although one could distinguish
nominally between a number of distinct *hamulas* (and within each of them
between individual *'ailahs*, or constituent extended families) the interrelations
between these corporate groups were formally and informally dense. While
any murder of Beit Sahouri by Beit Sahouri would be potentially explosive
in a town of approximately 11,000 in which almost all persons belong to one
of six *hamulas*, the murder of a Rishmawi by a Qumsiyyeh was particularly
divisive insofar as both are *'ailahs* of the al-Qazaha *hamula* (to which 40% of
the town's population belongs) and both families are almost exclusively
Greek Orthodox (the religious community to which two thirds of the town's
population is affiliated). Were extended family loyalties to be maintained a
wedge would be driven through the midst of one of the town's two major
clans and, insofar as intermarriage between members of the two *'ailahs* is not
uncommon, nuclear families would be riven as well. Furthermore, although
parallel cousin marriages continue to occur in Beit Sahour, marriages
between Christian families will often not only cross *hamula* boundaries but
also knit together couples (and thus families) across sectarian divides.[33] As
people pointed out to me, almost every Christian in the town, with the
possible exception of some of those who came — or were descended from
those who came — to Beit Sahour as refugees in 1948 and after 1967,[34] were
related in some way (directly, or through ties of god-parenthood, or both) to
both the Qumsiyyeh and Rishmawi families. The children of one of my
primary informants (who was of the Al-Jaraysah clan) were god-parented by
Rishmawis, while his brother's children were god-parented by Qumsiyyehs.

33. A Catholic informant told me: 'It is standard practice to take daughters from the
    Orthodox and return them to the Orthodox....In the past this was forbidden by the
    churches and an apostate was excommunicated, but this has changed and women,
    having switched religions, will often come back to their family's church after death or
    separation. The children, on the other hand, are raised in the religion of the father's
    family' (4.4.98). This arrangement, while not prescriptive, is quite common. Christian-
    Muslim marriages are extremely rare, and usually only involve Beit Sahouris 'outside'
    in the international Palestinian diaspora (but see below for a recent case and its conse-
    quences). Geertz 1979 explicates the logic and function of parallel cross-cousin
    marriage.
34. 376 households out of a total of 2306 (data collected December 1997).

A crisis leading to a feud between Rishmawis and Qumsiyyehs would impede if not block the operation of a number of kin and patronage networks linking Christian Beit Sahouris across a multitude of fields. Not only would the family networks detailed above be disrupted, but a feud would divide the Orthodox community, which currently shares a single church. A dispute between two important 'ailahs , representatives of which occupy many of the important positions in the Arab Orthodox Club, would render that forum for intra-communal sociality and decision at least temporarily inoperative and subsequently less representative. Finally, as I will discuss below, the involvement of the third man — who no one would name and many would not even indicate was Muslim — threatened to open a rift between Muslims and Christians which might prove catastrophic for a town with a minority Muslim population sited in the midst of a predominantly Muslim area.

As a result, when news of the 'second death' first circulated through the town and negotiators for the families of Faez and Sammer Qumsiyyeh[35] approached the Rishmawis in their diwan to state their clients's responsibilities and to request a truce so that negotiations over blood money could be initiated, a number of moves were made by townspersons and community organisations to bridge the gaps prised open by the violence of the events.

One of the first moves made was the renunciation of Faez Qumsiyyeh (and by implication the entirety of his immediate family) by the elders of other Qumsiyyeh families in the town and their reiteration of their 1988 rejection of the family of Bishara and Sammer.[36] Although El-Aref, in his study of tribal law, claims that such renunciations 'must have taken place well in

35. Although the murder had happened fourteen years earlier, the adult males of Faez's and Sammer's immediate families went into hiding since they - at least according to the rules of tribal law - were liable to vengeance killing by Rishmawis until the terms of a truce were reached (as long as, in the terms of Cohen's informants, 'the grave of the victim is still open' Cohen 1965: 139). Faez and, by then, Sammer were in prison (and Bishara was in Israeli-controlled Jerusalem), but the other adult males in their families were theoretically vulnerable. Haddad points out that all males from the killer's clan who are over twelve and not elderly are vulnerable to attack (Haddad 1920: 105), but in the Beit Sahouri instance the passionate renunciations of the act by other Qumsiyyehs were understood to absolve them of involvement. Furthermore, the ethos of the town militated against anything more than mere formal observance of the rituals of atwah.

36. Such a declaration by members of the extended 'ailah of their 'innocence' of, that is non-implication with, the killer is called i'l_n bar_'a (see Cohen 1965: 144, n. 1). Among the Bedouin with whom El-Aref worked it is called tulu' (El-Aref 1944: 88).

advance of the murders...[and] cannot be resorted to following a murder as a means of lessening the field on which vengeance can be taken' (El-Aref 1944: 87-88), Cohen in his discussion of the operation of tribal law in Palestinian villages within Israel in the late 1950s points out that in cases where persons are understood to have acted from clearly personal motives rather than in terms of any which can be seen as familial (he is, admittedly, here discussing the less significant case of adultery) responsibility will devolve to the individual involved (Cohen 1965: 139, n. 7). Four decades later, in the context of a town self-consciously organised in modernist terms (one man told me that 'since the early sixties we had been working to diminish the authority and influence of the *hamula*' [14.1.99]), it was generally held to be inconceivable that anyone other than a 'psychopath' (15.1.99) would think of taking vengeance on the families of the killers. Form was, nonetheless, followed, and the delegations approaching the Rishmawi elders to sue for peace did not include Qumsiyyehs but were composed of spokesmen from other Sahouri families through which the implicated Qumsiyyeh families had chosen to speak. The guarantors elected by the two Qumsiyyeh families confessed the guilt of their respective clients and promised that an agreement on blood money payment would be reached; in response elders from the Rishmawi family guaranteed that no revenge murder would be committed.

The response of the Rishmawis, who had gathered to hear the Qumsiyyeh admission of responsibility, was far from unanimous; questions of who would negotiate the settlement and what sort of settlement it would be had to be worked through. The Rishmawi *'ailah* is large, and the salon was crowded with representatives of the many households of which it was composed. Discussion went on far into the night over how the case was to be defined. The division effectively lay between two camps. One, which contained many of those who had been active participants in *intifada* mobilisation, said the killing of Basem had been a political act carried out against 'the nation' and should therefore be negotiated by 'the national front' — that is by a committee made up of representatives of the political parties active in the town. The other position was that of two groups with distinct agendas which nonetheless could both be satisfied by making the matter a family affair. One of these — the largest — was composed of family members who were simply concerned to ensure that Basem's family got the greatest possible settlement out of the negotiations. Basem, as the eldest son, would have been the chief support of his parents who had — since his death — been virtually impoverished by his father's subsequent non-fatal stroke. While a settlement between the Qumsiyyehs and a bloc made up of the national parties would serve to 'build bridges' and thus to end the threat of factionalisation within the town, it would result in only a nominal payment of blood money and therefore leave Basem's family little better off than it was at present. While the 'bridge-building' option was clearly the course the PNA authorities had wished the case to follow, it was argued against power-fully by many representatives on 'humanitarian' grounds (14.3.99), although, it is important to note, many of this 'party' would have preferred to see the matter settled both within a national idiom and with a satisfactory payment to Basem's family. The other party in the 'anti-national' bloc was that of the traditionalists, and although this was neither a popular nor a powerful position it was held by several of the old men who felt their authority had been eroded through the years of popular mobilisation. They simply wanted things done 'properly' after the long years of innovation, and were anxious to prevent yet another 'coup' by the political forces which had usurped power which they felt belonged in the hands of the community's traditional leadership.

As it was, this latter group 'settled' the issue by taking it out of the hands of the family. After a long night of unresolved argument, one or more of its members drove to the neighbouring Bedouin village of Ta'amra and reported there to the elders who traditionally would have been those approached to serve as *qudaa* (judges) that those elders had been insulted by the national bloc within the Rishmawi family. The old men (or *hatta* as one of my informants called them with derogatory and metonymic reference to the head coverings they traditionally wear) insisted that they were owed an apology, implying that without one they would not in future be available as *qudaa* for Beit Sahour. When this was reported to the representatives of the national grouping the next morning the group walked out of the negotiations in disgust.

Thus a discursive shift was effected whereby it became impossible to deal with the case directly in national political terms. Ironically, despite the fact that the affair had in effect been translated into the traditional familial idiom, the entirety of the community — including all the Beit Sahouri Qumsiyyehs not in the nuclear families of Faez and Sammer — remained mobilised in opposition to those implicated in the killing. The problem remained an explicitly political issue in Beit Sahouri eyes despite the fact that the machineries of presentation and negotiation which had been brought into play necessitated that it be dealt with as though it were an issue between two *'ailah* (family groups). Over the next several days men representing various non-familial collectivities in the town (the Orthodox Club, the various political parties, the churches, the unions, the scout groupings, and so on) met with the Rishmawi family's elders to familiarise them with the implications of the case for their groups, for the town, and for the national cause in general. In addition, one man — both a Beit Sahouri and a senior member of the PNA's Southern Region 'intelligence service' (*muhaabaraat*) — met at several points with the Rishmawis to inform them as to what the National Authority wanted to emerge from the negotiations.

One of the reasons for the escalating anxiety as the conditions for the *sulha* (reconciliation ceremony) were being discussed was fear that the amount of blood money the Rishmawis would demand might prove to be so high that the Qumsiyyeh families would refuse to pay it, thus instigating the breakdown of the truce and the imminence of feud. *Atwah*, tribal law, is — rather than a coercive system grounded in state power — a system of reconciliation grounded on the assumption that those who embrace it consider continued sociality to be more important than the occasional expenses accrued in maintaining it. Blood money payments ensure peaceful relations between groups placed in a state of potential war by an act of violence, and serve not only to disarm the warring groups by establishing emergent commensality between them but also to bind those groups by formal ties of obligation until these are replaced by other less onerous ties. As Peters points out in his work on the Libyan Bedouin, the initial payment at the *sulha* should be mutually agreeable, producing a context in which

the two hostile groups [can be] brought together again for the first time, [showing] that the cleavage between them has been narrowed sufficiently to permit them to eat round one bowl, and that, by virtue of this commensal meal, the way is (...) opened for the restoration of normal relationships. (Peters 1990: 64)

Peters furthermore indicates that the promise of a further amount to be given to the victim's family is made at this time, but notes that neither a schedule of fixed payment dates nor a quantification of how much will be paid at each installment is made. The agreement is that within a fixed time (usually three to five years) the remaining debt will be paid off. In fact, in most instances, after a year or so the debt begins to be deferred and reduced so that in time obligations to pay off blood money are gradually 'forgotten' and replaced by less onerous bonds between the families:

the payment of a debt in full means only one thing — hostility. 'Where there is no debt, there are no relationships.' Debt must be allowed to run between groups, for it is this which creates obligations and perpetuates social relationships. As the debt of blood money mounts, the social relationships between the groups improve. The cessation of payments and the absence of further demands are final, earnest that the relationships are again normal' (Peters 1990: 65, also 170 on the eventual replacement of debt for the bridewealth accompanying a bride given by the killer's family to that of the victim).

In the Beit Sahouri instance the intervention of extra-familial groups who considered the case in terms of the interests of wider communities was pro-voked by awareness of the severity of the crime (involving not only torture and the fatal spilling of blood but as well the intentional dishonouring of the corpse) as well as of the extremely long delay between the time the crime was committed and the time when the delegations from the families of Faez and Sammer Qumsiyyeh approached the Rishmawi salon. While the cal-culated infliction of pain and humiliation rendered the crime more heinous than either an undeliberated act of passion or, as is often the case behind blood money negotiations, a simple accident,[37] the long delay between when the murder was carried out and when its perpetrators confessed (or, as many suspected, were forced to confess) made it plain that the commitment of the perpetrators to peace with the Rishmawis was at best pragmatic (14.3.99). It was clear to all participants that the spirit of desired reconciliation which should bring about the working of *atwah* was absent on the part of the Qumsiyyehs, and the well-grounded fear of those who knew the implications for the wider Beit Sahouri community was that the Rishmawis would respond in kind with a demand for what would, in effect, be full compen-sation for the loss and dishonouring.[38]

37. Cohen (1965: 68-71) and Granqvist (1965: 117-23) provide examples of accidental deaths necessitating negotiations and payments.
38. Traditionally the representatives of the offender approach the family of the victim as soon as possible after the transgression, thus indicating not only a desire to prevent vengeance but also to re-establish balance in the community. In such cases the miscreant's willingness to put himself (or be put by his kin) in the hands of those he has rendered enemies (in one of Granqvist's examples a killer presents himself to the armed relative of his victim saying 'I am the meat and thou art the knife' [Granqvist 1965: 123]) is countered by the victim's family's respective sacrifice of prestige in their openness to making an arrangement. Black-Michaud points out that 'the victim's group, whose sacred duty it was to avenge their kinsman's death..., were, by accepting arbitration, diminishing somewhat their stature in the eyes of public opinion by this willingness to procrastinate for motives of a material nature" (Black-Michaud 1975: 92). Several among the Rishmawis - already committed to accepting compensatory blood money by agreeing to negotiations - argued that as there was no good will in the Qumsiyyeh approach the only honourable recourse was a demand for compensation sufficiently large to stand as a compensatory act of violence (12.3.99).

On the night of the *sulha*, which took place in the hall of the Greek Catholic convent, the 'whole town' gathered because 'everyone — even [other members of the Qumsiyyeh] family — had suffered badly under the league' and all were concerned about how the affair would be resolved (14.3.99, 15.3.99). The meeting was convened under the jurisdiction of a noted *sheikh* from Hebron, a major Palestinian city twenty miles to the south of Beit Sahour, who had been chosen to act as *qaadi* (judge) by the Rishmawis with the agreement of the representatives of the Qumsiyyehs.[39] The size of the meeting, its public character, and the prestige of its arbitrator were all unusual, as was the character of the negotiations. Usually, as one of my informants told me, the arbitration was simple, quickly effected, and, finally, convivial:

normally, even when a person was killed, the killer's representatives would go to the family of the person killed, apologise profoundly (how can you refuse when the old men are humbling themselves and the entire family is putting itself in your debt?...) and then work ritually through 'we need a million shekels', then 'and here is 100,000 for Mohammed and 100,000 for Jesus' until there was nothing to be paid. This is about goodwill and needs to be done within three days at most (14.3.99).[40]

Here, however, the good will was lacking. The Rishmawi family made an initial demand which, while high, would have allowed a series of reductions to a price which was more easily payable, particularly for Faez's family which — unlike Sammer's — was not well off. In response, however, the Ta'amri representatives of Faez's family and those negotiators speaking for

39. His reputation and provenance testify to the importance with which the local community viewed the case. His religious status is analogous to that of other blood money arbitrators such as the Cyrenaican *marabtin bi'l Baraka* (Peters 1990: 64) and the Berber *igurramen* (Gellner 1969). The victim's family choses the *qaadi* but the perpetrator's family must agree the choice and pay wages and expenses.

40. The delicate balancing of the requirements of status and the pragmatics of payment are clear in Granqvist's description of the negotiation following an accidental killing involving families from Artas and from the Ta'amre: 'In this special case the blood money demanded was 100 liras (pounds) which was high enough to allow bargaining ... 45 pounds was deduced: 10 for the sake of God, 15 for all the saints and the prophets, 10 for Mohammad il-Zir [the arbitrator], and 10 for those present — the men. It was still too high a sum however... And the Ta'amre women refused to eat of the food... For the sake of the women who refused to eat of the food, a further five pounds was deducted. By these deductions they finally came down to fifty pounds... And the Ta'amre people paid the 50 liras... and they ate and made merry' (Granqvist 1965: 122-23, see also Haddad 1920: 107).

Sammer and Bishara made a counter offer which was ludicrously low for intentional murder (i.e., 9000 Jordanian dinars). This form of bargaining breached convention and threatened the negotiations with breakdown, but it was eventually bridged by the interventions of those same extra-familial spokespersons who had earlier discussed the case with the Rishmawis during the preparatory period. A final agreement was eventually reached (and approved by the *qaadi*) that the families of the killers would each pay 20,000 Jordanian dinars[41] as a first payment with subsequent payments to be arranged and made at later dates adding up to no more than 18,000 further dinars. Faez's negotiators spoke with his father and returned to announce his agreement. Those who spoke for Sammer left the hall to relay to Bishara the *qaadi's* decision and returned a few minutes later to announce that Bishara had said that Sammer had been forced to confess by beating, that he'd not been involved, and that they would pay nothing (14.3.99 and *passim*).

The immediate response was one of near universal outrage. The delegation appointed by Bishara which had initially approached the Rishmawis, as well as the appointed negotiators who had subsequently spoken for Bishara and Sammer in the debates, had repeatedly admitted that the family accepted guilt and its responsibility for making blood payments. The last moment renunciation broke the truce, and while some of my informants said the *qaadi* anounced that any Rishmawi had the right to kill any of the males of Bishara's immediate family (14.3.99) others claimed there was no need to announce blood vengeance when the deal was refused since everyone took it for granted (15.3.99). *En masse* the crowd — including other Qumsiyyehs — broke from the church hall and headed for the house of Bishara and Sammer in order to burn it down. A local man, who lived between the church hall and the Qumsiyyeh house and who worked for the Palestinian security forces, knew that women were living in the house and, fearing they might be killed, hid himself in a field between his house and Bishara's and fired his machine gun in the air. The crowd — assuming Bishara and his supporters were in the house and armed — dispersed, and PNA forces came in to clear the house and ensure the rioters returned to their houses.[42] This

---

41. £17,866 or $28,170 at the September 1995 rate of exchange. This was a relatively low settlement, particularly considering the nature of the crime. It can be compared with a settlement of 12,000 dinars a local factory owner was forced by arbitration to pay one of his workers when his gun went off by accident and grazed the man's neck (15.12.99).

42. The story of the policeman dispersing the crowd was told to me by the man involved (16.12.97 and 19.12.99). Several other people have told me that Bishara was in the house and had fired on the crowd (*passim*).

was the moment when Basem's brother was arrested and beaten.

For the next couple of weeks Beit Sahour settled into an uneasy peace. Arrangements had been reached with the father of Faez Qumsiyyeh, and although he was unhappy about having had to sell land in order to pay a substantial quantity of blood money on his own (the other Qumsiyyehs had successfully renounced Faez and therefore cleared themselves of responsibility), there was no feud between his family and the Rishmawis. Bishara, from his sanctuary in Israel, sold his house to the husband of his daughter, therefore formally protecting it from being damaged in feud vengeance. Sammer was safe in prison although he, like his father, was liable to be killed by any Rishmawi that saw him (18.12.97).[43] No one — see below — spoke of the third man other than to say he was safe in a collaborators' village in Israel. Most, if not all, of the 20,000 dinars was given to the parents of Basem.

Two weeks after the debacle in the church hall Faez died in prison. The official version released by the PNA was that he died of natural causes, but no one in Beit Sahour believed that. The general belief among Beit Sahouris was that Bishara had had him killed in order to lift the onus from his son and, indirectly, from himself (16.12.97, 19.12.97 and *passim*).[44] Another version, that of Faez's father, was that — regardless of who it was who killed Faez, and he implied it was a Rishmawi — Faez's death satisfied the principle of 'blood for blood'; a death had been followed by a death and therefore all debts were off. Faez's father demanded, even before Faez's funeral, that the Rishmawis return his 20,000 dinars (15.3.99).

The Rishmawi response was furious. The negotiations in the church hall had left them substantially slighted, primarily by the initial Qumsiyyeh offer of 9,000 dinars and the violation of ritual that offer effected, but also by the relative smallness of the final agreed settlement. Faez's father's demand for the return of the 20,000 dinars paid was yet more violence against the concept of community which underlay both *atwah* and Beit Sahour: 'the point of blood money is not about the cost of a crime (for instance the medical care

---

43. Formally all the other adult males of Bishara and Sammer's family were also legitimate targets for vengeance killing, but people with whom I talked refused to analyse the situation in terms of tribal rules for vengeance but instead claimed, in the words of one informant, that only Bishara and Sammer were liable to be murdered 'because they have not attempted to resolve the case' (18.12.97).

44. That version is given credibility by the fact that within a week Sammer was released from prison, allegedly because there was no one alive and in reach of the PNA who could testify against him (he had never been formally charged with murder).

of a victim) but about making a statement of apology and reconciliation. Faez's family's demand for the money is an obscenity' (19.12.97). This event, for some of the Rishmawis, was the last in a series of provocations directed towards their family by the Qumsiyyehs. That interpretation — which operated in the idiom of family — effaced the wider political context which had given form to the earlier narratives around the death of Basem Rishmawi and pushed lineage identity to the foreground. Paul Stirling, in a 1960 article treating a feud in a Turkish village, wrote that 'lineages not only protect their members from quarrels, but also tend to encourage quarrels from which they will need protecting' (Stirling 1998: 11). While in this instance (as in any other) it would be difficult to argue that the lineage *per se* was an actor in the evolving difficulties, it was clear that lineage identity did provide a position allowing actors to respond to bewildering or threatening events with a strong and legitimate collective voice. As insult after insult seemed to emerge from the same *'ailah* which had earlier tortured a Rishmawi to death, a number of Rishmawis began increasingly to feel that the killing and the events which followed were neither political nor criminal but antagonistic expressions of one 'lineage' towards another. Although there were others — both within the Rishmawi *'ailah* and outside of it — who continued to struggle against this interpretation by arguing that the events were spawned and fostered by the antagonism of the Israeli state towards the Palestinian people as a whole and towards the townsfolk in particular, their voices began to be rendered inaudible by the growing inter-familial fracas.

One impediment to feud, however, was the presence of a substantial number of Qumsiyyehs in the bloc mobilised against Sammer, Bishara and Faez. Qumsiyyehs had been as much persecuted by the activities of the Village League as had other Beit Sahouris, and one informant in fact told me that Bishara — in the heyday of his powers — had made a particular point of refusing favours to other Qumsiyyehs precisely to show that he was beholden to no one in the town (14.3.1999). For the identity politics of the situation to move totally into the idiom of family and lineage such situationally-drawn delineations had to be effaced, and this erasure was effected during Faez's funeral by one of the Rishmawis (who a nationalist Rishmawi referred to as a 'criminal' [11.3.99]) who photographed all of the Qumsiyyehs who attended and then circulated the 'incriminating' photographs amongst the Rishmawis. According to the photographer, and those who took him seriously, the presence at Faez's funeral of a large percentage of the town's Qumsiyyehs was testimony to the fact that they were loyal to Faez despite having escaped responsibility for his participation in Basem's murder by renouncing him. The photographer's charges seemed to be given even

greater credence by the fact that those Qumsiyyehs who had been osten-
tatiously photographed leaving Faez's funeral were understandably nervous
about attending the funeral two days later of an elderly Rishmawi who had
recently died.[45] Those Rishmawis who were attempting to provoke hostilities
between Qumsiyyehs and Rishmawis were consequently able to claim that
the Qumsiyyehs had chosen to attend the funeral of a Rishmawi killer rather
than to offer condolences to the Rishmawis for the loss of one of their family.
Others in the town were incredulous about the photographer's behaviour
and the positive reception it was given by some of the Rishmawis, asserting
that it was a provocation and that the Qumsiyyehs who had gone to Faez's
funeral had attended not to pay respects to Faez but to offer comfort to those
left living; 'people go to funerals not for the dead but for the living' (16.4.98).

Nonetheless, and despite the fact that not all Rishmawis and Qumsiyyehs
accepted the reconfiguration of the social terrain, the charge served to
constitute two antagonistic camps made up respectively of all Rishmawis and
all Qumsiyyehs. Those Rishmawis who felt that family honour had suffered
in the course of the *Sulha* and what ensued were able, through mobilising a
rhetoric of hostility to 'those' who had humiliated them, to reassert the
strength and honour of the Rishmawis. The members of Faez's immediate
family, who felt resentment about the fact that they had been left to carry the
financial burden of paying off the Rishmawis, in turn found it in their
interest to implicate other Qumsiyyehs in the burgeoning feud with the
Rishmawis so that the 20,000 dinars Faez's father had been forced to pay
would be returned as a consequence either of a strong bloc of kin support
consolidating behind him or because an eventual outbreak of feud violence
would abrogate the terms of the settlement.

Over the subsequent three and a half years, violence has broken out on
several occasions between Rishmawi and Qumsiyyeh youths, and although
to date careful counsel has prevented these eruptions of underlying hostily
from developing into more extensive feuding, nothing has been resolved
(15.3.99 and *passim*). Faez's father continues to demand the return of his

45. Although informants claimed that in the past when the town was smaller all the
inhabitants of the town attended all marriages, baptisms, funerals and the like, it is
now assumed that people 'are required to go [only] to funerals' and that they can treat
the others as family affairs (16.11.93). Although observation shows that now only
friends, families, and members of the same religious community attend funerals, it is
the case that the Qumsiyyeh and Rishmawi families are both affiliated to the Orthodox
Church and that therefore failure to attend each other's funerals was a visible assertion
of division.

20,000 dinars, while the Rishmawi elders continue to assert not only that this demand is a violation of the *Sulha* agreement but also that the failure of Faez's family to make the final payment (*teyba*), programmed into the agreement, means that the reconciliation process has broken down. Things are, in effect, in abeyance, and although no substantial violence between Qumsiyyehs and Rishmawis has broken out and caused the suspended antagonisms to coalesce into open feud, neither has any move by nationalist or trans-familial forces in the town succeeded in breaking the deadlock and restoring commensality between those involved. The Rishmawi-Qumsiyyeh feud, like the Israeli Occupation, has withdrawn into the shadows but is far from forgotten. Both violences underlie the surfaces of everyday interaction within Beit Sahour, and an upsurge of violence from either of the two sites could serve to mobilise the town. If that violence were to come from the occupation — for instance out of serious and threatening confrontations over settler expropriation of Beit Sahouri land on *Jebel Abu-Ghneim* (or, as the Israeli press calls the planned site of a massive new settlement, *Har Homa*) — the town would be likely once again to sublimate its internal divisions and unite to present a consolidated front to a shared enemy. If, on the other hand, a Rishmawi or Qumsiyyeh youth should be badly injured or killed in a fight at school or in the streets, or if one of the Rishmawis were to resolve to take vengeance on a member of Faez's family insofar as the final reconciliation payment (*teyba*) has not been paid, an open feud would erupt within the town which would, at least temporarily, tear apart the structures of sociality which give form to Beit Sahour as a community.

I have attempted, in this long ethnographic account, to show the way in which each moment of sociality holds suspended within it a multitude of possible developments. The 'first death' of Basem Rishmawi articulated, for the majority of inhabitants of Beit Sahour, a model capable of giving shape to a Manichaean world made up of an imagined community and another grouping antagonistic to that community. It also impelled strategies of social consolidation and resistance appropriate to the maintenance of the community it helped to bring into conscious being. What I have attempted to show, however, is that just as the context in which that story circulated was transformed by political and social developments, so too did the meaning of the story shift. Although one might argue that what happened in 1995 was that 'people got their facts right' and therefore a 'true story' replaced a 'false story', what I have tried to show is that the rectification of the 'facts' — the realisation that Palestinian collaborators working for the Israelis killed Basem rather than Israelis themselves — would have had little if any effect had

there not already been a very substantial shift in the perspectives of Beit
Sahouris on issues of politics, identity, nation and community. Within the
terms of nationalist discourse the question of whether an Israeli soldier
following the orders of his superiors kills a Palestinian or whether a
Palestinian collaborator following the orders of his Israeli superiors does the
deed is moot; in each instance the deed is a political assassination carried out
by an agent of the national enemy in accordance with that enemy's plans to
eradicate the nation. That the 'second death' of Basem Rishmawi came
instead to be, for many, an expression of the antagonism of one Beit Sahouri
family grouping for another demonstrates the ascendency of a different
mode of interpretation and the — at least temporary — defeat of the first.
Antagonism, which I have argued serves to construct solidarities amongst
those who perceive it as threatening, came to be seen as inter-familial in the
post-Oslo context, and the ascendency of that idiom 'muted' interpretators
who continued to argue that the real antagonism came from the Israeli state.
That muting, however, was not simply a matter of silencing voices but was
furthermore a matter of engendering situations in which a nationalist
response could be seen to be inappropriate and extraneous.

The hegemonisation of the familial idiom of interpretation and the over-
turning of the nationalist idiom was not a simple matter of will, choice, and
the fickleness of interpreters. Through the details of the story of a story
which I have relayed above we can see the operations of the convoluted logic
of contingency. The contexts within which various interpretations of the
torture and murder of Basem Rishmawi are situated and elaborated are
themselves dense with the accretion of a multitude of other articulations as
well as with the institutional structures (some active, some latent) which
have taken shape as persons in the past and present have used those articulations as models for activities. An event in the process of being interpreted
and being fixed in its meaning by a consensus has — like a pinball dropping
through various channels and rebounding from flippers and barriers — to
'negotiate' a multitude of switching points, and at each of these shifts can be
effected in the way the event is interpreted and in the consequences it will
come to have. If the inequities of power underlying the Oslo Accords hadn't
led to the PNA's vow not to prosecute collaborators..., if the old men in the
Rishmawi family *and* the *hatta* of Ta'amra hadn't been resentful of the undermining of traditional structures of authority..., if Faez hadn't died in prison...,
if the photographer hadn't had the equipment or the will to photograph the
persons at the Qumsiyyeh funeral... things would not have developed as they
did. Some of those 'switching points' are more stable than others; the decision of the PNA to turn the case over to '*Atwah*, or tribal law, inserted the

deliberations on the significance of the case into a traditional structure which could only work with it in familial terms. The translation of the events into the idiom of family which that time-honoured institution had effected can in turn be seen to over-determine the far more idiosyncratic decision of the photographer to extend the borders of the antagonism to the limits of the Qumsiyyeh 'ailah. Although after more and more interpretative decisions are made the range of options which succeeds is substantially reduced, the force of contingency still prevails. In this case there is no way that the analyst, poring over this dense interweaving of interpretations and events, can assess how things will turn out. Although the logic of events has substantially closed down the ways in which the community can negotiate the implications of the murder of Basem Rishmawi, the historic context in which that logic operates still retains the power to transform its course and its meaning. If, in the near future, an Israeli settler or soldier building Jewish homes on the outskirts of Beit Sahour shoots a Beit Sahouri demonstrator things will develop very differently than if, in the course of a normal weekday, a Rishmawi or Qumsiyyeh schoolboy gets caught up in a schoolground argument over a girl and stabs a youth from the other family. Whatever happens — and it may be neither of these — the unfolding of future events will in turn scatter new stories, acts, and interpretations over those which have already been accreting around this event since 1981, and the commingling of these two bodies of stories will in turn engender new events and new configurations of sociality.

Postscript: the third man

Throughout my research into the way Beit Sahouris negotiated the dilemmas thrown up by the murder of Basem Rishmawi, none of my informants would tell me the name of the 'third man' who had been implicated in the killing. It is not that people didn't know who he was, or where he had lived, or where he was at present; it was just that people didn't want to talk about him. Generally, when I would ask for information about him to correspond with the very substantial amounts of information I was offered about Sammer or Faez, I would be told he wasn't important, either because he had lived outside of Beit Sahour in the Bethlehem suburbs or because he had disappeared and therefore couldn't be tried for the crime. Others however had told me, generally in passing, that he was a Beit Sahouri who had lived quite near to Bishara Qumsiyyeh and who had recently been seen living in a collaborator village on the road between Jenin and Afula. If I pointed that out to those with whom I was talking, or suggested that by the rules of

'*Atwah* it didn't really matter whether or not the culprit could be located if his family could, my informants would look uncomfortable and change the subject. The 'third man' was beyond the bounds of the story, and his family had not been called to account in the course of the *sulha* negotiations.

Nonetheless, in time, the salient facts about him began to emerge. One Rishmawi woman, enraged by what she felt was the town's relative indifference to the traumatic significance of Basem's murder (she is the one who told me that when the story came out in 1995 it was as though Basem had been 'killed again'), muttered about 'the PNA's refusal to acknowledge the Muslim-Christian element' (19.12.97). When I pressed her on this she would not elaborate, but later in the same conversation cursed a friend of mine for refusing to tell me 'that the other man was Muslim' (19.12.97). Others, later, acknowledged that the third man had lived within Beit Sahour and was a Muslim (12.3.99 and 14.3.99) but said, in effect, 'no one wanted to follow that up' (12.3.99). I have never been able to collect more information about this man, about whether and why the PNA refused to allow him to be implicated and tried in the case, or about the relations of his family with the rest of the Beit Sahouri community. The only things about him that people, under pressure, were willing to state was that he was Beit Sahouri, and a Muslim.

On the last day of my most recent research visit to Beit Sahour I met briefly with a Beit Sahouri university lecturer whom I knew, and in the course of gossiping he asked me if I'd heard about an episode which had occurred that winter which 'had the whole town in an uproar'? A Beit Sahouri woman — 'a bad woman, but Orthodox' — had surreptitiously married a Muslim man (whose provenance was not proffered, although the location of the place where they lived immediately after the marriage suggests strongly he was Beit Sahouri). When her family found out it was outraged and tried to get her back, but she and her husband fled to Ta'amra where they took shelter with a bedouin family. Elders from her family, along with the town mayor, went to the PNA in Bethlehem to complain and were told by the authorities (who are very sensitive to Muslim-Christian issues) that they had no right to interfere. My informant concluded his story with:

the Sahouris see this as an expression of the threat to them of the Muslims. It used to be that we were separated by the mountains from Obadiya [a neighbouring Muslim village] but now its mosques are on our borders, the Jews are on Jebel abu-Ghneim, and Bethlehem is mixed. Everyone is taking over, and now they are beginning to take the women (15.3.99).

In this discourse Beit Sahour has become a very different place from that described in the speeches reported in the first part of this paper. There, Beit Sahour was a Palestinian village made up of Christians and Muslims who shared in everything, and particularly in their solidarity in the face of the national enemy (who was 'Israeli', not 'Jewish'). Here, on the other hand, 'we — the Sahouris' are Christian and deeply threatened by other religious communities ('Muslims' and 'Jews') who are pressing on our borders from all sides and now, most frighteningly, 'are beginning to take the women'. What is invisible in this discourse is the Beit Sahouri Muslims who constitute a minority population within the borders of a largely Christian town of which the population itself constitutes a minority within the Palestinian nation. The man in this story, who has stolen the daughter of his Christian neighbours and, by marrying her, turned her into a Muslim, is, like the third man in the killing of Basem Rishmawi, the internal trace of an antagonism which Beit Sahouran Christians rarely discuss, and then only as something 'outside'. Neither of them, however, were pressing on the borders from outside; they were already inside, killing Christians and effacing Christian identity.

There is a shadow discourse throughout my notebooks, back as far as my earliest *intifada* work in Beit Sahour, which haunts Beit Sahouri assertions of strong commensality and communality between Muslims and Christians. Christian Beit Sahouris talk — in tones which in 1990 were hushed and somewhat embarrassed yet which, as my chronicle approaches the present day, get more open and assertive — of the threat of the Muslims elsewhere in Palestine, of their covetousness about Christian wealth, of their intolerance for religious and cultural difference, and of the impossibility of coexistence with them. This material was always there just under the surface, but it wasn't dominant and only served to organise perceptions (and assertions) at certain moments — and then only in relation to Muslims outside of Beit Sahour. Even now it is extremely rare to hear a Beit Sahouri Christian say something negative about a fellow townsperson who is Muslim, and when they do it is criticism of particular individuals which link them to a generalised *outside* collectivity (e.g., 'so and so is like a Khalili [Hebronite]'). I have never heard a Beit Sahouri Muslim criticise a Beit Sahouri Christian *as* a Christian.

The unnamed and unpursued 'third man', like the unnamed and unlocalised Muslim husband about whom everyone in Beit Sahour was allegedly talking — but not to me, are reminders of what must not be brought into the open. Although Beit Sahouris have always been Christian Beit Sahouris and Muslim Beit Sahouris, there is a chilling realisation growing increasingly more apparent as the threat of Israeli military dominion appears to recede. Without the presence of 'an enemy who is enemy to us both', forms of self and communal assertion which had previously been sublimated in the interest of asserting solidarity are coming increasingly to serve as 'models of' and 'models for' the social (see Geertz 1973: 93-94). To be reminded that the antagonism between Muslim and Christian which the ideologues of both religions increasingly assert is not simply an antagonism between an inside and an outside but even more saliently an antagonism inside Beit Sahour is to be reminded of the impossibility of community. That counterfactual knowledge is simultaneously known by all, and universally disavowed.

Bibliography

Abed, G. (ed.) 1988. *The Palestinian Economy. Studies in Development under Prolonged Occupation*. London: Routledge.

Aronson, G. 1990. *Israel, Palestinians, and the Intifada: Creating Facts on the West Bank*. London: Kegan Paul International.

Asad, T. 1975. 'Anthropological Texts and Ideological Problems: An Analysis of Cohen on Arab Villages in Israel'. In: *Review of Middle East Studies* I, 1-40.

Black-Michaud, J. 1975. *Cohesive Force: Feud in the Mediterranean and the Middle East*. New York: St. Martin's Press.

Bowman, G. 1986. 'Unholy Struggle on Holy Ground: Conflict and its Interpretation'. In: *Anthropology Today* II, 4-7.

Bowman, G. 1993. 'Nationalizing the Sacred: Shrines and Shifting Identities in the Israeli-Occupied Territories'. In: *Man: The Journal of the Royal Anthropological Institute* XXVIII, 431-60.

Bowman, G. 1994. 'A Country of Words': Conceiving the Palestinian Nation from the Position of Exile'. In: E. Laclau (ed.), *The Making of Political Identities*. London: Verso.

Bowman, G. forthcoming. 'Constitutive Violence and Rhetorics of Identity: A Comparative Study of Nationalist Movements in the Israeli-Occupied Territories and Former Yugoslavia'. *Social Anthropology: Journal of the European Association of Social Anthropologists*.

Cohen, A. 1965. *Arab Border-Villages in Israel: A Study of Continuity and Change in Social Organisation*. Manchester: Manchester University Press.

El-Aref, A. 1944. *Bedouin Love, Law and Legend: Dealing Exclusively with the Badu of Beersheba*. Jerusalem: Cosmos Publishing Company.

Frankel, G. 1994. *Beyond the Promised Land: Jews and Arabs on the Hard Road to a New Israel*. New York: Simon and Schuster.

Geertz, C. 1973. 'Religion as a Cultural System'. In: *The Interpretation of Cultures: Selected Essays by Cliffod Geertz*. New York: Basic Books.

Geertz, H. 1979. 'The Meanings of Family Ties'. In: C. Geertz, H. Geertz and L.

Rosen, *Meaning and Order in Moroccan Society: Three Essays in Cultural Analysis*. Cambridge: Cambridge University Press, 315-92.

Gellner, E. 1969. *Saints of the Atlas*. London: Weidenfeld and Nicolson.

Ginat, J. 1987. *Blood Disputes among Bedouin Rural Arabs in Israel: Revenge, Mediation, Outcasting and Family Honor*. Pittsburgh: University of Pittsburgh Press.

Granqvist, H. 1965. *Muslim Death and Burial: Arab Customs and Traditions Studied in a Village in Jordan*. Helsinki: Societas Scientiarum Fennica: Commentationes Humanarum Litterarum XXXIV: 1.

Haddad, E.N. 1920. 'Blood Revenge Among the Arabs'. In: *Journal of the Palestine Oriental Society* I, 103-12.

Hunter, F.R. 1991. *The Palestinian Uprising: A War by Other Means*. Berkeley: University of California Press.

Karpin, M. and I. Friedman 1999. *Murder in the Name of God: the Plot to Kill Yitzhak Rabin*. London: Granta Books.

Laclau, E. and C. Mouffe. 1985. *Hegemony and Socialist Strategy: Towards a Radical Democratic Politics*. Winston Moore and Paul Cammack (trans.). London: Verso.

Lustick, I. 1980. *Arabs in the Jewish State: Israel's Control of a National Minority*. Austin: University of Texas Press.

Mansour, A. 1988. 'The West Bank Economy: 1948-1984'. In: G. Abed (ed.), *The Palestinian Economy: Studies in Development under Prolonged Occupation*. London: Routledge, 71-99.

Mauss, M. 1969. *The Gift: Forms and Functions of Exchange in Archaic Societies*. Ian Cunnison (trans.). London: Routledge and Kegan Paul.

Morris, B. 1987. *The Birth of the Palestinian Refugee Problem 1947-1949*. Cambridge: Cambridge University Press.

Morris, B. 1990. *1948 and After: Israel and the Palestinians*. Oxford: The Clarendon Press.

Palestinian Central Bureau of Statistics 1999. *Population, Housing and Establishment Census 1997, Census Final Results — Summary: Bethlehem Governate*. Ramallah: Palestinian Central Bureau of Statistics.

Pappe, I. 1992. *The Making of the Arab-Israeli Conflict, 1947-1951*. London: Tauris.

Pena, G. 1984. *Christian Presence in the Holy Land*. Jerusalem: Christian Information Centre.

Peters, E. 1990. *The Bedouin of Cyrenaica: Studies in Personal and Corporate Power*. (Cambridge Studies in Social and Cultural Anthropology). Cambridge: Cambridge University Press.

Robinson, G. 1997. *Building a Palestinian State: The Incomplete Revolution*. (Indiana Series in Arab and Islamic Studies). Bloomington: Indiana University Press.

Schiff, Z. and E. Ya'ari. 1990. *Intifada: The Palestinian Uprising — Israel's Third Front*. New York: Simon and Schuster.

Shapira, A. 1992. *Land and Power: the Zionist Resort to Force, 1881-1948*. William Templer (trans.). Studies in Jewish History. Oxford: Oxford University Press.

Stirling, P. 1998 (1960). A Death and a Youth Club: Feuding in a Turkish Village. Unpublished paper on the University of Kent Anthropology Web Site at <http://lucy.ukc.ac.uk/Stirling/Papers/ADeathYouthClub/>.

Tamari, S. 1983. 'In League with Zion: Israel's Search for a Native Pillar'. In: *Journal of Palestine Studies* XII, 42-56.

CHAPTER 4

A Case of Identities:
Multiple Personality Disorder

Poul Pedersen

'My Dear fellow', said Sherlock Holmes as we sat on either side of the fire in his lodgings at Baker Street, 'life is infinitely stranger than anything which the mind of man could invent. We would not dare to conceive the things which are really mere commonplaces of existence. If we could fly out that window hand in hand, hover over this great city, gently remove the roof, and peep in at the queer things which are going on, the strange coincidences, the plannings, the cross-purposes, the wonderful chains of events, working through generations, and leading to the most outré results, it would make all fiction with its conventionalities and foreseen conclusions most stale and unprofitable' (Doyle 1981: 190f).

These are the famous opening lines of 'A Case of Identity' where Dr. Watson learns that life is stranger than fiction. Multiple Personality Disorder (MPD) might illustrate the master detective's point. Its history is full of queer things and strange coincidences, cross-purposes and wonderful chains of events, and associated as it is with bizarre and terrifying phenomena like sexual abuse, sadistic torture, Satanism, human sacrifice, cannibalism, and alien abduction, it is more scaring than the most repulsive horror fiction. It is, however, an ambiguous example because it questions neat distinctions between reality and fantasy: MPD is real but also made up.[1]

Multiple Personality Disorder (MPD)[2] is a serious mental disease referring

---

1. My discussion of the 'reality' of MPD owes much to Hacking's treatment of the issue (Hacking 1995: 8ff.).

2. The diagnosis of Multiple Personality Disorder was recognised officially by the American Psychiatric Association when it was included in its 1980 edition of the *Diagnostic and Statistical Manual of Mental Disorders* (known as *DSM-III*) (American Psychiatric Association 1980). In the fourth edition (*DSM-IV*) from 1994 MPD appeared under the name of 'Dissociative Identity Disorder [DID] (*formerly* Multiple Personality Disorder)' (American Psychiatric Association 1994). However, most people still use the

to an individual who develops two or more — and often many more — different personalities which recurrently take control over the individual's behaviour. In the United States in the 1980s it took on epidemic proportions, and over the last decade it has become the most controversial type of diagnosis in American psychiatry. Proponents and critics of the diagnosis fight a fierce battle over the reality of the disease. The bulk of the specialist literature 'is strongly biased toward proving its existence as a *real* psychiatric disorder, and much of the rest is devoted to claiming that *it doesn't exist*' (North *et al.*1993: ix, italics added). Proponents claim that the disease is caused by early childhood traumas, most often brought about by sexual abuse (Putnam 1989), while skeptics or critics say that it is either grossly over-diagnosed (Thigpen and Cleckley 1984) or iatrogenic — an artefact of therapy, something made up by therapist and patient (Piper 1997). Recently, further skepticism has been nourished by a number of sensational mal-practice cases against psychiatrists and other therapists who have recovered memories of traumatic childhood abuse in MPD patients who had no such memories before entering therapy. The most spectacular of these cases is — so far — that of Patricia Burgus against Dr. Bennett Braun which was settled out of court with $10.6 million in damages to Burgus. Treated by Braun, she became convinced she had more than 300 alternate personalities as a result of traumatic childhood abuse which included participation in ritual murders, cannibalism, Satan worship, and torture by family members. During therapy she was hypnotised and heavily medicated. She now says that during treat-ment 'reality and fantasy blended together' (FMSF 1997).[3] We should not, however, question the reality of the disease. Even if it is made up, if 'reality and fantasy blend together,' as Burgus said, it is still real. In this perspective, MPD fits well with anthropological notions of culture and identity. They, too, are made up, but are, nevertheless, real.

   This chapter is about the recent cultural history of MPD. I focus on disease dynamics, on the interaction of the disease with its wider social and cultural context. MPD involves a break-down of identity, 'a failure to integrate various aspects of identity, memory and consciousness' (American Psy-chiatric Association 1994: 484), but, paradoxically, it also has an amazing potential for generating identities in its wake. I follow Jenkins in his broad-term definition of identity as 'our understanding of who we are and who

   old name. To avoid confusion over terminology I will in this chapter only refer to
   Multiple Personality Disorder, or MPD, (cf. Piper 1997: 3, n. 1).

3. Before the case was settled, Patricia Burgus (appearing under the name of Anne Stone)
   told the story of her psychiatric treatment, see Ofshe and Watters (1994: ch. 11).

other people are, and, reciprocally, other people's understanding of themselves and of others (which includes us)' (Jenkins 1996: 5). What should be
emphasised here is that identity is about meaning, and as such it is
grounded in the individual's operation of cultural resources. In the present
context the main cultural resources involved in the creating of identity and
meaning are medical and biographical knowledge as it is framed by power
and interests of public and private life.

Medical knowledge has a complex and open-ended cultural potential.
When a new psychiatric disorder is created, says van Praag, 'it starts to live
a life of its own, possibly a dangerous life, at that' (Van Praag 1993: 209).
Likewise Micale has, in his outstanding historical study of hysteria, noticed
that 'once a disease concept enters the domain of public discussion, it
effectively becomes impossible to chart its lines of cultural origin, influence,
and evolution with any accuracy' (Micale 1995: 238f). Scientific, artistic, and
popular theories, images, and ideas become caught up with one another, and
this concoction of ideas, information, and associations forms a cultural
resource pool from which everybody may draw. Where some illness category
is recognised, it is 'deployed through the practical interests of experts, victims and others: as a concrete finding and also as a figuring and a pattern of
conduct through which new social interests emerge' (Littlewood 1996: 3). The
cultural historical study of MPD is the investigation into such dynamic
complexes of coincident cultural phenomena.

MPD — general features

Historically, the first case we may recognise by current standards as Multiple
Personality Disorder is reported by Paracelsus, the Swiss Renaissance physi-
cian and alchemist (1493-1541). It is a hostess of a Tavern near Basel who:

had accused her servants for many months of stealing the daily takings. One day
she found blood on her bedclothes and on the table, where there were also pieces
of broken glass. It then came out that her 'second self' as a sleepwalker pilfered her
own money, which her 'original self' found intact, hidden away in the roof. The
'original self' remembered nothing of this activity (Völgyesi 1966: 16).[4]

---

4. *DSM-IV* lists the main current diagnostic criteria as 1) the presence of two or more
   distinct identities or personality states 2) that recurrently take control of behavior, 3)
   an inability to recall important personal information (amnesia), the extent of which is
   too great to be explained by ordinary forgetfulness (American Psychiatric Association
   1994: 487). There is some confusion about the dating of Paracelsus' case. Bliss 1980,

More detailed accounts appear from the end of the eighteenth century, and though the cases become more frequent in the nineteenth century, it was always — until the 1980s — a rare disease.[5] Before the recent epidemic, most cases were seen in France and the United States in the period 1880 to 1920 after which it virtually disappeared for almost half a century. In the early 1970s the situation was changing. A growing number of cases were reported in the United States, and in 1982 Boor saw an 'epidemic of multiple personality' (Boor 1982: 302). Before 1980 there were less than 300 references to multiple personalities in the professional literature.[6] Since then, 'over 25,000 people have been diagnosed with the disorder' (Pendergrast 1996: 44). Ross, the influential Canadian MPD psychiatrist, claimed in 1992 that the disease was strongly under-diagnosed, estimating that more than two million people in the United States matched the diagnostic criteria.[7] The dramatic increase was followed by an intensive professional and public attention which stimulated still more cases.

Multiple Personality Disorder is first and foremost a Western, or North American, disease. It disappeared from England and France before 1920, and for a long time very few cases were reported outside of the United States and Canada. The first case outside the West was reported in India in 1956 (Alexander 1956). The increasing number of North American cases have been followed by the spreading of the disease to other Western and non-Western countries, and recently it has been found in Puerto Rico, England, Australia, New Zealand, the Netherlands, Norway, Sweden, Switzerland, and Turkey.[8]

Putnam 1989: 28, and North *et al.* 1993: 4, give the impression that it dates from 1646, but that is impossible as Paracelsus died in 1541. The confusion is caused by the authors' careless reading — or perhaps not reading — of Völgyesi 1966: 16, which clearly states that the quotation is from Paracelsus' 'Opera, Strasbourg, 1646; vol. 2, p. 553.' 1646 is the publication year of the source and not the year when the events took place. The first recorded MPD case is, in other words, more than a hundred years older than assumed. Another early candidate could be Benedetta Carlini, the visionary and lesbian nun in Renaissance Italy. Records of her life in the Pescia convent before 1620 suggest MPD (Brown 1986: 202, notes 23 and 24).

5. For the history of the disease, see, for example, Ellenberger (1970); Hacking (1995); Kenny (1981, 1986); Merskey (1992); Mulhern (1994). The most comprehensive bibliography is Goettman *et al.* (1994).

6. Calculated from the figures in Goettman *et al.* (1994: xii).

7. 'One percent of the population fits the [diagnostic] criteria for being a multiple personality,' quoted in Ofshe and Watters (1994: 206).

8. *Puerto Rico*: Martinez-Taboas (1991). *Australia, New Zealand, and England*: Pendergrast (1996); Warwick and Butler (1998). *The Netherlands*: Boon and Draijer (1993). *Norway*: Bøe *et al.* (1993). *Sweden*: Karilampi and Carolusson (1995). *Turkey*: Sar *et al.* (1996).

Multiple Personality Disorder is a highly dynamic disease. It interacts easily with its environment, and symptoms may change and diversify rapidly. In the following account of the main features of the disease I refer mostly to the situation in the late 1980s. The person suffering from MPD is called a 'multiple' or 'host' or 'primary' person, and the personalities 'inside' the multiple are known as 'alters' or 'alternate identities.' A multiple has several alters which at certain times take control over his or her behaviour. They frequently have different names and distinct personal histories, and they may differ in terms of, for example, age, gender, ethnicity, and sexual orientation. Amnesia, lack of memory or 'losing time,' is a recurring problem: the multiple will generally have no memory of the occasions when one or the other alter has taken control, they will be experienced as 'lost time.' This often leaves the multiple in awkward or embarrassing situations. Relations between alters are often marred by competition and conflict which may provoke self-mutilation and suicide. Multiples appear to be highly hypnotisable and especially vulnerable to suggestive influences. Samples show that up to 90% of those diagnosed with MPD are women[9] (American Psychiatric Association 1994: 484-87). The early cases of MPD involved only one or a few alters. Today 'it is no longer unusual for there to be more than 10 alter personalities, and over 100 have been 'discovered' in several cases' (Orne and Bates 1992: 247).[10] In cases with many alters, they appear less distinct and more like identity fragments. Previously, MPD was a relatively benign condition, but now it has become one of the more grim mental illnesses, and 'patients tend to be severely disturbed and dangerously unpredictable: nearly half engage in self-mutilation; close to 50% are alleged criminals; approxi-

Switzerland: Modestin (1992). Takahashi (1990) and Allison (1991) speculate about the presence of MPD in *Japan* and the *Soviet Union*, and Darves-Bornoz *et al.* (1995) ponder why so few are diagnosed in France.

9. The prototype for a multiple in the 1980s is a middle-class white woman in her thirties (Hacking 1995: 33).

10. The psychiatrist Richard Kluft is said to have identified 4,500 alters within one patient (Pendergrast 1996: 150), but the world record no doubt belongs to Richard Seward of the Spring Shadows Glen mental hospital in Houston who 'estimated that Shanley [an MPD patient] had up to 10,000 alters' (Mark Smith in the *Houston Chronicle*, 'Hypnosis Becomes Pivotal Issue in Fraud Trial', 22 October 1998, quoted in <FMS-News@saul. cis.upenn.edu> 22 October 1998). It is not only the number of alters which has changed. Now alters may be infants ('littles'), teenagers ('middles'), males, females, animals, vegetables, dragons. Even Satan has shown up as an alter. Some years ago, Johnson — tongue in cheek — diagnosed a cat with MPD (Johnson 1994). Now a French psychologist is reported to have discovered that Kiki, a chimpanzee, has MPD, see Piper (1998).

mately 13% report committing a homicide; and over 90% have threatened suicide' (ibid.). When multiples some years ago entered therapy they presented a number of non-specific symptoms like depression, anxiety, eating and sleeping disorders, or substance abuse, and the diagnosis was only established after a long time. The average time period 'from first symptom presentation to diagnosis [was] 6-7 years' (American Psychiatric Association 1994: 486). However, Thigpen and Cleckley, veterans in the diagnosis and treatment of MPD, stated in 1984 that patients had come to them with the

desire or belief that they had the illness [...] It seems that in very recent years there has been even a further increase in the number of persons seeking to be diagnosed as multiple personalities — *some patients move from therapist to therapist until 'achieving' the diagnosis* [11] — and similarly, among some patients who ostensibly have the disorder there is a competition to see who can have the greatest number of personalities. (Unfortunately, there also appears to be a competition among some therapists to see who can have the greatest number of multiple personality cases) (Thigpen and Cleckley 1984: 63-64, italics added, see also Thigpen and Cleckley 1954 and 1957).

One should add that therapists, too, competed over the number of alters they could discover in their patients.

MPD is assumed to be the result of repeated trauma in early childhood, almost always involving sexual abuse. The formation of alters is supposed to be the child's way of coping with the particular abuse experience: the events are disconnected, or dissociated, from conscious awareness and passed on to unconsciously created alters which, so to speak, become the carriers of the pain. The alters represent, in other words, repressed traumatic memories of which the patient is unaware. The treatment focuses on the recovering of these memories and on integrating them into the patient's conscious life. The therapist establishes contact to the individual alters, which are 'called out' and made to tell their story about the abuse. This re-living of the traumatic experience is especially painful to the patients, because they knew nothing about the horrifying childhood memories. When all alters have been identified and all repressed memories of the abuse recovered, the treatment seeks to make the alters and the host person aware of each other and to negotiate a *modus vivendi* which will establish a *co-conscious* identity system. Finally, the alters are fused into one identity, the host person, and the patient is 'integrated,' cured (Putnam 1989).

---

11. This is known as 'doctor shopping'.

Etiology

There are two important questions to ask about the MPD epidemic in the early 1980s. One is why it appeared, and the other why the disorder was causally connected to child sexual abuse. The answers are found in the combination of media influence and a growing concern over child abuse.

In America there had been little interest in MPD since the 1920s, but this changed suddenly in 1957 when the psychiatrists Thigpen and Cleckley published the best-selling account of a multiple with three alters, *The Three Faces of Eve*. The same year the book was made into a film which reached a still wider audience.[12] In 1973, another sensational book, *Sybil*, presented the psychiatrist Cornelia Wilbur's work with a young multiple woman who had 16 alters and who had been sexually and sadistically abused by her mother (Schreiber 1973).[13] *Eve* and *Sybil* stirred a new professional and public interest in MPD and provided templates for thinking about the disorder for therapists as well as for patients[14] (Attwood 1978; North *et al.* 1993; Victor 1975). *Sybil*, in particular, had a major influence on ideas about the etiology of the disorder. Since the 1880s MPD had been understood as a 'bizarre' kind of hysteria and like hysteria it was assumed to be caused by psychological trauma (Hacking 1995: ch. 13).[15] Trauma, however, could be the result of any sort of painful event. With *Sybil*, traumatic experiences which might explain MPD were narrowed down to child physical and/or sexual abuse — suggesting a very dark side of American family life. *Sybil* was a single case but it acquired wider and much more general importance because it appeared at a time when the feminist movement was growing and child abuse was being recognised as a frightening national problem in the United States.[16] Most child sexual abuse victims were female and so was the majority of multiples. *Sybil* suggested an association between these two observations, and around 1980 it was considered a causal relationship. One of the first authoritative statements of this new theory of MPD was given by the

---

12. Thigpen and Clegley (1957). The film was directed by Nunnally Johnson and Joanne Woodward played Eve.

13. In 1977 *Sybil* appeared in a TV film version starring Sally Field as Sybil. It won four Emmys and became very popular. Woodward, of *Eve*, played Sybil's therapist (North *et al.* 1993: 117).

14. For an informative account of the media context of MPD, see North *et al.* 1993. On the relation between MPD and fictional literature, see Carroy 1993.

15. '[B]izarre' is Hacking's word (1995: 5).

16. For accounts of the relationship between MPD, child abuse, and the feminist movement, see Hacking (1986, 1991, and 1995).

psychiatrist Richard Kluft at a meeting of the American Psychiatric Association in 1979, six years after *Sybil*:

Multiple Personality is a syndrome which follows child abuse. Most multiples, as children, have been physically brutalised, psychologically assaulted, sexually violated, and effectually overwhelmed. A small number may have only experienced one of these forms of personal desecration (quoted in Aldridge-Morris 1989: 45-46).

In the early 1980s, feminists began to use the word 'survivor' as a general term for a person who had been traumatised by being sexually and/or physically abused as a child (most often involving incest), and it would also include multiples. Modelled on 'Holocaust survivor,' it evoked images of American childhood as a gigantic Auschwitz of patriarchy. Over the next decade there appeared multiple survivors with new and terrible abuse stories about satanic ritual torture performed by international satanic organisations, and about being abducted by aliens and having horrifying experiences in outer space (Mulhern 1991, 1994; Schnabel 1994). The context of trauma and the localisation of evil expanded from the family and society and took on global and intergalactic dimensions.

In the late 1970s the annual meetings of the American Psychiatric Association had workshops on MPD. The first professional newsletter dedicated to the disease appeared in 1979 (Hacking 1995: ch. 3). In 1980 two books added new aspects to the popular ideas of MPD. Michelle Smith and Lawrence Pazder's *Michelle Remembers* associated it with satanic ritual abuse, and Ralph Allison's *Minds in Many Pieces: The Making of a Very Special Doctor* introduced possession and exorcism. It was also in 1980 that MPD was included in the third edition of the *Diagnostic and Statistical Manual of Mental Disorders* (*DSM*, 'the Bible of Psychiatry') of the American Psychiatric Association. Pendergrast points to the economic aspects of the official recognition of the diagnosis. 'Because American insurance companies will pay only for mental illnesses sanctioned by the *DSM*,' he says, 'multiple personalities suddenly became lucrative and acceptable in the United States and Canada. The 1980s witnessed a veritable explosion of MPD cases in North America' (Pendergrast 1996: 43).[17] The first professional organisation, The International Society for the Study of Multiple Personality and Dissociation, was formed in 1983, and in 1983-84 four major professional journals devoted entire issues to MPD. In 1985 a multiple began to circulate the newsletter 'Speaking for

17. On the politics of *DSM*, see Kirk and Kutchins (1992, 1997); Wilson (1993); Healey (1997: ch. 7).

Ourselves,' and the professional journal, *Dissociation*, was founded in 1988 (Hacking 1995: ch. 3). At this time, MPD looked well established. It seemed to have come to stay.

In the 1980s, the causal understanding of MPD was circulated widely outside the specialists' journals and conferences. Millions learned about MPD from watching soap operas and talk shows on TV[18] and the booming genre of self-help books for survivors was particularly efficient in spreading the knowledge to a highly motivated audience. One of the most popular of these is Ellen Bass and Laura Davis' *The Courage to Heal: A Guide for Women Survivors of Child Sexual Abuse* (1988) which — according to Pendergrast (1996: 16) — has sold more than 750,000 copies in three editions. Bass and Davis write:

Virtually everyone who is diagnosed as being multiple has been severely abused — sexually, physically, or psychologically — as a young child. To cope with this trauma, the child blocks the feelings and memories from consciousness and another self, the 'alter', takes over and functions. If there is no chance for nurturing healing experiences, the child continues to split as a way to deal with stress and pain. Over time, the alternate personalities assume an independent existence (Bass and Davis 1988: 424).

The memory wars

In the early 1990s MPD, and in particular recovered memory therapy, was involved in what has been called the 'Memory Wars'. In therapy, a large number of patients recovered previously unknown and unverifiable memories of being sexually abused as children by parents and other close relatives who were subsequently presented with abuse charges. In March 1992 a group of accused parents and university professionals formed the False Memory Syndrome Foundation (FMSF) which informs about the dangers of recovered memory therapy and works in support of people accused on the basis of false memories recovered in therapy.[19] Survivor supporters responded in kind and formed the advocacy organisation 'Silent No Longer'

---

18. North *et al.* (1993) have interesting information about the media influence.

19. 'The FMSF Scientific and Professional Advisory Board', <http://www.FMSFonline.org/advboard.html>. Since 1992 related organizations have been established in a number of countries outside the United States: Canada, Australia, Israel, Netherlands, New Zealand, Sweden, and United Kingdom (FMS Foundation Newsletter (e-mail edition), vol. 7, no. 9, November 1998).

(Lindsay and Read 1995: 850). When the consequences of the diagnosis and treatment became known to a wider public, recovered memory therapy and MPD were associated with personal tragedies, professional scandalisation, and sensational lawsuits involving malpractise, of which the Burgus case is but one example. Critics and sceptics of MPD expect that this will go on for some time and eventually bring an end to the diagnosis. Be that as it may, the present climate *has* influenced the advocates of MPD, as can be seen from recent cautious remarks on recovered-memory therapy (see International Society for the Study of Dissociation 1997; Royal College of Psychiatrists' Working Group on Reported Recovered Memories of Child Sexual Abuse 1997).

The most striking feature of the patients entering therapy is that hardly any of them have dissociated identities or memories of having been abused. This is, however, not surprising, because it follows directly from the disease theory: memories of the traumatic events are repressed, and if there are no signs of alters (the memory keepers), it is just because they are hiding (Piper 1997: 5-7). Absence of symptoms confirms theory and guides therapy. Recovered memory theory is based on the belief that traumatic events must be re-lived and worked through to be integrated into the patient's conscious life. The patient must, in other words, come to remember the repressed memories, which are believed to be stored as faithful and stable records of the events. It is the therapist's job to assist in this memory work. It is significant that recovered memory therapy was developed on the basis of therapists' clinical experience and not on cooperation with memory researchers, because it explains why the assumptions behind the therapy go against almost anything known by modern memory research. To be brief, memory researchers agree that it is *not* the rule that traumatic events are repressed, and it is highly unlikely that repeated abuse could *ever* be repressed. No memory researcher thinks of memories as a fixed imprint on the mind which can be retrieved unchanged after decades of repression.[20] Critics of recovered memory therapy claim that the recovered memories are illusory memories created by suggestion by the therapist. Read and Lindsay (1994: 415) go a step further and refer not only to false memories, but also to 'therapy-induced false beliefs'.

Confidentiality considerations often make it impossible or very difficult to acquire precise knowledge of the therapeutical process. However, a number of studies demonstrate that many therapists are highly suggestive or

---

20. For an excellent state of the art discussion of these issues, see Schacter (1996: ch. 9).

insisting when their patients claim not to have any memories of being abused (Crews 1997; Lindsay and Read 1994, 1995; Loftus 1993; Loftus and Ketcham 1994; Mulhern 1994; Ofshe and Watters 1994; Pendergrast 1996, Read and Lindsay 1994; Showalter 1997).[21] If the patient persists in not remembering, the therapist can rely on a veritable armoury of techniques to trigger memory and to call out the alters: drug supported hypnosis, age regression, visualisation, artwork, dream analysis, and many more (Lindsay and Read 1994). The therapist's probing is helped by the fact that today, 'popular writings have been so fully absorbed by the culture that these too can serve as a source of suggestion that can greatly influence what happens in therapy and outside it' (Loftus 1993: 533). Therapists often recommend that the patients read books like Bass and Davis' *The Courage to Heal* and join support groups where they will be given direct experience of how it is to be a multiple. All this adds up to an aggressive and often highly successful attempt to change the patient's belief system.

The theory and therapy of MPD offer numerous examples of circular reasoning, lack of independence between theory and evidence, loose criteria for diagnosing cases and recognising symptoms, absence of controls for the effects of suggestion and projection, and general inability to confirm or falsify patient testimony about childhood trauma (Lynch 1995: 121). Coercion in therapy is well documented (Pendergrast 1996: ch. 4), but it would probably not work without the patient's compliance. Many of those diagnosed with MPD are known to be highly hypnotisable and especially vulnerable to suggestive influences, but perhaps more important is the patient's urgent need of explanation, of a sense of meaning in the new phenomena he or she encounters during therapy: the disturbing proliferation of alters, the haunting memories, the break-down of identity. To accept the diagnosis — to accept to be a multiple — is a conversion process. It is to understand one's life course as framed by certain previously unknown events. It is to get a new identity by acquiring a new biography.

21. Following the now defunct criminal fraud prosecution against psychiatrists at the Spring Shadows Glen mental hospital in Houston (see note 10 above), several hundred pages of transcripts of actual therapy sessions have become accessible on the Internet. This material strongly supports previous criticism of recovered memory therapy. The transcripts can be read at this address, <http://www.FMSFonline.org/therapy.html>.

Alternatives

Critics say that MPD is a iatrogenic disorder — an artefact of therapy. Perhaps one should not be too categorical about this. Schacter reports on two cases where MPD 'was evident prior to any therapy' (Schacter 1996: 242). This does not, however, necessarily support the idea that MPD is caused by sexual and/or physical abuse. In fact, there is no convincing evidence for this claim. It is impossible to tell from available data 'whether there is a relationship between sexual abuse alone and MPD, between physical abuse alone and MPD, and between both kinds of abuse together and MPD. That is, the data are consistent with the possibility that sexual abuse has no causal role in the production of MPD' (Read and Lindsay 1994: 419). Present knowledge seems, in other words, to suggest on the one hand that MPD is not always iatrogenic, and on the other that there may be other causes than sexual and/or physical abuse.

If there are no clear answers to the questions of etiology, the situation is no better when it comes to diagnosis. In their critical survey of the literature, North *et al.* (1993: 183) emphasise that '*[c]urrent knowledge does not at this time sufficiently justify the validity of MPD as a separate diagnosis*'(italics orig.). Fundamental assumptions about the disorder are, in other words, not based on firm knowledge, and we should, of course, call for further research. At present, however, we can pay notice to two obvious facts. First, there are extremely few cases of MPD established before the onset of therapy, and, second, the vast majority of cases are diagnosed long after symptom presentation (6-7 years, says *DSM-IV*). How should we understand this? Is it possible that pre-therapy MPD is the 'real' disorder, and that MPD developing after initiation of therapy is iatrogenic? This is probably too crude a distinction, because some multiples, who have a thorough knowledge of the disorder, are known to have 'chosen' MPD as an idiom of distress before they seek treatment. Social and cultural factors may at this early stage play a role in the patient's self-diagnosis, and the disorder may be seen as a result of self-therapy. It is clearly impossible to determine whether a patient is or is not 'contaminated' by media presentations of MPD, but if we allow for the possibility that a few pre-therapy cases are not produced by self-suggestion, we still have a problem with the large number of cases which are first discovered in therapy. If they *are* created by suggestion, how should we understand the therapeutical process and in particular the patient's role? The most fruitful line of research addressing this question was started by the late Nicolas Spanos in the mid-1980s.

Spanos' approach was radically critical, questioning everything about

MPD, diagnosis, etiology, and therapy, but also the fundamental idea of psychology and psychotherapy that present conditions are explained by past experiences. He pursued what he called a 'sociocognitive perspective,' which suggested:

that patients learn to construe themselves as possessing multiple selves, learn to present themselves in terms of this construal, and learn to reorganise and elaborate on their personal biography so as to make it congruent with their understanding of what it means to be a multiple. These patients are conceptualised as actively involved in using available information to create a social impression that is congruent with their perception of situational demands, with the self-understandings they have learned to adopt, and with the interpersonal goals they are attempting to achieve (Spanos, Weeks, and Bertrand 1985; quoted in Spanos 1996: 3).

Multiple identities are established, legitimated, maintained, and altered through social interaction, and neither childhood trauma nor a history of severe psychopathology is necessary for their development or maintenance (Spanos 1996: 4). The dynamics of MPD, and in particular the sudden change in the number and character of alters, are difficult to explain with a theory assuming that alters are symptoms 'caused by past traumas.' Such changes are better understood 'as expectancy-guided, goal-directed displays that change as a function of new information concerning role demands' (Spanos 1996: 302). In Spanos' view patients are troubled persons, but also creative cultural agents who, in Kenny's words, 'have learned to act and interpret their experience in dissociative terms and reconstructed their autobiographies accordingly' (Kenny 1998: 450).[22] Interestingly, some multiples share Spanos' aversion to the abuse argument and its implicit celebration of victimhood, as we shall see shortly.

From disorder to culture

In 1993 Richard Kluft, one of the leading MPD psychiatrists, worried that many patients instead of fighting the disease had turned it into a way of life. He said:

Part of the socially prescribed role of being ill is working to recover and leave your illness behind. We are in a position where many of our MPD patients and some of ourselves are not necessarily bearing this in mind. Instead we are giving licence to

---

22. For a critical response to Spanos sociocognitive approach, see Gleaves (1996).

a lot of MPD patients sitting around learning how to deal with an MPD environment, making MPD friends, talking MPD all day... I think we are giving the
implicit message to many MPD patients that MPD is forever... The wish to be
validated and not to be alone with one's illness is understandable... We all understand the wonderful forces that group cohesion and group membership can bring.
However, it is important to realise that one's commonality should not be to have
MPD, but to get rid of it as soon as possible and to go on with one's life (quoted
in Hacking 1995: 38).

To Kluft and the other MPD psychiatrists, the diagnosis was never an end
in itself. It offered the patient the necessary knowledge with which to go on
with the treatment. If the patient became preoccupied with the newly
acquired survivor identity it was thought of as a transitory phase on the way
to becoming integrated. However, a number of multiples accommodated to
their illness by turning their history as abuse victims, their survivorship, into
a resource for self-empowerment. This was part of a wider recent cultural
movement in North America, 'an emerging 'culture of victimhood' in which
people tend to attribute their problems to the harmful actions of powerful
others rather than viewing them as their own responsibilities' (Lindsay and
Read 1995: 847; cf. Kaminer 1992; Haaken and Schlaps 1991). Schnabel has
suggested that in some cases a claim of child abuse served as 'the medically-
acceptable complaint through which the role of MPD victim is adopted by
a self-victimising individual' (Schnabel 1994: 58). Living the MPD way of life
in an MPD ghetto and nourished by the 'wonderful forces' of group cohesion
and group membership, mentioned by Kluft, the multiple may get a range
of new and attractive social opportunities which will work against efficient
therapy and a return to a pre-MPD life (Schnabel 1994: 59).

I think the most important aspect of Kluft's observation was an implicit
fear that doctors and patients were drifting apart, that the multiples were
walking out on the doctors and setting up quarters in their own therapeutic
communities. This was not exactly what happened in the 1990s — the
development was more complex — but there was among the multiples a
movement towards autonomy which went in two directions. One emphasised
the etiology, that MPDs were victims of incest or other kinds of abuse, and
linked up with other victims under the broad survivor identity, as mentioned
above. The other focused on multiple identity as the most important aspect
of MPD and would eventually question the pathology of multiple personality
and promote a new multiple role, a development which would turn the
disorder into culture. This, again, offered new roles to the multiples. To find
the roots of this development we must go back to the mid-1980s.

High-functioning multiples

Not all multiples are severely disturbed. In the mid-1980s psychiatrists discovered what they called 'high-functioning' multiples. They were individuals 'of high accomplishment whose pathology was extremely well disguised in both their lives and in their clinical presentation' (Kluft 1986: 722). They were often successful professionals who were not aware of their disorder and only wanted psychiatric or psychoanalytical assistance to work through personal problems in their professional or marital life. The therapy resulted in the MPD diagnosis. In 1986 Kluft presented three cases of high-functioning multiples who had all integrated, and he found that given the proper treatment such patients had an excellent prognosis (Kluft 1986: 726).

In the early 1990s appeared a new type of high-functioning multiples who knew themselves as multiples and who lived with their alters in a generally stable, cooperative, and protective way and with no wish to integrate. 'Dee', who belongs to this second high-functioning generation of multiples, explains her situation in the following letter:

I am MPD and would like to say that as long as all the parts [i.e. alters] work collectively and in full harmony, a multiple can lead a very normal life. I am in data processing and have been since 1979. I am very successful at what I do. I am fortunate though to have parts who do choose to work harmoniously together. I also understand that some multiples don't necessarily have that privilege. I know how difficult it is for us even with everyone's cooperation. I can only imagine the confusion that other multiples have to face. I am successful but I struggle each and every hour of every day. And I go home at the end of the day mentally and emotionally exhausted. Then I relax and let the others out to play. I slump my body into a chair for a while and say, 'OK, guys. Go ahead. I'm all yours'. We visit. We re-group. We iron out any problems of the day. We listen to gripes and/or concerns. And then when everyone has been heard, we put me back together again and get back into life. Like, getting dinner, doing laundry, and helping the kids doing their school work, etc... As long as all of the parts are respected and treated, as the individuals that they are, they are more than happy to continue in harmony. When they are threatened with 'integration', which is like dying to them, then they become difficult, uncooperative, and belligerent. Therefore, as long as we can work as a multiple, we will stay that way. *Don't rock the boat, huh?*[23]

23. 4 September 1997, <http://www.nosscr.org/connect1/messages/7104.html>, italics
    added. See also Beth's story in Antze 1996, and the letter from Faith Christophe,
    <http://www.asarian.org/~astraea/household/die.html>.

Members of the House of the Moon, a high-functioning household,[24] have urged other multiples to consider alternatives to getting integrated. They 'don't need to be "cured"' for they have 'chosen the cooperation [of alters] path and feel very strongly that this is the best path for [them].' Their account of how they move along this path adds interesting details to Dee's letter above:

How does cooperation work for us? Well, we basically generally work by majority vote when we have decisions to make. We carefully listen to those who object to something that the system [household] as a whole has decided to do, and take their objections into consideration. We communicate, verbally and more often non-verbally, amongst ourselves and try our best [...] to look after each other and make sure everyone in our system is doing all right. Our system largely communicates non-verbally, which is a concept it is probably hard for 'singletons' to understand. We communicate most often via emotions, mental pictures, intuitive feelings, and other ways that are harder to express via language.[...] As we noted previously, we readily admit that the path of cooperation is not always an easy path. Sometimes we are 'switchy' (many people coming 'out' to the front position of the system in a short period of time) when we need to get something done and can't afford the lack of concentration that is generally the result of being switchy. Sometimes members of our system vehemently disagree on what the best decision in a given situation is, and this leaves us very indecisive and unsure of whose wishes to abide by or how to compromise. Sometimes the member of our system that is best at dealing with/doing does not come 'out' and someone who's not as good at dealing with it/doing it has to do so instead. Sometimes one of us chooses to deal with a situation in the way the system as a whole would not have chosen, without consulting the rest of us beforehand. Despite all these problems, we are glad that we are we, and we do not want to stop being a we.[25]

Dee and other high-functioning multiples emphasise that 'multiplicity' need not be a debilitating condition. Multiples can be successful and creative people with a high achievement level. Their multiplicity provides them with resources for coping with a wide range of tasks and challenges, and they 'can accomplish a great deal in a short period of time, such as receiving a six year law degree from Harvard in three years'.[26] It is significant that a growing number of multiples are opposed to the stigmatisation of the MPD label and

---

24. 'Household' refers to the ensemble of host and alters.
25. <http://www.geocities.com/Wellesley/5719/gift.html>.
26. 'Learning about DID [MPD]':
    <http://www.geocities.com/HotSprings/Spa/2550/whatis.html>.

the forms of therapy which seek to do away with the alters by integrating them with the host person. They do not see themselves as abnormal, as suffering from a disorder, but as specially gifted persons who differ in positive terms from the so-called 'normals,' whom they often refer to with some condescension as 'singletons', or 'simpletons',[27] a viewpoint Faith Christophe brings out in a long and angry letter from which I quote:

I can see myself as part of a whole if I think of this household as a group of people living in this house [body] and we help each other, make our decisions and stuff. And sometimes 2 or more of us cooperate to do something we couldn't do alone. And maybe we even have thought transference with each other, but we don't lose our IDENTITIES!! I can't see a gestalt or see each person in the household as just a part of a 'greater' person. It's fascist. It means I (and the others in this household) only exists as a cog in a machine. It means my (any of our) individuality doesn't count. This is more abuse. You are always told in abuse that your feelings and emotions are not real. What a bunch of bullshit, can't anyone see integration is just another scam.[28]

Singtibles

MPD is a dissociative disorder, and dissociation is supposed to be a continuum running from the 'normal' dissociation of day dreaming and absent-mindedness of singletons to the 'pathological' and extreme dissociation of MPD of multiples (Putnam 1989: 9-11; Hacking 1995: ch. 7). Some people think they are somewhere in between, '"neither fowl nor fish", neither clearly multiple nor clearly singleton'.[29] They are in the mid-continuum and call themselves *singtibles*. They do not fit the diagnostic criteria for MPD, but, still, they feel multiple. To them it is not a question of having the diagnosis, but of their own authentic experience of multiplicity. In 'Confessions of a MP-Wanna be', Kirsti — sometimes appearing as Inanna, Lilnannas, Nan, or Books — movingly explains why she is attracted to the multiple identity in its singtible form. Her story points to the complex and ambiguous relation-

27. Many members of the House of the Moon, 'Multiplicity Is Not a "Disorder", AKA Integration Isn't the Only Choice':
 <http://www.geocities.com/Wellesley/5719/gift.html>.
28. <http://www.org/~astraea/household/die.html>.
29. 'Welcome to the Wonderful World of the MidContinuum!'
 <http://www.asarian.org/~vickis/continuum.html#doubts>.

ship to other types of multiples, to the 'altering' of objectified moods and feelings, and to the online forum as an emerging moral space:

When I came here [i.e. online], about 2 years ago I was in a place in my healing where I was looking at the different parts inside me. I had found a small girl, the classic 'inner child' work, through studying something about Transactional Analysis I became aware of the parental voice inside me. I was also discovering my inner teenager, and here in Sanctuary [an online forum for abuse survivors], I found a place where I could create characters for them; give them descriptions, names; find their voices, listen to them, let them speak and be heard, all of which was incredibly healing and important to me. However, there was the temptation for me [...] to take those parts and make them even more separate and distinct than they in fact are [...] It was also a wonderful chance to become something special, different, rare, interesting — not just another survivor, but someone who was plural, ... if my distress needed a reason, a label, a diagnosis to justify it, part of it may well have been due to influence from people around me who I thought were incredibly cool and who were members of households, wanting to be like them, to fit in, to be part of the cool crowd too [...] Let me clarify — I never claimed to lose time, to fit the classic DID [MPD] diagnostic criteria. But there were times when I wished that I did do so, that I would have some neat explanation for everything I was going through [...] I still come here [i.e. online] as Lilnannas, or Nan, or Books sometimes when I feel the need to get in touch with those parts of me, or I am feeling totally teenagerish for whatever reasons. I am sorry if my doing so causes offence to any 'true' households or midcontinuum people here. I am also sorry if I have misled people in the past — and say that it was not out of ignorance, not out of a desire to hurt or invalidate what you went through, but it was because I was still struggling to understand myself.[30]

Politics of the multiple personality condition

Dee worried about her parts. Faith Christophe shouted at the psychiatrists and their integration abuse. There is among these second generation high-functioning multiples an awareness of the political implications of MPD.[31] Anthony Temple (also known as Andy) is one of the most articulate representatives of this new and strongly politicised turn of MPD. He is part of the

30. 'Confessions of an MP-Wannabe':
    <http://www.geocities.com/Wellesley/1520/post.html>.
31. Interesting Internet sources about MPD from this non-mainstream perspective can be found at:
    <http://www.asarian.org/~astraea/household/>.

Astraea household, and in a number of Internet instalments he has (some-times in cooperation with Jade Greenwillow from the same household) developed what we might call 'the politics of the multiple personality condition'.[32] He emphasises that Western thought and society work with very rigid standards of reality which marginalise and stigmatise multiples, and he accuses the psychiatric establishment and the media of destroying even highly functioning multiple identity systems in the name of improving them and normalising them:

The American Psychiatric Association calls multiple personality a disorder, imply-ing chaos and being out of control. Since the mental health industry dictates legal standards of normality, all multiples are considered abnormal. This encourages media morbidity and focus on lurid details [...] Multiples are perhaps the last minority which can be safely persecuted and discriminated against.[33]

In 'Multiple Personality Condition: Political and Social Reform' Temple and Greenwillow compare the multiples' situation with that of the homosexuals some decades ago:

For multiple households, the situation today is roughly equivalent to that of a gay or lesbian forty or fifty years ago. If you're discovered to be multiple, you will find your legal rights have all but vanished...Those who are outed, or who simply find it difficult to hide the fact of their many selves, are victimised again through discrimination.[34]

---

32. 'Multiple Personality and Cultural Trance':
    <http://www.asarian.org/~astraea/ household/trance.html>.
    The terminology used by the multiples is a fascinating topic, which clearly brings out the cultural identity aspect of MPD. For other works by Temple, see 'Is Multiple Personality Natural?':
    <http://www.asarian.org/~astraea/household/theory.html>.
    'On Integration':
    <http://www.asarian.org/~astrae a/ household/integrate.html>.'
    How and Why MPC?':
    <http://www.asarian.org/~astraea/household/why.html>.
    'Multiple Households, the Net, and Reality':
    <http://www.asarian.org/~astraea/household/mpreality.html>.
    And 'There is no Model for Non-Pathological Multiplicity in Western Society':
    <http://www.asarian.org/~astraea/household/theory.html>.
33. <http://www.asarian.org/~astraea/household/trance.html>.
34. <http://www.asarian.org/~astraea/household/manifest.html>.

Interestingly, Temple also argues against the strong New Age influence in the new self-conscious thinking of MPD, which turns multiple personality systems into:

something like supernatural deities... By writing that multiplicity, a microcosm created as an alternative to barely living within an oppressive cultural myth, is either drastically above or beneath society's standards, the media is able to subtly blot out our willingness to learn from the all-important wisdom of some of the world's most distinctive individuals.[35]

Temple's most interesting contribution is his questioning of the established etiology of MPD which may take the discussion beyond abuse, trauma, and disorder. 'Multiple Personality is a natural state of mind,' he and Green-willow declare,[36] and elsewhere he adds:

Many in our household believe firmly that had there never been any abuse, had the birth person [the host person] lived in conditions of loving harmony, this household would still exist. My theory is that multiple personality occurs spon-taneously and naturally. It is a way of perceiving and relating to the world. Not everyone is multiple, just as not everyone has blue eyes or an aptitude for mathematics.[37]

The abuse argument has come under attack on two fronts. Spanos launched his critique from a scholarly, sociocognitive perspective, and Temple his from a participating, household perspective. Most recently, Temple has, with Jay Barnes, announced the 'Astraea Research Service':

As of October 1998, Astraea's Web is offering personal research and editing services for people writing papers or preparing presentations on Multiple Personality. Bear in mind, that we do not regard multiple personality as a disorder or a mental disease; we see multiplicity as natural, with possible genetic origins, not as something caused by childhood trauma. These views will be reflected in our work. Astraea is a multiple household. No member of this household is a mental health professional.[38]

---

35. <http://www.asarian.org/~astraea/household/trance.html>.
36. <http://www.asarian.org/~astray/household/manifest.html>. Temple might (without saying so) be inspired by the suggestion that hypnosis, trance, possession, and multiple personality may express a universal human ability to dissociate. See Crabtree 1985.
37. <http://www.asarian.org/~astraea/household/theory.html>.
    See also the two letters about 'Multiple Without Abuse':
    <http://www.asarian.org/~astraea/household/letters.html>.
38. 'Astraea Research Service', <http://www.asarian.org/~astraea/info.html>.

Temple and other high-functioning multiples have taken MPD far beyond the agenda of the early 1980s when the epidemic took off. Once MPD was a pathological condition, a break down of identity, or, in Hacking's words, 'a new way to be an unhappy person [...], a culturally sanctioned way of expressing distress' (Hacking 1995: 236). Now — to some people — being a multiple is *an* identity in its own right, a new way to be a *happy* person. Non-abused multiples have no need of doctors, and they have carved out a foothold of their own from where they speak confidently about their utopian vision of a multiple world.[39]

Multiple personality culture and the Internet: 'see you in cyberspace!'[40]

All types of multiples can be found on the Internet, classical MPDs, high-functionings, singtibels, multiples with or without trauma. One of the most interesting net sites is 'Astraea's Web: Multiple Personality Resources'. It presents itself as a web site about Multiple Personality 'from a non-main-stream perspective', which does not consider Multiple Personality as patholo-gical or as a 'highly sophisticated coping mechanism' for dealing with child-hood abuse. Multiple personality is, in this perspective 'just something as natural as having brown or blue eyes [...] just a group of people sharing a single body'. The site is not about abuse survivorship, it is 'about multiple households connecting and communicating with each other, [sharing] stories and [having their] reality validated by people like [themselves]. It is about multiple personality from a political, social, and philosophical perspective'. It is a site for members of multiple households who 'don't fit in, whose experience doesn't tally with what is "supposed" to happen according to the

---

39. In 1983, Hacking compared the situation of homosexuals with that of multiples. He believed that multiples would never be able to liberate themselves from 'the medico-forensic-journalistic labeling' like the homosexuals had done. 'At the risk of giving offense' he said, 'I suggest that the quickest way to see the contrast between [...] homosexuals and [...] multiple personalities is to try to imagine split-personality bars. [Multiples], in so far as they are declared, are under care, and the syndrome, the form of behavior, is orchestrated by a team of experts. Whatever the medico-forensic experts tried to do with their categories, the homosexual person became autonomous of the labeling, but the [multiple] is not' (Hacking 1986: 233). In 1995, he still doubted the multiples' possibilities of autonomy, though he admitted to be 'well aware of how things change'. He even suggested he might 'yet come to eat those words' [of 1983/1986] (Hacking 1995: 38). Perhaps he should prepare for the meal.

40. 'Hannah's Hideaway', <http://www.geocities.com/HotSprings/8432/hanabana.htm>.

mental health industry'. It questions 'the authority of mental health pro-
viders, legal systems, and governments, to dictate to [multiples] what [their]
reality is or should be'. 'Astraea's Web: Multiple Personality Resources' is the
'flagship webpage of the *"First Person Plural* Webring" which hopes to
'generate interest in and awareness of plurality as possibly a variant natural
human condition [...] Associated with plurality are persistent reports of
transpersonal experiences. While these are scientifically unverifiable, they are
a permanent feature of the multiple-personality *culture*'.[41]

The people and households behind these websites offer a strong argument
for their collective identity. They talk about *the* multiple-personality culture
and refer to 'people like themselves,' to 'connecting and communicating,' to
'awareness', and the 'sharing of stories'. Challenging the pathologising
representation of the mental health industry they insist on representing
themselves to be defined in their own cultural terms. They are multiples *für
sich*.

However, this is not what one should expect. The multiple condition does
not by itself encourage collective manifestations. Multiples have difficulties
in forming larger and stable interest groups because they have problems in
attending meetings. If 'one person switched into an aggressive alter during
a meeting, everyone else felt threatened. Unless there is a nonmultiple
facilitor present, more switching may occur, and pandemonium can break
out' (Hacking 1995: 37). Self-help groups guided by experienced therapists
have appeared in all major American cities, but they are probably often
unstable arrangements, and not all multiples would feel safe in such a place.
The disease has many anti-social aspects, and social isolation is probably
more the rule than the exception among multiples. 'It's a lonely life being in
the world of MPD', as Shiloh said.[42]

On the other hand, multiples do share some knowledge about MPD. Since
the late 1950s there has existed a rich MPD-lore in the media. Books, films,
soap operas, and talk shows have dissipated information about the disorder,
and it is common knowledge that 'MPD is associated with amnesias for the
alternate personalities and an assortment of dramatic clues such as changes
in voice or physical appearance when the personalities switch.' The intense
media attention has been followed by imitative behaviour, and many
multiples' performance has been modelled on *Three Faces of Eve*, *Sybil*, or

---

41. All quotations are from <http://www.asarian.org/~astraea/household/>, italics
    added.
42. <http://www.golden.net/~soul/shiloh2.html>.

some soap opera (North *et al.* 1993: 115-59). Besides, 'MPD patients have been meeting together for years in group therapy, in hospital settings and at conferences that focus on MPD' (Mulhern 1991: 157), and quite a few demonstrate an intimate knowledge of the professional literature. If multiples appear alike, it is not just because they share the same diagnosis, but also because they share the same cultural resources for the expression of the disease. The popularity of the Internet has, I believe, added a new dimension to the shared awareness of being a multiple.

It is no coincidence that many of my sources are taken from the Internet. Indeed, it is possible that the Internet has been a major force in promoting multiple personality culture. In 1997 the editor of the Mental Health Net Website noticed that many multiples were active on line. He suggested a number of reasons for this. For example, the Net is an easily accessible information source, it is a convenient media for establishing electronic support groups, and it offers a safe place for people who fear close social contact.[43]

The Internet is, indeed, the ideal communication environment for socially inhibited people like multiples. As 'Mia' told her co-members of an MPD virtual support group, ' I never had such a group of friends before, most of us avoid people ... thank you all'.[44] The Net facilitates quick and almost unrestricted communication without the risk involved in face to face encounters. Because the Net is always available, the multiple has optimal control of the communication situation. He or she can sit safely at home and log in and out whenever it is convenient. This means that it is possible for multiples to build up the long-term emotional relationships that are so difficult to establish by other means. However, I think there is more to it than just the emotional side. The virtual support groups become very real cultural reference groups. My hunch is that the multiple section of the Net is a high-activity area. As a part of my research for this chapter, I joined an electronic discussion group for a brief period in which I daily received about a hundred messages. This relatively stable and frequent communication is a continuous processing of cultural resources which foster collective awareness

---

43. Grohol, J.M. 'The Prevalence of Multiples Online. [Online]. *Mental Health Net:* <http://www.cmhc.com/archives/editor21.htm>, 1 July, 1997.
    See also the interview with Lisa Varhola, who developed *TimePassages*, a website for abuse survivors:
    <http://mentalhealth.miningco.com/library/weeklyaa092297.htm>.
44. 'Sexual Abuse, Dissociative Identity Disorder/MPD Support Group': <sadm@maelstrom.stjohns.edu>.

and belonging to a virtual community. The information exchanged feeds into
the lives of the participants and influences their interpretation of their own
situation. Multiples' personal home pages, for example, with their elaborate
and often beautiful graphic representations of households, may well serve
as models for other multiples' understanding of their own personality
system. Simultaneously, there is a development of conventions and standards
of communication, design of home pages, specialised language and vocabu-
lary, which serve as group or identity markers. The Net has become a field
of intense cultural creativity, and this would, surely, also be the case for that
part of it where multiples are active.[45] It has played a major role in promoting an awareness of a multiple personality culture.

Multiples of the future

Hacking has offered a rough periodisation of the recent development of
Multiple Personality Disorder. It 'germinated in the sixties, emerged in the
seventies, matured in the eighties, and is adapting itself to new environments
in the nineties' (Hacking 1995: 39). It has been four decades with a dramatic
increase in the number and kind of multiples and alters (and of professionals
specialising in the disease). What about the next decade? It seems safe to
think that the growth has peaked and to predict a substantial decline in the
number of cases. The MPD 'industry' (Piper 1997: xiii) profited enormously
from the link with child abuse, but was later trapped in the scandals of
recovered memory therapy. As more and more malpractice cases are won by
former MPD patients, the industry and its insurance companies realise that
it is risky business to invest in the disease. All this should encourage
diagnostic reticence, and MPD might cease to be 'a culturally sanctioned way
of expressing distress' (Hacking 1995: 236).[46]

If MPD is phased out in the next decade, it will be a second demise and
an example of what Micale has called 'the strange cyclicity of psychopathological forms through time' (Micale 1995: 174-75). The first dis-

---

45. Leonard Holmes found that these 'sites are among the most creative of consumer
    mental health sites.' See, 'Have a Disorder? Build a Web Site - Part Three: Dissociative
    Disorders':
    <http://mentalhealth.tqn.com/library/weekly/aa040797.htm>.
46. This is confirmed by a recent survey of American board-certified psychiatrists' attitudes
    towards the current DID (MPD) diagnosis which showed that only about one-quarter
    of the respondents felt that the diagnosis was supported by strong evidence of scientific
    validity (Pope et al. 1999).

appearance took place less than a century ago. MPD was understood as a hysterical disorder. Due to fundamental changes in diagnostic theory and practice around the turn of the century the classic hysteria diagnosis disintegrated and its various symptoms were linked to other diagnoses like epilepsy, syphilis, and a number of mental disorders (Micale 1995: 169-75). Hysteria disappeared — its symptoms becoming part of other diseases — and MPD, as a special case of hysteria, went with it. The coming and going of MPD is, as Micale has showed for hysteria, 'part and parcel of the larger historical phenomenon of the "rising" and "falling" of nervous diseases' (Micale 1995: 174; cf. Shorter 1992, 1994). It is interesting to ponder the second demise of MPD. We should remember that most people diagnosed as multiples first present non-specific symptoms like depression, anxiety, eating and sleeping disorders and that the diagnosis of MPD only comes up after several years of treatment. Therapists have ample time to consider differential diagnoses, and I believe there is a growing pressure to do so. Presumably, many of the future borderliners, somatisers and other distressed people would, if diagnosed on the same symptoms, in 1990 have ended up as multiples.[47] We can expect MPD, like hysteria, to disintegrate and its various symptoms to be covered by other and even new disease categories. Perhaps the next millennium will benefit from Anthony Temple's efforts and only see multiples of the non-abused kind, demonstrating, once again, Sherlock Holmes' words that life is stranger than fiction. Real, yes, but also made up.

Acknowledgements

I would like to thank Peter Freyd of the False Memory Syndrome Foundation for generously providing information on a number of occasions. I owe a special debt to Sherrill Mulhern who shared her important work on MPD with me. Friends and colleagues commented on a previous draft of this article or helped me in various other ways. I am particularly grateful to Gretty Mirdal, Richard Jenkins, Mark le Fanu, Jens Seeberg, Andreas Roepstorff, Judith Asher, and George Ulrich. Finally, the assistance of Henk Driessen and Ton Otto, model editors, is much appreciated.

47. This retrodiction is based on the observation that 'DID [MPD] overlaps substantially with several psychopathological conditions, including borderline personality disorder (BPD) and somatization disorder' (Lilienfeld et al. 1999: 509; Spanos 1996: 247-64).

Bibliography

Aldridge-Morris, R. 1989. *Multiple Personality: An Exercise in Deception*. Hove and London: Lawrence Erlbaum.

Alexander, V.K. 1956. 'A Case Study of Multiple Personality.' In: *Journal of Abnormal and Social Psychology* 52, 272-76.

Allison, R.B. (with T. Schwartz) 1980. *Minds in Many Pieces: The Making of a Very Special Doctor*. New York: Rawson, Wade.

Allison, R.B. 1991. 'Travel Log: In Search of Multiples in Moscow'. In: *American Journal of Forensic Psychiatry* 12, 51-66.

American Psychiatric Association 1980. *Diagnostic and Statistical Manual of Mental Disorders*. Third edition. Washington, D.C.: American Psychiatric Association.

American Psychiatric Association 1994. *Diagnostic and Statistical Manual of Mental Disorders*. Fourth edition. Washington, D.C.: American Psychiatric Association

Antze, P. 1996. 'Telling Stories, Making Selves. Memory and Identity in Multiple Personality Disorder'. In: P. Antze and M. Lambek (eds.), *Tense Past: Cultural Essays in Trauma and Memory*. London: Routledge, 3-23.

Attwood, G.E. 1978. 'The Impact of *Sybil* on a Patient with Multiple Personality'. In: *American Journal of Psychoanalysis* 38, 277-79.

Bass, E. and L. Davis 1988. *The Courage to Heal: A Guide for Women Survivors of Child Sexual Abuse*. New York: Harper Perennial.

Bliss, B.L. 1980. 'Multiple Personality: A Report on 14 Cases with Implications for Schizophrenia and Hysteria'. In: *Archives of General Psychiatry* 37, 1388-97.

Bøe, T., J.H. and H. Knudsen 1993. 'Multippel personlighet — et fenomen også i Norge?' [Multiple Personality — a Phenomenon also in Norway?]. In: *Tidsskrift for Norsk Lægeforening* 113, 3230-32.

Boon, S. and N. Draijer. 1993. *Multiple Personality Disorder in the Netherlands: A Study on Reliability and Validity of the Diagnosis*. Amsterdam: Swets and Zeitlinger.

Boor, M. 1982. 'The Multiple Personality Epidemic. Additional Cases and Inferences Regarding Diagnosis, Etiology, Dynamics, and Treatment'. In: *Journal of Nervous and Mental Disease* 170, 302-4.

Brown, J.C. 1986. *Immodest Acts. The Life of a Lesbian Nun in Renaissance Italy*. Oxford: Oxford University Press.

Carroy, J. 1993. *Les personnalités doubles et multiples: Entre science et fiction*. Paris: Presses universitaires de France.

Crabtree, A. 1985. *Multiple Man: Explorations in Possession and Multiple Personality*. Toronto: Collins.

Crews, F. 1997. *The Memory Wars. Freud's Legacy in Dispute*. London: Granta Books.

Darves-Bornoz, J.-M., A. Degiovanni and P. Gaillard 1995. 'Why Is Dissociative Identity Disorder Infrequent in France?'. In: *American Journal of Psychiatry* 152, 1530-31.

Doyle, A.C. 1981. 'A Case of Identity'. In: *The Penguin Complete Sherlock Holmes*. London: Penguin Books, 190-201.

Ellenberger, H. 1970. *The Discovery of the Unconscious*. New York: Basic Books.

FMSF 1997 (False Memory Syndrome Foundation Newsletter, 1997, e-mail edition). 'Malpractice Suit Against Dr. Bennett Braun Scheduled for Trial in November' 6(10), November.

Gleaves, D.H. 1996. 'The Sociocognitive Model of Dissociative Identity Disorder: A Reexamination of the Evidence'. In: *Psychological Bulletin* 120, 42-59.

Goettman, C., G.B. Greaves and P. Coons 1994. *Multiple Personality and Dissociation, 1791-1992. A Complete Biography*. Second Edition. Lutherville, MD: The Sidran Press.

Haaken, J. and A. Schlaps 1991. 'Incest Resolution Therapy and the Objectification of Sexual Abuse'. In: *Psychotherapy* 28, 39-47.

Hacking, I. 1986. 'Making Up People'. In: T.C. Heller *et al.* (eds.), *Reconstructing Individualism: Autonomy, Individuality and the Self in Western Thought*. (The paper was first presented in 1983). Stanford: Stanford University Press, 222-36.

Hacking, I. 1991. 'The Making and Moulding of Child Abuse'. In: *Critical Inquiry* 17, 253-88.

Hacking, I. 1995. *Rewriting the Soul. Multiple Personality and the Sciences of Memory*. Princeton: Princeton University Press.

Healey, D. 1997. *The Antidepressant Era*. Cambridge, Mass.: Harvard University Press.

International Society for the Study of Dissociation 1997. *Guidelines for Treating Dissociative Identity Disorder (Multiple Personality Disorder)*. Internet edition: <http://www.issd.org/issdguide.htm>.

Jenkins, R. 1996. *Social Identity*. London: Routledge.

Johnson, S.P. 1994. Feline MPD: Cats with Suspected Multiple Personality Disorder. <http://www.inner-sanctum.com/grotto/humr0012-html>.

Kaminer, W. 1992. *I'm Dysfunctional, You're Dysfunctional*. Reading, Mass.: Addison-Wesley.

Karilampi, U. and S. Carolusson 1995. 'A Single Case Study of Multiple Personality'. In: *Nordic Journal of Psychiatry* 49, 133-39.

Kenny, M.G. 1981. 'Multiple Personality Disorder and Spirit Possession'. In: *Psychiatry* 44, 337-59.

Kenny, M.G. 1986. *The Passion of Ansel Bourne*. Washington, D.C.: Smithsonian.

Kenny, M.G. 1998. 'Disease Process or Social Phenomenon? Reflections on the Future of Multiple Personality'. In: *Journal of Nervous and Mental Disease* 186, 449-54.

Kirk, S.A. and H. Kutchins 1992. *The Selling of DSM: The Rhetoric of Science in Psychiatry*. New York: Aldine De Gruyter.

Kirk, S.A. and H. Kutchins 1997. *Making Us Crazy: DSM: The Psychiatric Bible and Creation of Mental Disorders*. New York: The Free Press.

Kluft, R.P. 1986. 'High-Functioning Multiple Personality Patients: Three Cases'. In: *Journal of Nervous and Mental Disease* 174, 722-26.

Lilienfeld, S.O. *et al.* 1999. 'Dissociative Identity Disorder and the Sociocognitive Model: Recalling the Lesson of the Past'. In: *Psychological Bulletin* 125, 507-23.

Lindsay, D.S. and J.D. Read 1994. 'Psychotherapy and Memories of Childhood Sexual Abuse: A Cognitive Perspective'. In: *Applied Cognitive Psychology* 8, 281-338.

Lindsay, D.S. and J.D. Reed 1995. '"Memory Work" and Recovered Memories of Childhood Sexual Abuse: Scientific Evidence and Public, Professional, and Personal Issues'. In: *Psychology, Public Policy, and Law* 1, 846-908.

Littlewood, R. 1996. 'Reason and Necessity in the Specification of the Multiple Self'. In: *Occasional Paper* 43. London: Royal Anthropological Institute of Great Britain and Ireland.

Loftus, E.F. 1993. 'The Reality of Repressed Memories'. In: *American Psychologist* 48, 518-37.

Loftus, E.F. and K. Ketcham 1994. *The Myth of Repressed Memory*. New York: St. Martin's Press.

Lynch, M. 1995: 'Narrative Hooks and Paper Trails: The Writing of Memory'. In: *History of the Human Sciences* 8, 118-28.

Martinez-Taboas, A. 1991. 'Multiple Personality in Puerto Rico: Analysis of Fifteen Cases'. In: *Dissociation* 4, 189-92.

Merskey, H. 1992. 'The Manufacture of Personalities: The Production of Multiple Personality Disorder'. In: *British Journal of Psychiatry* 160, 327-40.

Micale, M. 1995. *Approaching Hysteria: Disease and Its Interpretations*. Princeton: Princeton University Press.

Modestin, J. 1992. 'Multiple Personality Disorder in Switzerland'. In: *American Journal of Psychiatry* 149, 88-92.

Mulhern, S. 1991. 'Satanism and Psychotherapy: A Rumor in Search of an Inquisition'. In: J.T. Richardson, J. Best and D.G. Bromley (eds.), *The Satanism Scare*. New York: Aldine de Gruyter, 145-73.

Mulhern, S. 1994. 'Satanism, Ritual Abuse, and Multiple Personality: A Sociohistorical Perspective'. In: *International Journal of Clinical and Experimental Hypnosis* 42, 265-88.

North, C.S., J.-E. M. Ryall, D.A. Ricci and R.D. Wetzel 1993. *Multiple Personalities, Multiple Disorders: Psychiatric Classification and Media Influence*. New York: Oxford University Press.

Ofshe, R. and E. Watters 1994. *Making Monsters: False Memories, Psychotherapy, and Sexual Hysteria*. New York: Charles Scribner.

Orne, M.T. and B.L. Bates 1992. 'Reflections on Multiple Personality Disorder: A View From the Looking Glass of Hypnosis Past'. In: A. Kales, C.M. Pierce and M. Greenblatt (eds.), *The Mosaic of Contemporary Psychiatry in Perspective*. New York: Springer-Verlag.

Pendergrast, M. 1996. *Victims of Memory: Incest Accusations and Shattered Lives*. (First published in USA 1995). London: HarperCollins.

Piper, A. 1997. *Hoax and Reality: The Bizarre World of Multiple Personality Disorder.* Northvale, N.J.: Jason Aronson.

Piper, A. 1998. 'News Flash', *FMS Foundation Newsletter* (e-mail edition) 7(9), November.

Pope, H.G. *et al.* 1999. 'Attitudes Toward DSM-IV Dissociative Disorders Diagnoses Among Board-Certified American Psychiatrists'. In: *American Journal of Psychiatry* 156, 321-23.

Putnam, P.W. 1989. *Diagnosis and Treatment of Multiple Personality Disorder.* New York: Guildford.

Read, J.D. and D.S. Lindsay 1994. 'Moving Toward the Middle Ground on the "False Memory Debate": Reply to Commentaries on Lindsay and Read'. In: *Applied Cognitive Psychology* 8, 407-35.

Royal College of Psychiatrists' Working Group on Reported Recovered Memories of Child Sexual Abuse 1997. 'Recommendations for Good Practice and Implications for Training, Continuing Professional Development and Research'. In: *Psychiatric Bulletin* 21, 663-65.

Sar, V., L.I.Yargic and H. Tutkun 1996. 'Structured Interview Data on 35 Cases of Dissociative Identity Disorders in Turkey'. In: *American Journal of Psychiatry* 153, 1329-1333.

Schacter, D.L. 1996. *Searching for Memory: The Brain, the Mind, the Past.* New York: BasicBooks.

Schnabel, J. 1994. 'Chronic Claims of Alien Abduction and some Other Traumas as Self-Victimization Syndromes'. In: *Dissociation* 8, 51-62.

Schreiber, F.R. 1973. *Sybil.* Chicago: Regnery.

Shorter, E. 1992. *From Paralysis to Fatigue: A History of Psychosomatic Illness in the Modern Era.* New York: The Free Press.

Shorter, E. 1994. *From the Mind into the Body: The Cultural Origins of Psychosomatic Symptoms.* New York: The Free Press.

Showalter, E. 1997. *Hystories: Hysterical Epidemics and Modern Culture.* London: Picador.

Smith, M. and L. Pazder 1980. *Michelle Remembers.* New York: Pocket Books.

Spanos, N.P. 1996. *Multiple Identities and False Memories: A Sociocognitive Perspective.* Washington, D.C.: American Psychological Association.

Spanos, N.P., J.R. Weeks and L.D. Bertrand 1985. 'Multiple Personality: A Social Psychological Perspective'. In: *Journal of Abnormal Psychology* 94, 362-76.

Takahashi, Y. 1990. 'Is Multiple Personality Disorder Really Rare in Japan?'. In: *Dissociation* 3(2), 57-59.

Thigpen, C.H. and H.M. Cleckley 1954. 'A Case of Multiple Personality'. In: *Journal of Abnormal and Social Psychology* 49, 135-51.

Thigpen, C.H. and H.M. Cleckley 1957. *Three Faces of Eve.* New York: McGraw-Hill.

Thigpen, C.H. and H.M. Cleckley 1984. 'On the Incidence of Multiple Personality Disorder: A Brief Communication'. In: *International Journal of Clinical and Experimental Hypnosis* 32, 63-66.

Van Praag, H.M. 1993. *'Make-Believes' in Psychiatry or The Perils of Progress*. New York: Brunner/Mazel Publishers.

Victor, G. 1975. *'Sybil*: Grande Hystérie or Folie à Deux?'. In: *American Journal of Psychiatry* 132, 202.

Völgyesi, F.A. 1966. *Hypnosis of Man and Animals*. London: Baillière, Tindall, and Cassel.

Warwick, M. and J. Butler 1998. 'Dissociative Identity Disorder: An Australian Series'. In: *Australian and New Zealand Journal of Psychiatry* 32, 794-804.

Wilson, M. 1993. 'DSM-III and the Transformation of American Psychiatry: A History'. In: *American Journal of Psychiatry* 150, 399-410.

World Health Organization 1992. *The ICD-10 Classification of Mental and Behavioural Disorders: Clinical Descriptions and Diagnostic Guidelines*. Geneva: World Health Organization.

CHAPTER 5

Ritual and Conflicting Identifications:
The Case of a Female *Bricoleur*

Louise Thoonen

Introduction

This essay deals with the female initiation rite *fenia meroh*, which is performed among the Meyhabehmase tribe inhabiting the north Ayfat region in the interior of Irian Jaya's Bird's Head. The *fenia meroh* rite (literally meaning 'woman comes down') aims at transforming individual novices into adult women who, especially by internalising ancestral laws, fit within the socio-cultural group and who share a common identity. Despite the profound ritual effects, however, initiated women sometimes experience that the group identity they are supposed to have internalised during initiation (social identification in accordance with tribal modes of life), is inconsistent with their sense of self. The tension between these conflicting identifications forms the focus of this chapter.

I will focalise some particular aspects from the life-history[1] of one woman, Maria Baru, who has been coping intensively with these conflicting individual and collective identifications after her initiation. When Maria was about 15 years old, in the 1960s, she had been a novice in the *fenia meroh* rite. At the time I recorded her life-history, in 1994 and 1995,[2] Maria had become a

1. In this paper I have also borrowed research material from Ien Courtens, with whom I conducted the fieldwork in close cooperation: the parts on healing are mainly taken from Courtens 1998. Ien conducted anthropological field research on female ritual healers. Although we carried out separate projects, in practice our research paths frequently crossed because of the cognate nature of our research themes. Among other things, we exchanged fieldwork materials which we considered significant for each other's project. I am grateful to Ien for giving me such valuable data and for providing critical comments on earlier drafts of this paper.

2. I conducted field-research in the northwest Ayfat for thirteen months, as PhD Research Scholar of the Centre for Pacific Studies (Department of Anthropology) of Nijmegen University. The fieldwork was financed by the Netherlands Foundation for the

prominent person within northwest Ayfat society. Currently she is still a leading woman in the sphere of indigenous cultural practices and local Christianity, both of which have influenced the initiation rite to a large extent.

In this chapter, selective parts of Maria's life-history are provided to explore the ritual's purpose for (re)constructing the self of young persons in relation to the ways Maria coped with this purpose in practice. I will discuss, first, the tensions Maria experienced after initiation, between her sense of self and the social identity as connected to her tribal group. Second, I will discuss how Maria coped with these conflicting identifications in the remainder of her life-course by seeking to reconcile these (and other) identifications. While doing so, she acted as a pioneer and *bricoleur*.

The two major theoretical starting points of this chapter are taken from Ewing (1990), who argues that persons who deal with conflicting identities seek to achieve reconcilement. Ewing further states:

When we consider the temporal flow of experience, we can observe that individuals are continuously reconstituting themselves into new selves in response to internal and external stimuli.[3] They construct these new selves from their available set of self-representations, which are based on cultural constructs (ibid: 258).

When using this latter perspective, I argue, we will be able to show that the ritual's aim of transforming the self of novices into a social identity is not automatically effected and may even result in conflicting identifications. To put it differently: rather than perceiving initiation rites as processes which establish society's rights over the individual, in which the 'authorial selves' of initiates are absent (Cohen 1994), we have to consider the flow of experience of initiated persons and their 'authorial self'. So, I will use an actor oriented perspective by exploring personal experience and self-determination. In this way, we will be able to understand that 'internal stimuli' such as personal desires and character traits as well as 'external stimuli' such as

---

Advancement of Tropical Research (WOTRO) and the Department of Anthropology of Nijmegen University. The preparation of the fieldwork was carried out in close co-operation with the NWO (Netherlands Organization for Scientific Research) priority programme 'The Irian Jaya Studies: a programme for Interdisciplinary Research' (ISIR) financed by WOTRO.

3. Jenkins (1996: 50) made a similar point by stating that the self 'is constructed within the internal-external dialectic (...)'. Contrary to Ewing, however, Jenkins emphasises the role of the 'external social environment' as he is convinced that 'selfhood is absolutely social'.

processes of cultural change, affect the ways and the intensity in which initiated persons utilise their initiation experience.

Before I present Maria's life-history, let me explain that the distinction between '(sense of) self' and 'social identity' does not suggest a stringent boundary between the individual and society. Above all, the distinction serves analytical purposes, precisely meant to explore the interaction between individual persons and society. First, it focuses on the process of social interaction and, herewith, identification, by means of which persons construct a self. To quote Lutkehaus (1995: 14) in a volume on female initiation in Melanesia: '(...) a person's identity is an aggregate of social relations, the links he or she has to other individuals'. Second, the distinction highlights the importance of individual persons as leaders and *bricoleurs* within the process of social identity formation. So, I agree with Jenkins (1996) that the self arises within social interaction and that a dialectical relationship exists between individual and collective identities. While focalising this interaction and Maria's *bricolage*, I will examine Stephen's and Herdt's (1989: 11) argument that it is in the 'gap between cultural representation, and subjective necessity and desire, that we find the impetus for creativity and innovation'. I will further show that, as Tuzin (1989: 188) remarked, 'only in the minds of individuals are religious ideas created'.

In order to gain insights into how Maria coped with the presumed impact of the *fenia meroh* ritual, it is necessary to juxtapose the later stages and the preceding stage, so I will start by referring shortly to Maria's early childhood. From the initiation period itself I will highlight only a few aspects: those to which Maria referred as being central to her experience, and those which have to be known for comprehending the significance of *fenia meroh* for her later life. In order to keep this chapter short, the remainder of Maria's life-history concerns a selective representation too.

Maria Baru's life-history

Maria Baru was born in Tabamsere, a small settlement in the north Ayfat region where, just one year before, the Dutch Roman Catholic mission had been introduced. As Maria frequently and proudly mentioned during our conversations, Tabamsere's village-head, her maternal uncle, was the first person in the entire Bird's Head region to accept the Catholic mission (Thoonen 1998).

From her sixth year onwards, Maria attended primary school at the local mission. She was a talented pupil which made a missionary priest select her for continuing her education at the missionary boarding school in Senopi (north Ayfat). At the time, Maria was 11 years old. She wanted further education and acted with determination to pursue this personal desire. However, her parents did not want to give their permission and prevented her from leaving them, but Maria ran away. She said to the priest, 'Just start walking [to Senopi], I will follow you in the late afternoon', and so she did. That night, however, her father caught up with Maria and the priest. He entered into a discussion with the priest and stated that his daughter had to stay. As Maria told me:

Then, the priest said, 'Enough! Maria stays with you'. So, I went back home with my father. Back to Tabamsere. I felt constantly grieved. And I thought to myself, 'Why am I not allowed to be educated?'. I went to school again in Tabamsere. (...). Later, Father Jonker returned to the village and baptised me and other children as a Christian.

In her retrospective self-representation, it appears that Maria already knew what she wanted when she was a young child, and that she simply did not obey the opinion of the elderly. In other words, even as a child, before her initiation, Maria had a strong sense of self from which she tried to accomplish her major personal wish: leaving her home settlement for Western education. Moreover, it appears that she tried to accomplish this wish by self-determination, namely taking control of her life by running away. In our conversations Maria emphasised: 'I wanted to be educated, but my parents insisted that I would join *adat* (tradition). I did not want to join *adat*, I longed to take part in development'. Up to this stage in her life, however, Maria did not actually succeed in challenging the tribal life by realising her personal wish. Moreover, staying in her home settlement meant that Maria would be initiated soon. She was on the threshold of the early stage of her adult life which, according to indigenous rules, implied that she was obliged to participate in the *fenia meroh* ritual as a novice. After the description of her initiation, as given below, we shall see how Maria coped with her personal wish for Western education later on.

'Becoming a social self': Maria's participation in *fenia meroh*

When Maria was about 15 years old, she reached menarche which marked the beginning of her initiation. Her mother summoned her to leave the village. Maria obeyed her and walked into the forest, where she initially remained in a menstrual hut (*akasikos*). After the bleeding had stopped, a female relative took her to the secluded cult house, a pile dwelling also called *fenia meroh*, which, meanwhile, had been built by male relatives. At the time, Easter had just passed. At Easter time the following year, Maria was to end her initiation.

Maria was initiated collectively with three other novices, also members of the Baru clan. When they entered the cult house an important element was that they received a new, symbolic name. As Maria told me:

I stayed in *fenia meroh* together with Anselma, Magdalena and Faustina. (...) The three of us received the name of *Aka*. My name was Maria, but when I entered *fenia meroh* it was no longer allowed to call me Maria. Throughout our stay in *fenia meroh* we all had to be called *Aka* (...). *Aka* is a flowerbud, a flower that has not opened up yet. We had become a bud already, a flower that still was closed. Soon, however, the bud would open up.

When Maria recounted the meaning of *Aka* in the above passage, she expressed the importance of the *fenia meroh* ritual in relation to her gendered self in this particular stage of life: entering the cult house was compared with entering the first stage of womanhood. In Maria's experience the symbolic naming meant further that, during seclusion, her previous identity (as connected to her personal name) was stripped off and had to be transformed into a collective identification. As we will see below, being initiated implied that Maria had to subordinate personal interests and opinions. During this liminal stage, which aims at depersonalising the initiates, there was hardly any space for autonomy.

Each morning, Maria and the other novices were obliged to get up some hours before sunrise and prepare taro at the fire-place. Next, they had to listen to a deluge of ancestral laws and good advice (*watum*) which the female cult leader, a senior relative, recited during the rest of the day:

My teacher, *Ibu* (Mrs.) Ndam, she talked, and talked, and talked... We just sat down and listened with our head bowed. We had to listen attentively, so we would know the rules and warnings by heart.

By listening to her teacher, Maria learned about proper female behaviour and social intercourse. In particular she learned that she had to take care of her parents, other elderly people, her future husband, and her future children, among other things by providing food for them. She further learned about female secrets such as the female life-giving forces of menstruation, fertility, pregnancy, giving birth to children and child-raising.

Another domain Maria referred to as being highly important concerned indigenous healing methods. In particular, Maria gained knowledge of the therapeutical effects of a wide range of plants and trees, and the application of leaves, roots and tree-bark. She also learned the secret magical formulas by means of which ancestral spirits could be requested to cure diseases and to stimulate female fertility. The majority of the healing methods concerned 'female matters' such as fertility, pregnancy, and giving birth (Courtens 1998).

On other days, when her teacher left the cult house and returned to the village for some days, Maria was allowed to walk into the surrounding forest to gather vegetables and go fishing. She did not eat the gathered food herself, but presented it as a gift to her teacher when she returned. Maria herself complied with the stringent food taboos to which she was submitted. Once initiated, these food taboos had to be maintained during several years, although in altered, less stringent forms.

The happy days of foraging in the surrounding forest occurred less frequently, however, than the days of listening to the ancestral laws and advice her teacher recited. Above all, Maria experienced the secluded period of her initiation as becoming immersed in ancestral laws while living isolated from village-life. She frequently referred to these aspects while recounting her initiation, and once in a striking way she said to me: 'We were hidden as if we were dead. My face was filled with traditional laws'.

After a year, the period of seclusion came to end. Cheerfully, Maria told me about the transitional phase that followed. She narrated that, first, she was purified by a washing ritual. Next, her teacher as well as her mother and other older female relatives decorated her with objects such as a headband, feathers of a bird of paradise, a skirt, woven bracelets, and *kain timur* (cloth). The decorations she received during this dressing rite were blessed by her teacher with magical formulas which transmitted protective ancestral powers. As Maria explained to me: '*Ibu* Ndam told us that we had to wear the decorations day and night, until one of the bracelets would break spontaneously'. This represented the sign that the ancestral powers which imbued the decorations, had penetrated the body optimally. The ancestral powers would protect Maria and enable her to stand up for herself in her adult life, especially within social relationships with men and within the domain of *kain timur* (cloth) exchange.

Another important experience at the end of the seclusional phase was that Maria received five sacred symbols which expressed central cultural values. By receiving these symbols, Maria told me, she became 'connected to the symbols'. The symbols first were blessed by Maria's teacher with magical formulas and then handed over to her. Here, I will highlight just one[4] of these symbols, of which Maria explained the meaning as follows:

Tafoh (fire) is the principal thing, because where people live there is fire. Without fire we would be hungry, we would die. The laws the elderly people gave to us, are like the fire: we have to use it. The fire must not be extinguished, but has to stay permanently (...). It must be passed on to next generations within the family.

After she had received the sacred symbols, Maria finally left the cult house at nightfall and went to the dance house. There, a three-day ceremony started during which she once more received protective ancestral powers. Further, she had to listen attentively to a deluge of good advice from female and male relatives, based upon ancestral laws and their own and other people's experience of life. During this phase of the closing ceremony Maria felt exhausted. Deep into the night, she stood upright while listening to the laws and advice. When she fought sleep and closed her eyes for just one moment, her teacher got angry with her because she lost concentration.

During the closing ceremony the importance of names as vehicles of identity formation came to the fore. Maria, like her fellow-initiates, received the name of *Ita*, 'flower in bloom', which referred to womanhood: the flowerbud that Maria had been when she entered the cult house, had been opened up by the *fenia meroh* rite. Maria also received the indigenous first name of her maternal female ancestor Huf. From then on, Maria had to be called 'Ita Huf', at least till she would give birth to a child.

The final ceremony in particular gave Maria a feeling of pride, because so many relatives had travelled to Tabamsere for the celebration. Maria's *fenia meroh* rite, however, was the last initiation rite to be performed in the village of Tabamsere. From then on, female and male initiation rites (*wuon*) were abandoned in her village (and in several other baptised northwest Ayfat communities), due to missionary and governmental prohibitive orders. Missionaries regarded the practice of initiation as undesirable because it kept limited children's participation in the missionary schools. This would hinder the process of conversion as schooling formed the major missionary method.

Through initiation Maria had become a full member of the clan as well as a gendered person. Now, she had inherited the ancestral laws, knowledge,

---

4. The other symbols concerned *etuoh* (string), *tah* and *kwir* (wood), *awiah* (taro), and *tabam* (soil). In this paper, it is not neccessary to elaborate on these symbols for comprehending the significance of *fenia meroh* for Maria's later life.

symbols, and protective powers which had guided her into the first stage of adulthood. In particular, she had reached the first stage of full womanhood, especially by inheriting the ancestral secrets and spiritual powers concerning female fertility, by inheriting the names of her female ancestors, and by learning the rules for proper female behaviour. However, what impact did the ritual actually have? Was Maria, by the *fenia meroh* rite, transformed into a person who shared the social identity of the tribal group without any problems? Or did she still long for Western education? In short, how was Maria to cope with the ritual purpose in practice?

Experiencing tensions: struggling for self-determination

Some days after the closing ceremony of *fenia meroh*, Maria met a missionary priest who visited Tabamsere for the celebration of Easter. She said to the priest:

Father, I shall go with you. I am now wearing my decorations which I may not take off soon. Wait until I am allowed to take them off, so I can join you.

Two months later, the priest returned. In the meantime, Maria's bracelet had broken spontaneaously. Only then she felt free to accompany the priest to the village of Senopi and in this respect she obeyed the laws of *fenia meroh*. Her fellow-novices, on the other hand, broke the laws as they had already followed the priest immediately after the closing ceremony. Yet, Maria violated the rules of behaviour in another respect: she did not ask for the permission of her parents, nor did she inform them that she was going to leave. Instead, she sneaked away. By running away from her native village, Maria followed her most ardent wish: further education. In my opinion, we can perceive this as an act of standing up for herself, which she had learned during initiation. However, she did so for the sake of another purpose than the ancestral powers initially were intented for. Her story runs as follows:

I followed Father Van der Kraan in July. On 7 July 1967, after the mass: *tàk*! I went together with Petronella Titit, a daughter of uncle Hauch. (...) Before, we had informed a relative that we were going to leave, and instructed her to inform our parents no sooner than the next day.
    We set off. On 8 July, we spent the night in the village of Zoon. (...) The headman (...) said to the father, 'Petronella and Maria must not go along with you, they have to stay here. Tomorrow I will bring them back home'. (...) But the father replied, 'That won't be possible'. And the two of us, we said to the priest, 'Do not listen to him, father. We do not want to go back, we will join you'.

(...) On 11 July, we arrived in Senopi. We directly went to the house of the sisters, whom I had met before. (...) Oh, the sisters were glad! They already knew our names. They had been informed about our arrival.

The next day, I went to school. I entered the fourth grade.

In the above passages, as from Maria's decision to leave her native village, the theme of self-determination once more comes to the fore and more vigorously than in the period before her initiation. Further, the passages show that her personal desire for Western education was closely connected to the 'external stimulus' of the missionary process. Maria's life-history as continued below will show that this 'external stimulus' was to become of overriding importance for the ways in which Maria, as an individual actor, coped with her initiation-experience in the remainder of her life-course.

In Senopi, Maria stayed at the missionary boarding school which was managed by Dutch missionary sisters. After school, the sisters instructed her in Western household work like ironing cloths and using a sewing-machine. Maria felt happy at the boarding school, especially on the days she assisted the nurse in the missionary hospital.

The *tafoh* (fire) of her *fenia meroh* experience, however, had started to extinguish when she moved from Tabamsere to Senopi. As Maria explained:

I was not able to use what I had learned in the *adat* [traditional] house because I went to school already. (...) So I abandoned all the methods the older people had shown me (Quoted from Courtens 1998).

Nevertheless, when Maria narrated her life-history it appeared that she did not actually abandon her initiation knowledge. In fact, she submerged a considerable part of the knowledge but, simultaneously, integrated a part of it in her daily life. For instance, contrary to the indigenous rule she did not call herself 'Ita Huf' but 'Maria'. On the other hand, however, she still complied with the food taboos as she feared the consequences of violating them: becoming seriously ill or menstruating continuously. Further, she did not apply the indigenous healing methods she had learned during her initiation, but usually used the medicines from the local hospital. There was one important exception. As Maria told me: 'Whenever I suspected that I had become ill by evil spirits, I said to the sisters, "Your medicines are not sufficient to cure this kind of disease"'. Maria, however, did not deepen her knowledge of ancestral laws. Instead, she moved further into the Christian sphere. In 1968, she received the sacrament of confirmation. After some time, she started studying the Bible the bishop had given to her during the ceremony.

It took three years before Maria was to meet her parents again, but during those years of separation she did not forget them. She showed her parents that she cared for them in a manner which was appropriate for women, as she had learned during *fenia meroh*: by means of food. She regularly sent food to them via missionaries who were going to visit her native village. Maria's first reunion with her parents had been an emotional event. When she narrated this part, she showed that the condition of living separated from her parents actually had been hard for her. Nevertheless, she pursued living her life in far-away places: she moved to the town of Manokwari to attend the domestic science school (*SKP*).

After Maria finished her education, she got married and moved to the West Ayfat region. Her husband, Paulinus Bame, was in the service of the Catholic mission as a carpenter. Maria and Paulinus were among the first couples who celebrated their wedding in Church.

The next year, Maria gave birth to her first child. She did not name her daughter after a female ancestor according to indigenous practice, but named her Josephine after her favourite missionary sister. By means of motherhood, Maria had reached the stage of full womanhood. Maria indeed felt that she had become a full adult woman. And, now, the food taboos had finally come to an end. In the years that followed Maria gave birth to two more children. In those years, her parents passed away.

Through the years, Maria had become a devout Catholic. She read the Bible every day and perceived the scriptural passages as a guideline within her personal life. Praying to God and attending mass also took a central place within her daily life. In fact, being a Christian had become an integrated part of her sense of self. All those years, though, she still followed specific indigenous customs, in particular worshipping her ancestors. Her major aspiration, however, was to live her life as a devout Christian.

Maria receives visions: re-valuation of *fenia meroh*

So far, we have seen that undergoing initiation, in Maria's case, did not result in a radical shift within her sense of self. Despite the profound ritual effects, Maria experienced that the social identity she was supposed to have internalised during initiation, in a way was inconsistent with her sense of self. Through the ritual Maria had been initiated into the indigenous female domain and she indeed internalised some of these aspects in her sense of a gendered self. The ritual, however, did not subvert Maria's desire for personal development by means of Western education. She moved into the missionary domain, selected to be initiated into Western notions and practices regarding women and, herewith, into the social identity of the mission. Simultaneously, the incorporation into the missionary sphere marked an important transition in her sense of self. From then on, Maria became a devout Catholic and above all she wished to live as a Christian. At the same time, however, she adhered to selective indigenous religious notions and practices as connected to her initiaton experience. Up till then, Maria did not refer to the coexistence of the various identifications as being conflicting. In the remainder of her life-history, however, it appears that Maria, in a later stage, experienced tensions between these identifications.

When Maria was in her thirties, the phase in which she had supressed her *fenia meroh* experience for the greater part was disrupted by some events. This took place during a critical situation in her personal life: she had given birth to three children, yet her husband wanted her to bear another baby. Maria herself did not long to have more children. Nevertheless, she tried to get pregnant again, but without result. Then, Paulinus threatened to leave her for another woman. Maria was seized by panic and prayed to God and called the spirits of her deceased parents for help. In my view, the disruption of the 'submerging-period' was closely connected to this personal crisis, which touched the core aspect of *fenia meroh*: female fertility. Maria herself, however, foregrounded the need of curing sick persons in explanation of what happened to her in that stage of life: she received visions in which the knowledge of healing she had gained in *fenia meroh* was revealed to her once more. Maria emphazised the following:

(...) special things happened to me. I had visions, I heard the voices of *Yefun* [God] and my deceased parents. The voices repeated what I had learned as a child about the use of leaves, trees. The visions showed me what I had lost. The knowledge I had gained in *fenia meroh* (...) (Quoted from Courtens 1998).

First, the voice of God spoke to Maria after she had requested his help to cure sick persons:

God said to me, 'Maria, you requested strength to pull me. But I already gave this strength to your elders, and they handed everything over to you. You already know everything, all about the application of leaves, roots, and tree-bark. You already gained the knowledge' (Quoted from Courtens 1998).

Some time later, when her husband became very ill, Maria called the spirits of her deceased parents. They instructed her to cook specific leaves for Paulinus. Shortly after, Maria received more supernatural messages. When she was praying by means of her rosary and her statuette of the Virgin Mary, the voice of God spoke to her again. When Maria was asleep, God manifested himself through her dreams, and once in the shape of a blazing ray (Courtens 1998). Although the visions appeared in various forms, the messages all revealed the same assignment: they summoned Maria to apply the knowledge on healing she had received during initiation, so she could help sick people by curing them.

When she received the visions, Maria initially felt confused and did not know how to deal with this assignment. After it had been repeated several times within various forms, she realised that she no longer should neglect the ancestral knowledge she had gained during her initiation:

(...) when I was young I learned about curing in *fenia meroh*. But I did not take it to heart, except some things. The older people wanted to give it to me, but temporary I had a small heart. However, I might not forget, it all had to live on. (...) I prayed to God, *Yefun*. He gave me back what the elderly people already had shown me. He gave it to me directly, I heard his voice (Quoted from Courtens 1998).

Only after these visions Maria 'dared to use' the ancestral knowledge and 'pulled' herself 'together' to cure sick people. In the period that followed, Maria cured some seriously ill persons in a way that by others was perceived as a miraculous feat. Maria herself also took the indigenous medicines. She got pregnant again and her husband stayed with her.

However, the holy messages did not only guide Maria towards applying parts of the knowledge she had gained during initiation; at this stage of her life Maria's role of pioneer and *bricoleur* came to the fore. While acting as a healer, Maria combined indigenous ways with Christian notions and practices because she had become a devout Catholic. It was of crucial importance to her, for instance, that she had received the messages directly from God. In practice, therefore, she united the indigenous ways of healing with the application of Christian symbols such as the crucifix, a statuette of the Virgin Mary, and a painting of the apostles Peter and Paul. During the healing sessions, she muttered the ancestral formulas she had learned during *fenia meroh* as well as Christian secret formulas and prayers (Courtens 1998).

So, some fifteen years after Maria had been initiated she finally breathed new life into the *tafoh* (fire) of *fenia meroh* and, herewith, into her social identity as connected to tribal modes of life. As it occurred within a phase of life in which Christianity had grown important to her, in Maria's experience the ancestral knowledge had become inextricably bound up with

Christian notions and practices. Therefore, in reaction to both internal and external stimuli, she sought to achieve reconciliation: she re-interpreted both domains and (re-)incorporated them into a more coherent self. As Maria stated:

Now I use everything, everything what I got from the Church to cure sick people. And what I learned from our tradition, everything, everything till the end (Quoted from Courtens 1998).

Maria continued healing sick people, and from the early 1980s onwards she became one of the most renowned healers in the northwest Ayfat region. The fact that Maria had been the first person in the area to receive divine messages, which she used to cure seriously ill people in miraculous ways, led other villagers to request that she take them under her wing and share her spiritual ancestral and Christian knowledge with them. Finally, in this way Maria became the founder and leader of a special Christian prayer group which, at present, is made up of members from all parts of the Bird's Head region. Members of the group perform healing rites in the creolised forms as taught to them by Maria (Courtens 1998). So, through reconciling her identity as connected to initiation with her identity as connected to Christianity, Maria did not just achieve a more coherent self: while uniting both domains, she simultaneously created new, creolised, rituals which are popular in present-day north-western Ayfat society. In this regard she acted as a pioneer and *bricoleur*.

In the 1990s, Maria even united both domains in a more radical way: she went beyond revitalising selective parts of the *fenia meroh* rite through healing and re-instated the entire initiation rite. This time, the major driving force was formed by 'external stimuli'.

The central stimulus was formed by the fact that, at the time, Maria and some of her close relatives who belonged to the last generation of initiated persons were growing old. They were expected to pass away within a few years. As Maria put it, with regard to her eldest brother: 'If Agus passes away before he has transmitted his ancestral knowledge and powers to his son, we will be ruined'. The threat of the passing away of the last initiated family-members was connected to a renewed interest for their tribal identity.

In order to 'save' the identity of her clan and tribal group, Maria decided to re-instate the *fenia meroh* rite. Again, it was of crucial importance to her that the indigenous and the Christian domain would 'walk together'. As Maria underlined, Christian girls (and boys) had to be initiated and only when they received both ancestral and Christian spiritual knowledge and powers, their personal development would be 'complete'. From this perspective Maria, as a ritual specialist, performed a *fenia meroh* rite in a drastically shortened and simplified form which fitted within local Christianity and modern ways of life. By doing so, she once more acted as a pioneer and *bricoleur*. As Maria referred to during our conversations, she had now realised her major life task: 'uniting *adat* (tradition) and *agama katolik* (Catholicism) in an equivalent measure'.

Concluding remarks

This case illustrated that the *fenia meroh* rite's aim of forcing the self of individual group members into a social identity according to tribal modes of life, is not automatically effected. Despite the profound ritual effects, Maria experienced that the social identity she was supposed to have internalised during initiation in a way was inconsistent with her sense of self. On the one hand, Maria indeed internalised some aspects in her sense of a gendered and tribal self. On the other hand, however, the ritual had not subverted Maria's desire for personal development by means of Western education. By including personal experience and self-determination into the analysis, we have seen that 'internal stimuli' as well as 'external stimuli' affected the ways and the intensity in which Maria utilised her initiation experience: she continuously constructed new selves in reaction to internal and external stimuli. Herewith, she played along with continually changing personal desires, opinions and interests as well as the ever changing socio-cultural context. The importance of the different kinds of stimuli varied throughout Maria's life-course.

Maria's case has further shown that it is not only in the gap between social identification and sense of self (as referred to by Stephen and Herdt), but also in the gap between different social identifications (both striving at reconciliation) that we can find the impetus for creative agency and innovation such as *bricolage*. Especially when these gaps or conflicting identifications involve crises. Initially, Maria did not experience tensions between her tribal and Christian identities. Later, however, she did and it was at this stage in her life that her role as a pioneer and *bricoleur* was expressed. It happened for the first time during a personal crisis (an internal stimulus) during which she received divine visions. Through reconciling her social identity as connected to initiation with her social identity as connected to Christianity, Maria not only achieved a more coherent self but also, in uniting both domains, she simultaneously created new, creolised, healing rituals and became a religious leader. The second time her role as pioneer and *bricoleur* was expressed occurred about one decade later, not during a personal crisis but during a collective crisis of her clan and tribal group. It is interesting that Maria emphasised the necessity of Christian girls (and boys) being initiated: only when they received both ancestral and Christian spiritual knowledge and powers would they become 'complete' persons. From this perspective, Maria reinstated an altered version of the *fenia meroh* rite and acted as one of the ritual leaders. By doing so, she not only realised her major life-task project of reconciling tribal and Christian identifications but, once more, she acted as a pioneer and *bricoleur* who created a new, creolised ritual.

Bibliography

Borsboom, A. 1987. 'Riten en Emoties. Gedragingen rond het Sterven bij Australische Aborigines'. In: P. van der Grijp et. al (eds.), *Sporen in de Antropologie. Liber Amicorum Jan Pouwer*. Nijmegen: Instituut voor Culturele Antropologie, Katholieke Universiteit.

Cohen, A.P. 1994. *Self Consciousness. An Alternative Anthropology of Identity*. London and New York: Routledge.

Courtens, I. 1998. '"As One Woman to the Other". Female Ritual Healers in Northwest Ayfat'. In: J. Miedema, C. Odé and R. Dam (eds.), *Perspectives on the Bird's Head of Irian Jaya, Indonesia. Proceedings of the Conference Leiden, 13-17 October 1997*. Amsterdam: Rodopi, 33-50.

Ewing, K. 1990. 'The Illusion of Wholeness: Culture, Self, and the Experience of Inconsistency'. In: *Ethos* 18(3), 251-79.

Jansen, W. 1993. 'Creating Identities. Gender, Religion and Women's Property in Jordan'. In: M. Brügmann et. al (eds.), *Who's Afraid of Femininity? Questions of Identity*. Amsterdam: Atlanta, 157-69.

Jenkins, R. 1996. *Social Identity*. London and New York: Routledge.

Lutkehaus, N. 1995. 'Feminist Anthropology and Female Initiation in Melanesia'. In: N. Lutkehaus and P. Roscoe (eds.), *Gender Rituals. Female Initiation in Melanesia*. New York: Routledge, 3-30.

Myerhoff, B. 1982. 'Rites of Passage. Process and Paradox'. In: V. Turner (ed.), *Celebration. Studies in Festivity and Ritual*. Washington: Smithsonian Institution Press. Cambridge, Oxford: Polity Press, 109-36.

Otto, T. 1991. *The Politics of Tradition in Baluan. Social Change and the Construction of the Past in a Manus Society*. Nijmegen: Centre for Pacific Studies, University of Nijmegen.

Poole, F.J.P. 1982. 'The Ritual Forging of Identity. Aspects of Person and Self in Bimin-Kuskusmin Male Initiation'. In: G. Herdt (ed.), *Rituals of Manhood. Male Initiation in Papua New Guinea*. Berkeley: University of California Press, 99-154.

Stephen, M. and G. Herdt 1989. 'Introduction'. In: G. Herdt and M. Stephen (eds.), *The Religious Imagination in New Guinea*. New Brunswick and London: Rutgers University Press, 1-15.

Thoonen, L. 1998. '"We Have Accepted the Father First". The Arrival of the Catholic Church in Northwest Ayfat'. In: J. Miedema, C. Odé and R. Dam (eds.), *Perspectives on the Bird's Head of Irian Jaya, Indonesia. Proceedings of the Conference Leiden, 13-17 October 1997*. Amsterdam: Rodopi, 51-79.

Thoonen, L. n.d.. 'Life-history and Female Initiation. A Case-study from Irian Jaya'. In: P. Stewart and A. Strathern (eds.), *Identity Work: Constructing Pacific Lives*. Pittsburgh: Pittsburgh University Press, (forthcoming).

Tuzin, D. 1989. 'Visions, Prophecies, and the Rise of Christian Consciousness'. In: G. Herdt and M. Stephen (eds.), *The Religious Imagination in New Guinea*. New Brunswick and London: Rutgers University Press, 187-211.

White, G.M. and J. Kirkpatrick (eds.), 1985. *Person, Self, and Experience. Exploring Pacific Ethnopsychologies*. Berkeley: University of California Press.

CHAPTER 6

Indigenous Struggles and the Discreet Charm of the Bourgeoisie

Jonathan Friedman

Introduction

Since the mid-Seventies there has been a massive increase in the activities of indigenous minorities in the world. Their struggles have become global news and they have entered numerous global organisations so that they have become an international presence. This, I shall argue, does not mean that they have been globalised and that they are just like everyone else in today's globalising world. They have been part of many a national scene for many decades. They have been marginalised in their own territories, boxed and packaged and sometimes oppressed even unto death. But this has changed in many parts of the world, because the indigenous is now part of a larger inversion of Western cosmology in which the traditional other, a modern category, is no longer the starting point of a long and positive evolution of civilisation, but a voice of Wisdom, a way of life in tune with nature, a culture in harmony, a *Gemeinschaft*, that we have all but lost. Evolution has become devolution, the fall of civilised man. But there is a social reality to this change as well, since the voices of the Other are the voices of real people struggling for control over their conditions of existence, conditions that have been denied to them at the very least. This struggle is not about culture as such, but about social identity of a particular kind, indigenous identity, which is constituted around cultural and experiential continuities that are only poorly mirrored in Western categories, not least, in anthropological categories. Fourth world struggles have been partially — and in some cases very — successful, but they do not operate in a simple structure where the only larger context is the nation state or some other kind of state. They are also part of a dynamic global system, one that is multiplex and contains a number of related processes. There has been a more general inflation of cultural politics and ethnic conflict in the world, but there are also substantial increases in class stratification, economic polarisation and major shifts in capital accumulation. All of these changes constitute a field of analysis that must, I believe, be our central focus of understanding.

We need always to struggle to gain and maintain a perspective on reality, especially in periods, like this one, when it seems to be escaping at such great speed. This is a period of rapid change. It is heralded as the age of information, the age of globalisation. Anthropologists have been much taken by the current transformations but have not done much in the way of research on them. This is unfortunate because the changes or experienced changes have certainly impacted on the discipline. What is going on? Is culture dead? Is consumption where 'its all at' (Miller 1995). Are we entering a new urban civilisation in which hybridity is the rule and the indigenous interesting primarily because it can be incorporated into a larger global celebratory machine, like world-music incorporates its various themes. It is necessary to step back, take it easy, look at the contours of the world we inhabit and investigate seriously the mechanisms that seem to be steering our history. What may appear as chaos, or as 'disjuncture' is truly an appearance, the starting point and not the end point of our attempt to grasp the nature of social reality.

On globalisation

The first appearance that strikes many of us today, is captured by the slogan 'globalisation', which is bandied about in business economics (where it really developed), to cultural studies and even anthropology. Some work on globalisation is analytically and theoretically significant, but much more of it consists in simple opinions and reflections on the immediate. Cultural globalisation thinking is based on a rather myopic view rooted in intellectual experience of the media, internet and travel. It correctly understands that the world has become smaller (but this is always relative: Braudel (1984) made speed of transport a key to his notion of world 'systems', a theme also well developed among geographers, not least Harvey (1989), whose concept of 'time-space compression' does enough to account for much of what globalisation consciousness is all about). Robertson (1995) who was one of the first out in these discussions, places globalisation at the turn of the 20th century, although he has now pushed this back to the ancient world. He is primarily interested in consciousness of a larger world and the way in which people increasingly identify with a larger global unity as well as the way the local expresses the global. The establishment of the League of Nations and many of our new global cults are examples of globalisation, but so is the

Meiji Restoration's importing of European concepts of governance. Cultural form moves and is adopted into increasingly larger places. Now of course this has been going on for quite a long time. Even the conceptual apparatus of globalism is present in the universalism of the Enlightenment or the ecumenism of the late Mediaeval Church, to say nothing of Alexander the Great. So, the historical demarcation of globalisation does not hold water since there is no historical disjuncture involved, or on the contrary, there may be innumerable such breaks. Robertson, at least, explores the ideological structures of globalisation, although without any concrete research material to support his interpretations.

In anthropology, globalisation discourse is even more limited in historical and intellectual scope. It usually refers to a very recent period, the 70's perhaps, and is closer to CNN in its intellectual breadth, the latter having been first with much of the jargon. Here it is used, very much following cultural studies arguments, to dislocate and deconstruct common notions of culture. The latter is no longer anchored in territory. Nor is anything else, according to Appadurai (1993). Instead we are all in movement, not just our migratory selves, but our meanings, our money and our products. And all of these various 'scapes' seem to have gotten lives of their own, leading to a chaotic disjuncture. More pedestrian approaches, such as that of Hannerz (1987), make no clear statements, except that the world has suddenly become culturally hybridised because of the various movements of cultural things, including here, subjects. This is indeed a global vision of matter out of place. Mary Douglas should have seen it coming. But it is also an enjoyable chaos of variable mixtures that has become an identity among certain intellectuals and non-intellectuals that are part of the reason that a larger perspective is needed. Globalising intellectuals, and significant actors in the world today, and they do not seem like indigenous movements. Kelly (1995) after citing Appadurai to the effect that, 'we need to think ourselves beyond the nation' (1993: 411), goes on to make his case against the indigenes:

Across the globe a romance is building for the defense of indigenes, first peoples, natives trammeled by civilisation, producing a sentimental politics as closely mixed with motifs of nature and ecology as with historical narratives... In Hawaii, the high water mark of this romance is a new indigenous nationalist movement, still mainly sound and fury, but gaining momentum in the 1990's... This essay is not about these kinds of blood politics. My primary focus here is not the sentimental island breezes of a Pacific romance, however much or little they shake up the local politics of blood, also crucial to rights for diaspora people, and to conditions of political possibility for global transnationalism (Kelly 1995: 476).

This is an issue of class or elite position to which I shall return. As an introduction to the issue it should merely be noted that globalising cosmopolitan
identity appears to be very much intertwined with the discourse of
globalisation, and that is not a scientific way to go about understanding the
global.

Let us take a step backward here and ask a few questions. Has the world
become globalised so recently? Is everything really different today? Are there
no territorial practices or (God help me) 'cultures' anymore? In much of the
discourse the answer is normative. There are plenty of nationalists and
ethnics and indigenous radicals around, but they have got it all wrong! They
haven't caught up with progress! And progress is globalisation, the formation
of a global village, and the village is really a world city. Oh what fun! ... but
for whom?

There is another side to this, and another approach to the global as well.
That approach is not, I would argue, so caught up in the categories that it
posits, but maintains an old fashioned distance to them. First, globalisation
is not new at all, according to those who have actually researched the
question. While there is much debate, there is also an emergent argument
that the world is no more globalised today than it was at the turn of the
century. Harvey (1989) who has done much to analyse the material bases of
globalisation puts the information revolution in a continuum that includes
a whole series of other technological time-space compressions. Hirst and
Thompson (1996) go much further in trying to de-spectacularise the phenomenon.

Submarine telegraphy cables from the 1860s onwards connected intercontinental
markets. They made possible day-to-day trading and price-making across thousands of miles, a far greater innovation than the advent of electronic trading today.
Chicago and London, Melbourne and Manchester were linked-in close to real time.
Bond markets also became closely interconnected and large-scale international
lending — both portfolio and direct investment — grew rapidly during this period
(Hirst 1996: 3).

Foreign direct investment which was a minor phenomenon relevant to portfolio investment reached 9% of world output in 1913, a proportion that was
not surpassed until the early 1990's (Bairoch and Kozul-Wright 1996: 10).
Openness to foreign trade was not markedly different in 1993 than in 1913.
In the 1890s the British were very taken with all the new world products that
were inundating their markets — cars, films, radio and x-rays and lightbulbs
(Briggs 1996).

As in the late 20th century trade was booming, driven upwards by falling transport costs and by a flood of overseas investment. There was also migration on a vast scale from the Old World to the New.

Indeed, in some respects the world economy was more integrated in the late 19th Century than it is today. The most important force in the convergence of the 19th Century economies was mass migration, mainly to America. In the 1890s, which in fact was not the busiest decade, emigration rates from Ireland, Italy, Spain and Scandinavia were all above 40 per thousand. The flow of people out of Europe, 300,000 people a year in mid-century, reached 1 million a year after 1900. On top of that, many people moved within Europe. True, there are large migrations today, but not on this scale (*Economist* 1997-1998, 20 Dec.-2 Jan., 73).

This was a period of instability, to be sure, of enormous capital flows, like today. It was also a period of declining British hegemony and increasing British cultural expansion. Britain had no enemies as such, except those that it was helping to create by its own export of capital. Arrrighi argues on the basis of historical research that massive financial expansions have accompanied all the major hegemonic declines in the history of the European world system.

To borrow an expression from Fernand Braudel (1984: 246) — the inspirer of the idea of systemic cycles of accumulation — these periods of intensifying competition, financial expansion and structural instability are nothing but the 'autumn' of a major capitalist development. It is the time when the leader of the preceding expansion of world trade reaps the fruits of its leadership by virtue of its commanding position over world-scale processes of capital accumulation. But it is also the time when that same leader is gradually displaced at the commanding heights of world capitalism by an emerging new leadership (Arrighi 1997: 2).

This kind of argument has been central for the kind of historical global systemic analysis that I have engaged since the mid 1970's. If our argument dovetails with Arrighi here, it is due to a certain equifinality of research results and not a mere theoretical similarity. In this model East Asia should be the next centre of the world system, but, many are arguing today that what historically appears as a periodical globalisation may be becoming a permanent state of affairs (Sassen 1998, Friedman 1998a, 1998b). As a result of speed-up, the cycles of accumulation may have so decreased in periodicity as to make geographical shifts a mere short lived tendency rather than process that can be realised. This should not detract from acknowledging the degree to which East Asia has grown to a dominant economic position. It might even be argued that the current crisis is a result of precisely this region's rapid growth in a period of shrinking real world markets.

The purpose of starting with all of this is to set the stage for a perspective. Globalisation has occurred previously. It does not necessarily indicate that we are entering a new era in evolutionary terms, and it is certainly structurally comprehensible in terms of what is known about the world system. Globalisation is a structural phenomenon in the terms set out here. In economic terms, it refers primarily to the decentralisation of capital accumulation. The unification of the world in technological terms is a process that is financed by decentralising capital investment, not by some autonomous cultural or even technological process. And while it certainly generates a global perspective for those who travel along the upper edges of the system, there are other processes that are equally global in terms of their systematicness, but exceedingly local/national/ethnic/indigenous in terms of their constitution. This is the crux of the problem: the current situation is one which is producing both globalised and localised identities. Now in sociological terms both of these phenomena are local. Globalisation is in fact a process of local transformation, the packing in of global events, products and frameworks into the local. It is not about de-localising the local but about changing its content, not least in identity terms. A cosmopolitan is not primarily one who constantly travels the world, but one who identifies with it in opposition to his own locality. That is why so many working class border-crossers in the world are so blatantly innocent of such an identity. They are less interested in celebrating their border crossing than in avoiding precisely the borders which are so deadly dangerous in their lives. The true cosmopolitans are, as always, members of a privileged elite, and they are not so in objectively cultural terms, if such terms make any sense, but in terms of their practices of identity.

Fragmentation and indigeneity

In global perspective, there is not that much disagreement today concerning the fact that the world is pervaded by a plethora of indigenous, immigrant, sexual and other cultural political strategies aimed at a kind of cultural liberation from the perceived homogenising force of the state. In a certain perverted sense this is as true of the new elites as of the regional minorities, but in very different ways. The rise of indigenous movements is part of this larger systemic process, which is not to say that it is a mere product in a mechanical deterministic sense. There are two very different but related aspects to this process. The social process consists in the disintegration of homogenising processes that were the mainstays of the nation state. This has led to increasing conflicts about particular rights and about the rights of 'particular' people, a real conflict between individual vs. collective rights and of the national vs. ethnic. Cultural politics in general is a politics of difference, a transformation of difference into claims on the public sphere, for recognition, for funds, for land. But the differences are themselves differentiated in important and interesting ways, not least in relation to extant structures of identification. Both regional and indigenous identities in nation states make claims based on aboriginality. These are claims on territory as such and they are based on a reversal of a situation that is defined as conquest. Roots here are localised in a particular landscape. There are important ambivalences here. All nationals can also be regionals and many nationals can identify as indigenes. All of this is a question of the practice of a particular kind of identity, an identity of rootedness, of genealogy as it relates to territory. It is in the very structure of the nation state that such identities are prior identities. No nation can logically precede the populations that it unified in its very constitution. This, of course, is a logical and not an empirical structure. There is no guarantee that the nation state did not itself generate regional identities. In fact much of the 'Invention of Tradition', tradition, consists in arguing precisely in such terms. Just as colonial governments created regional and state-to-be identities in Africa, so did nation states create regional minorities at home. What is overlooked in this intellectualist tradition is the way in which identities are actually constituted. The latter consist in linking a matrix of local identifications and experiences to a higher order category which then comes to function as a unifying symbol. The logic of territorial identity is segmentary. It moves in terms of increasing encompassment and it depends on a practice of creating fields of security. It expresses a certain life-orientation, an intentionality, that cannot be waved away by intellectual flourishes.

The differential aspect of indigeneity is not a mere social struggle for recognition of difference. It is about the way difference must be construed and incarnated in real lives. There are extreme examples of this process that are expressive of the deep structures of the nation state. It has led the Afrikaners of South Africa to apply for membership in the World Council of Indigenous Peoples. One of the most spectacular is the formation referred to as the Washitaw nation. The Washitaw according to Dahl (1997) are a self-identified tribe, inhabiting the Louisiana, Mississippi, Oklahoma area. They are black and are affiliated with the extreme right 'Republic of Texas'. They claim to be descended from West Africans who moved to America when the continents were still joined, i.e. before the Indians:

We are the aborigines — the dark-skinned, bushy-haired original inhabitants of 'so-called' north and south America (Muu, Afrumuurican) (Bey 1996: 4).

They have an empress who claims not only land but also an aristocratic descent for her tribe. Dahl shows that there are early references to Indians from the early 19th century that indeed describe the Choctaw as somehow different than their neighbours, but it is not clear that they were black. On the other hand, there are Black Indian tribes in Surinam who are descendants of runaway slaves and it is not unlikely that blacks may have been adopted into the Indian tribes of the area. What is more important is the fact that there is a local identity that may well be one that resulted from historical relations between blacks and Indians, but that it has been transformed into a tribal identity in which the African is paramount and more indigenous than (previous to) the Indian. The structure of the identity is what is important here and its association with the Republic of Texas is significant. For such groups, the major enemy is the state, representative of the cosmopolitan and anti-popular, oppressor of real people, imperial and posi-tively against the kind of aboriginal difference represented by the Washitaw and similar organisations. Their political aim is control over territory and governmental autonomy. They make their own licence plates (as do certain Hawaiian groups) and refuse the entire tax system of the United States.

The structure that is constructed here is one whose logic is organised by the very structure of nationhood, a relation between cultural identity and territory opposed to the territorial state which is perceived as usurper and conqueror. This kind of a structure emerges in conditions in which the state is clearly not representative of the people involved. Such conditions are variable, not only in space, but in time as well. The logic linking peoplehood and indigeneity to the constitution of the nation state is the same logic as well as a structure of opposition. Kapferer, in his discussion of Singhalese and Australian forms of nationalism (1988) suggests that Australia, as a variant of the modern nation state, is one based on an absolute distinction between nation and state. The people identify as separate and subordinate to the state, which is perceived as a foreign body. Australia is exemplary in that it is the history of a country that was not just a colony, but a penal colony, peopled by the powerless and clearly not associated in an organic way with statehood, not any more than prisoners can be said to own the prison that they inhabit. Australia is pervaded by an ambivalence that is quite complex. The core of the country, the nation, is alienated from the state which it has tried to capture. Its relation to both territory and empire places it in a fragile position. If its primary identity is established in relation to its main country of origin as a penal colony, it is also, by definition, an immigrant country. Not only alienated from the state, but even from Nature associated with the savage and uncontrollable outback that can only be conquered but not adapted to or understood (Lattas 1987). The nation, caught between and opposed to the state, the Aborigines and the new immigrants, constitutes a potentially volatile structure of identification that produces both primitivist and anti-primitivist ideologies. It may help to account for a State organised multiculturalism whose policy expressed in *Creative Australia* is aimed at recreating a new national identity based on a notion of combined differences which are not weighted in any clear way, thus alienating both a significant core of Australians and the Aborigines as well. It might also help account for the particular racism directed against Aborigines and which places immigrants and Aborigines in the same category of threat-to-the-nation (Blainey 1995).

The other extreme is represented by 'homogeneous' countries like Germany and even more so by the Scandinavian countries, where peoplehood, nature and the state are fused, and in which the modern state can be said to have been captured by the people, at least until quite recently. Now of course this is a historical process as well. In Sweden, the patriarchal structure was not imbued with a strong notion of representativity until the working class movements transformed its patriarchal organisation into an anti-state of sorts.[1] Where the early patriarchal structure was one in which the ruling class attempted to own the people, its capture inverted this relation. This is of course more complicated, since the state itself is essentially a representative governmental body and not a class. The real conflict relates to the control of the state as a political instrument. The social democratic state, the 'peoples home' became an 'anti-power' in itself, just as Clastres' (1977) anti-chief. The latter is the transparent instrument of peoplehood, but also an instrument of violent control and leveling. The Swedish state reorganised much of social and economic life in striving to create the 'good society' in the name of the people. This representativity was maintained until recently at the same time as state functions were defined actively as extensions of the will of the people. As Clastres and others also have pointed out, such a structure accords an enormous potential for the transformation of the state into an autonomous and self-directed organism. The practice of homogeneity

---

1. It should be noted, however, that the patriarchal state was strongly oriented to the 'people' and to the formation of a national unity of an organic type based very much on the responsibility of the national elites towards the people.

in Sweden was successful largely because it resonated with local identities. The ruling class was in important respects, and excepting here the nobility, an outgrowth of the 'people'. Indigeneity is only fragmenting when it is a separate identity within the state (as with the Saami). The indigenous as a general form of intentionality is about rooting. In certain conditions it produces alternative identities against the state, in other conditions it can produce extreme nationalism within the state. This accounts for the strange fact that the ideology of the New European Right is so similar to that of some indigenous movements. As a strategy it is more general than indigenous movements as such. Self-directedness is what makes such movements distinct. There is no logical way that national states and indigenous movements can co-exist without a change within the larger structure of the state itself, or by concluding compromises that simply accentuate the ambivalence in the situation. The articulation of indigeneity and the world system produces a whole set of new contradictions that are becoming salient in the current situation.

This simplified continuum is a continuum of positions in the global system as well as a continuum of logical variation. It is not a static or general typology but refers to an organisation of identification that can itself change over time. The globalised identities of today are those that have stressed the superiority of hybridity and then of multiculturalism which, from their point of view, is an encompassment of difference, that depends on 'being above it all'. But such positions are only possible with reference to the nation state itself. They are those who define themselves as going beyond the nation state and who declare that the latter is a dying or dead institution and even blame it for the major ills of the world, usually summed up in the word, 'essentialism'. But this is merely one position in a spectrum of possibilities that I cannot explore here. At the other end of the spectrum is indigeneity itself. The relation between national elites and the nationalist position is highly ambivalent insofar as it is ideologically egalitarian at the same time as it is hierarchical in practice.

I suggested that the major operator in this continuum is the dynamics of class formation in the global system. Globalisers are those who identify with the top of the system, while localisers tend to identify with the bottom. There is more to this, however, than mere identity politics. Dirlik (1994) among others (Friedman 1998a, 1998b) has argued that the logic of much postcolonial discourse is the expression of the formation of new globalised cultural elites and Van der Pijl (1998) has suggested interesting historical parallels in the development of the Free Masons. The tendency to redefine the nation or the locality as backward-looking and conservative is a principle

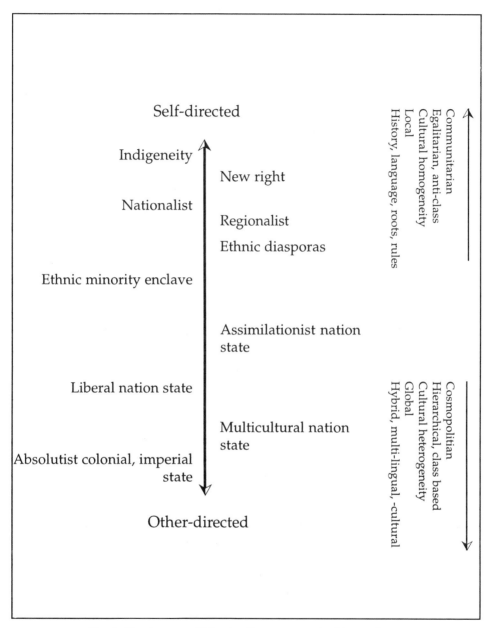

Fig. 1. Continuum of Identity Strategies in the Nation State

self-identifying aspect of the cosmopolitan. In the contemporary situation this seems to be occurring simultaneously with increasing class polarisation and downward mobility among middle and lower classes. Some of the components of this process are discussed below.

Global process and the unification of fragments under capitalism: the new classes

In a recent and very important thesis, Elizabeth Mary Rata, has described what she refers to as the emergence of tribal capitalism. Her hypothesis is that a new class has emerged, a post industrial class, whose wealth and power are based in the new sectors of economic development, the media, Internet and other software sectors, and the professions surrounding these sectors. This class is the bearer of a new ideology, one that must, at first, oppose itself to old capitalist elites. This class occupies an ambivalent position, a combination of particular elite status and a universalistic ideology of equality used in the struggle against the old hegemonic class. This leads to the emergence, out of a guilt complex typical for this class, of a bi-cultural ideology for New Zealand, the idea that We are all both White and Maori, we are special. This is very interesting insofar as it captures the notion of hybridity that is common in other elite ideologies, i.e. Australia, Canada and now, increasingly, among a certain similar cultural elite in the United States (not least academics). This is the global-orientation that I described above in relation to the establishment of globalisation as an ideology. Rata traces the way in which this class ideology articulated with the strengthening of Maori identity via the establishment of a separate cultural project, language schools, a national cultural revival and then land rights and access to capital on established tribal lands. This is a movement from cultural identity to tribal property. The Waitangi Amendment Act established the tribes as corporate political and economic entities and the later Maori Fisheries Commission became the means of transfer of property rights and funds for the establishment of fishing enterprises. The effects of juridification were increasing potential conflicts within the tribes as people struggled to define their genealogical rights to means of production. The issue of exclusion versus inclusion with respect to such rights is an expression of the tendency to class division among the Maori. This is a theme that appears throughout the rest of the thesis and is interesting to compare to peoples such as the Saami in which access to Reindeer and herding territories is a basis of privilege that severely divides the population, even though the colonial history is somewhat different. The combination of tribal organisation and capital accumulation and transfers is important in understanding the way a local movement can become reorganised into the global system. The class structure that seems to be emergent is one in which those who control capital within the tribes introduce wage labour among lower ranked kin turning them into a sub-ordinate class if these relations are reproduced. The second class division emerges between those with and without access to tribal property; more than half of the Maori who still inhabit urban ghettos. Rata makes use of Marxism and especially Regulation Theory to develop her thesis that there is a new form of accumulation emerging here, the 'tribal capitalist mode'.

There is a third process which Rata touches on as well, the formation of a Maori middle-class based on the control of specialised knowledge in the matrix linking the new National cultural class, referred to above, the cultural apparatuses of the state and the reconstruction of Maori society. These are intellectuals who played and continue to play key roles in the Maori move-ment, but also function as consultants to both tribes and government, as mediators and teachers. It is, of course, to be expected that intelligentsia should emerge within such movements and that they should become increas-ingly established as the movements become institutionalised. They are, after all, the focal points for political unity, and often sources of political action as well as pivots in the competition for funding and rights. It would be a sign of incomprehension, not untypical of anthropologists, to criticize such developments on the grounds that they deviate from the anthropologist's conception of traditional culture. Even the class aspect of this development is quite logical in terms of the process of integration itself. On the other hand, such divisions are bound to be sources of potential conflict within the emerging political community.

But there is more to this development that has everything to do with the state of global capitalism today. This is related to the extreme decentralisa-tion of capital accumulation and the spectacular shift from real investment to fictitious accumulation. Sassen (1996) estimates that there are at least 75 trillion dollars in financial circulation. Since the 80's financial assets have grown 2.5 times faster than the gross domestic product of the richest nations and they are continuing to grow logarithmically in this period of real over-production, as evidenced by the Asian crisis. Much of this money is trans-ferred in the form of porkbarrels to firms dealing with all kinds of non-productive activity, not least among the so-called consultancies and NGO's that have developed explosively in the past decade. There are of course many NGO's that are engaged in productive activities or in genuinely effective activities related to the survival of indigenous peoples, but there is no hindrance to the massive development of carpetbaggers and treasure hunters. One of these is the recent history of an organisation calling itself Uhaele, which approached the Office of Hawaiian Affairs (official state representative body for Hawaiian claims) with an offer to help them manage the approaching Hawaiian sovereignty for a sizeable fee. A contract was almost consummated but came to light suddenly and the whole affair was called off in a throttle of scandalous accusations concerning who had signed the agreement with the firm. The same organisation had some earlier dealings in Vanuatu where, after signing a lease for a small island, it proceeded to advertise the place as a tax haven for people of superior intelligence and sold shares in the island that was soon to be declared the independent country of Aurora. Nevels and his family were to be the royalty of this constitutional monarchy.

It is intended to create an independent country called AURORA, with minimal government, maximum personal freedom and a laissez-faire economy... It is intended that the population of Aurora will be very cosmopolitan; admission as first citizens will be based upon needed skills, professions and talents and belief in the political and economic principles upon which the country is founded. Men and women of numerous races, of varied religions, will be invited to apply (Nevels n.d. 1).

Needless to say, the independence never materialised. Vanuatu stopped it with military threats. Nevels disappeared and his investors lost their money. Nevels is a lawyer and when Uhaele surfaced, its home base was Reno, Nevada... of course. The group entered into elaborate negotiations with the Office of Hawaiian Affairs (OHA) which was scheduled to receive several hundred million dollars as reparations from the federal government and other funds from the State government for a historical series of acts which deprived Hawaiians of their political rights and their land base. These entailed ultimately that Uhaele would by and large control the administration of OHA's economy in exchange for 20% of the net proceeds. Now, as Uhaele had no capital, no employees, no equipment, this was clearly a goldmine for them, a challenge to their talent for getting a piece of the action. 'Uhaele was a letterhead and a telephone' (*Ke Kia'i* 1991: 8).

   The world is full of firms like this, on the hunt after the mass of financial wealth that is circulating into 'good causes', whether at the national or international level. In all of this there is always a tendency to class formation, however little this may be manifested. It has certainly led to the formation of global elite representatives of various groups who are immediately implicated in a field of tension, between their very rooted places of origin and the inordinate power of global funds to incorporate them into the global cocktail circuit. The United Nations and a host of other mega-organisations have been gathering places for the formation of global identities, places, as well, for the destruction of local accountability. The vitality of certain indigenous movements is measurable by the degree to which indigenous peoples manage to capture or replace their representatives in such situations. But this is truly a field of contradictory forces. The process of fragmentation via indigenisation is subject to processes of social *verticalisation* that are related to the institutions and funds that circulate in this period of globalisation of capital.

Verticalisation, fragmentation and the social transformation of the global system

Verticalisation, or class polarisation, is a vector of the global system and it effects all of the forms of fragmentation that represent the other major vector in the system. Ethnification and class formation are the paired processes that characterise this simultaneous development. The transformation of the nation state into a modern form of the Absolutist state is an expression of the same process. The increase in clientelism in European States, and between the states and regions and the Union, is part of the disintegration of the homogeneous nation state. The notion of a Europe based on regions rather than states is part of this and would transfer power to Brussels while undermining the relation between states and their subregions. Thus, the notion entertained by some of the cultural globalists, that we have somehow moved beyond the obsolete nation state and are entering a new world of the postnational, is a misconstrual of a more complex situation. While it is true that global capital exercises increasing power over national conditions of reproduction, this does not spell the end of the nation state as such, but its transformation, from a homogeneous entity in which common goals link the 'people' and their state, to a separation of the state from the nation. The state itself, according to ongoing research is becoming increasingly oriented to international capital flows, to the regulation of such flows as they relate to conditions of maintenance of territorial economic units. The recent Asian crisis has made this resoundingly evident. George Soros apparently lost over 100 million dollars in Asia, and he has, more generally, clamored for increasing international controls over financial flows.

Although I have made a fortune in the financial markets, I now fear that untrammeled intensification of laissez-faire capitalism and the spread of market values to all areas of life is endangering our open and democratic society. The main enemy of the open society, I believe, is no longer the communist but the capitalist threat... Too much competition and too little cooperation can cause intolerable inequities and instability... The doctrine of laissez-faire capitalism holds that the common good is best served by the uninhibited pursuit of self-interest. Unless it is tempered by the recognition of a common interest that ought to take precedence over particular interests, our present system... is liable to break down (Soros 1997: 45, 48).

This expresses a desire, at present being implemented by many states, for a stronger regulation of the conditions of equilibrium in the world market. Work by Sassen (1998) indicates that Nation State functions are increasingly shifting from national to international issues. This is what might be called the lift-off of the State. In Europe it is related in its turn to the emerging relation between nation states and the European Union. European governmental organs are not tied to constituencies as are national organs. They have experienced problems of corruption, in uncontrolled use of power, in inordinately high remunerations for their members, but this is also reflected in the many 'credit card' crises at the national level: there is a general accountability crisis in the nation state which is expressed in declining respect for politicians who are considered increasingly to be a class with their own interests. Politicians, on the other hand, have in various ways expressed their distaste for ordinary people whom they often accuse for being red-necked and nationalist. That this can occur in a country like Sweden is ample evidence of the forces involved. Carl Bildt, European Bosnia negotiator and former leader of the Conservative Party, has written that a European government is the ultimate solution for the continent and that it could well take a form reminiscent of the Habsburg Empire. Similar statements have come from social democrats and others. Sweden, which is officially multicultural, has stated categorically in a government bill that it no longer has a common history since so many different immigrant groups were present on Swedish soil (where does that put the United States or Canada?). The bill goes on to formulate a new structure for the state that moves clearly in the direction of a plural society, based on the association of different cultural groups. There are tendencies in the media elite and in the state to classify any opposition to this planned transformation as racism. The overall impact of the transformation of the global system is one that places the state in a new kind of vortex of global forces, one where it becomes a focal point for an association of different groups rather than the representative of what one comedian has called 'that special interest group, the people'. This structural tendency is one in which the political class and the other cultural elite class factions identify increasingly with the global, in which, as has been said of the American situation,

They have more in common with their counterparts in Brussels or Hong Kong than with the masses of Americans not yet plugged into the network of global communications (Lasch 1995: 35).

Now the state, transformed in this way, becomes the focal point of certain distributions of favours, funds and positions to an increasingly fragmented former unity. The clientelism to which I referred above is very much the product of this transformation. Regional, immigrant and indigenous minorities all become subject to this changing field of forces. The field tends to create new elites that move within the global sphere, ranked lower than the real big-shots, since they are clients to the real sources of power and money. They may have global spheres of their own, like the U.N. based World Council of Indigenous Peoples, and they sometimes mingle with higher ranked elites, but they are primarily local clients in the global mesh of neo-feudal dependencies.

The rise of indigenous movements was part of a general process of transformation in the world system, one in which the weakening of the Western nation state took the form of the rise of cultural politics. This was, as suggested, at the start, part of a common decline in hegemony which was also expressed in a rapid increase in economic globalisation. Whether this is a temporary or permanent change cannot be determined here because the general periodicity of accumulation has increased, because globalisation has become more rapid, cheaper and increasingly institutionalised. It has, in any case, produced major transformations of class relations; the emergence of a new cosmopolitan elite or congeries of elites that have been sucked into the globalisation process and who are the producers of globalising representations of the world, understandings that challenge the very existence of the nation state and proclaim a new post-national era at the same time as fragmentation and cultural conflict are more pervasive than ever at lower levels of the system. The articulation of verticalising and fragmenting process produces the paradox of class division at all levels, including movements that begin in urban ghettos. It is important to take these contradictions into account when trying to understand the trajectory of indigeneity in today's world.

Making the world safe for capitalism

The processes of vertical and horizontal polarisation that I have discussed here dovetail with the work of many other authors who have written about the cultural state of the world. Appaduarai (1993), as I have indicated, has noted a certain aspect of this transformation which he understands as an increasing confrontation between new diasporic and old national structures. His position, however, is more ideological than scientific. He does concede that the future may indeed entail a bloody conflict, but he assumes that the result of the conflict will necessarily be a new world of 'cultural freedom'. Others have stressed the marvels of cultural mixture and multiculturalism and have transformed former progressive ideologies of 'socialism' into a struggle for cultural plurality and cultural mixture. The new transnational ideology is certainly a force in the world, but it does not come from the grassroots. Its source is the world's various political and cultural elites. The forces involved in the processes of polarisation entailed the conversion of status from local to global for many; for rising middle classes and even indigenous representatives. For the latter, of course, such a shift implies a contradiction in identity, a contradiction between the rootedness of indigeneity and the cosmopolitan life of the higher circulating elites of the world arena. But even the economic forces involved here can easily lead to a stratification of indigenous groups within more restricted arenas where porkbarrels and state funding can be used to cement hierarchical control over the resources won over by indigenous movements. This is an important issue for indigenous movements themselves and many of the participants in such movements are acutely aware of these issues.

Much new research is needed and this is not merely a statistical question. The understanding of new social connections, new circles of friends and increasingly relatives[2] is in order. The role of the intellectuals is also crucial in understanding these developments. When Tony Giddens becomes an important advisor for Tony Blair in the name of the return of a socialist agenda, we might take a closer look at the agenda itself, the fact that Clinton, Blair and Prodi have joined forces leaving more 'traditional' socialists such as Jospin out in the cold. When George Soros calls for a new global regulation of capitalism, he is not calling for socialism but for a stability program to make the world safe for his investments. The new alliance of the left might well be a new example of the structural adjustment of the elites.

---

2. Kinship in such networks emerges through marriage and the extension of privileges to relatives and children.

Reflecting on actors, identities and resources

The image of the world conjured up in the preceding pages is one in which there is an interplay between a redistribution of resources as a result of systemic change, and a scramble — and even struggle — for advantage for some and survival for others. But I would also argue that the conditions of action are also very much determined by structural transformations that the various actors involved cannot access or transform directly. This is a Kafkaesque world whose actors may know what they are doing, but do not know what they are doing is doing. That is, they are largely unaware of the hidden processes that form their array of choices and which even structure their intentionalities. These processes are, in this discussion, the global processes that are currently reorganising conditions of existence throughout most of the world. When new cultural identities appear in which people opt for roots, where national, ethnic, indigenous and regional populations become entrenched and opposed to one another, this is not a mere question of rational actors. I argue here that these new identities are part of a process of indigenisation that is quite general, one that is produced by a failure or reversal of modernism and is ultimately related to the dislocations occuring as a result of globalisation. This strategy of rooting is generalised enough to produce the strange bedfellows referred to above in which there is a total collapse of left and right and the emergence of a mixed bag of peoplehoods often allied to one another.

Similarly the formation of cosmopolitan elites can only be understood in the transformation of motivational structures that informs the lives of elites. Globalisation is itself a crucial part of this, and the technological speed up that increases the rate of global access might be said to supply the modality for the new cosmopolitanism. But the vertical polarisation in which new elites are emerging whose identities are being separated from their territorial bases is the core of this transformation. The formation of identity is a process that cannot be reduced to manipulation and entrepreneurship. Collective identity is a more pervasive process based on strong resonance and shared experience of changing conditions which in its turn can be used and even exploited by leaders, and even here the emergence and the power of new leaders and elites depends very much on the social forms within which they appear. The cosmopolitanisation of indigenous movements occurs in the conjuncture of the two processes that I have discussed and produces paradoxes in which new positions are established and in which identities may become contradictory. Here the way in which actors function as group representatives is crucial in understanding final outcomes. While some have indeed found their place in United Nation Circles, others have not and have lost the support of their constituencies in the process. The specific cases need to be understood as ethnographic and historically specific phenomena, and here ethnography, one informed by the understanding of large scale process becomes absolutely decisive.

Conclusion: routes versus roots

I have tried to suggest that there is a certain systematicity in the world arena that can adequately account for concrete manifestations of globalisation as well as the many discourses that have seriously misrepresented them. Some years ago it was suggested by Arif Dirlik (1994) that the new post-colonial discourse was engendered within a particular class position, that of the new post-colonial elites themselves, and that it was extraordinarily adequate to the current phase of globalised capitalism. I suggested in another article that the ideologies of hybridity were integral parts of an emergent cosmopolitan perspective that combined an anti-modernist culturalism with an experienced globalisation of identity producing an ideology of global cultural encompassment (Friedman 1998a). If former internationalists and cosmopolitans were primarily modernists and not terribly concerned with their cultural identities, the new variety is just as concerned as all others to discover roots. For the cosmopolitan the roots become necessarily multiple and entwined in their worldly journeys; roots with routes. Clifford's (1997) collection of essays, *Routes*, expresses — but also explores — the interaction of roots and routes, even if he is primarily concerned with the identities of objects. Diasporas, for example can certainly be understood as the culturalisation of migration, but as identities they usually imply some form of placedness or point of origin. This is the rather trivial paradox in the notion that somehow we can move from the national to the transnational in the sense of superceding the former, when it is, of course, impossible to even conceive of the transnational without the national. The only non-rooted cosmopolitans are the older variety of internationalists who identified entirely with social projects, such as socialism, or with some other form of future orientation, but never with any form of culturally framed identity. The unease in the identity of today's cultural cosmopolitans may account for their obvious disliking for the indigenous identities that, numerically at least, are clearly on the rise and in the great majority.

My argument is that all of these emergent identities are existentially authentic, true to themselves. They have an experiential force that accounts for their ability to attract new members. From cosmopolitan hybrids to

Chiapas, all are true to themselves, even taking account of the complexities and variations of such identities. And in order to understand these real identities, which are not mere products of inventions and manipulations, we must try and understand the social conditions in which they arise. These are conditions that shape experience and, thus, channel cultural production. On the other hand we must also be cognizant of the nature of ideological struggle in the present conjuncture. This is one that is being waged in different ways and from different positions. While indigenous struggles are primarily locally focused, they have been globalised in the channels of international political organisations that have amplified their voice. While this produces a formidable contradiction in opening up a field of social identity for global representatives of the local, the latter has continuously produced forms of resistance to the formation of a new global power structure within the indigenous political sphere. Indigenising identities and ideologies make no pretensions to re-organising the world. The cosmopolitan struggle is quite different insofar as it is based in a rising elite faction, a globalised elite that self identifies as encompassing the cultural variety of the world. This struggle concerns ideological hegemony, an attempt to re-envision the world as a multicultural based yet hybridised unity-in-diversity. Elites are well placed to assert such a vision, but this placement is one that is increasingly questioned by those who do not occupy nor wish to occupy such positions. Lest we be taken in by the curious logical fallacy that would encourage us to move 'beyond place' to shift our thinking from roots to routes, it might be noted that routes connect places, that they have origins (roots) as well as end points and that to move beyond place entails the question, 'and where do we end up then'?

Bibliography

Arrighi, G. 1997. 'Globalization, State Sovereignty, and the "Endless" Accumulation of Capital' (manuscript).

Appadurai, A. 1993. 'Patriotism and its Futures'. In: *Public Culture* 5(3): 411-29.

Bairoch, P. and R. Kozul-Wright 1996. 'Globalization Myths: Some Historical Reflections on Integration, Industrialization and Growth in the World Economy'. UNCTAD Discussion Paper 113.

Bey, U.S. 1966. 'We are the Washitaw. Columbia via USA': The Washitaw Nation (manuscript).

Blainey, G. 1995. 'The New Racism'. In: *The Australian*. 8 April.

Braudel, F. 1984. *The Perspective of the World*. New York: Harper and Row.

Briggs, A. and D. Snowman 1996. *Fins de Siecle: How Centuries End, 1400-2000*. New Haven and London: Yale University Press.

Clastres, P. 1977. *Society Against the State*. Oxford: Blackwell.

Clifford, J. 1997. *Routes: Travel and Translation in the late Twentieth Century*. Cambridge, Mass.: Harvard University Press.

Dahl, G. 1997. 'God Save our County! Radical Localism in the American Heartland' (manuscript).

Dirlik, A. 1994. 'Post-colonial Aura: Third World Criticism in the Age of Global Capitalism'. In: *Critical Inquiry*, Winter, 328-56.

Economist 1997-98. 'The Century the Earth Stood Still' vol. 346, 71-73.

Friedman, J. 1998a. 'The Hybridization of Roots and the Abhorrence of the Bush'. In: M. Featherstone and S. Lash (eds.), *Spaces of Culture: City, Nation, World*. London: Sage, 230-56.

Friedman, J. 1998b. 'Class Formation, Hybridity and Ethnification in Declining Global Hegemonies'. In: K. Olds, P. Dickin, P. Kelly, L. Kong, and H. Yeung (eds.), *Globalisation and the Asia-Pacific*. London: Routledge, 183-201.

Hannerz, U. 1987. 'The World in Creolization'. In: *Africa* 57, 546-59.

Harvey, D. 1989. *The Postmodern Condition*. Oxford: Blackwell.

Hirst, P. 1996. 'Global Market and the Possibilities of Governance'. Paper presented at the Conference on Globalization and the New Inequality, University of Utrecht, November 20-22.

Hirst. P. and Thompson, G. 1996. *Globalization in Question*. Cambridge: Polity.

Kapferer, B. 1988. *Legends of People, Myths of State: Violence, Intolerance and Political Culture in Sri Lanka and Australia*. Washington: Smithsonian Institution Press.

Ke Kia'i 1991. 'The Odd Couple: Uhaele and OHA'. In: *Ke Kia'i* [The Guardian] 2 (9).

Kelly, J. 1995. 'Diaspora and World War, Blood and Nation in Fiji and Hawai'i'. In: *Public Culture* 7, 475-97.

Lasch, C. 1995. *The Revolt of the Elites*. New York: Norton.

Lattas, A. 1987. 'Aborigines and Contemporary Australian Nationalism: Primordiality and the Cultural Politics of Otherness'. In: G. Cowlishaw and B. Morris (eds.), *Race Matters*. Canberra: Aboriginal Studies Press, 223-55.

Miller, D. 1995. 'Consumption and Commodities'. In: *Annual Review of Anthropology* 24, 141-61.

Nevels, L.N. n.d. *The Aurora Corporation*.

Rata, E. M. 1997. Global Capitalism and the Revival of Ethnic Traditionalism in New Zealand: The Emergence of Tribal-Capitalism. Ph.D. thesis, University of Auckland.

Robertson, R. 1995. 'Glocalization. Time-Space and Homogeneity-Heterogeneity'. In: S. Lasch, M. Featherstone and R. Robertson (eds.), *Global Modernities*. London: Sage, 25-44.

Sassen, S. 1996. *Losing Control: Sovereignty in an Age of Globalization*. New York: Columbia University Press.

Sassen, S. 1998. 'Servicing the Global Economy: Reconfigured States and Private Agents'. In: K. Olds, P. Dicken, P. Kelly, L. Kong, and H. Yeung (eds.), *Globalisation and the Asia-Pacific*. London: Routledge, 149-62.

Soros, G. 1997. 'The Capitalist Threat'. In: *The Atlantic Monthly* 279(2), 45-58.

Van der Pijl, K. 1998. *Transnational Classes and International Relations*. London: Routledge.

CHAPTER 7

Dissimulations: Representing Ladakhi Identity

Martijn van Beek

Now the strange thing about this silly if not desperate place between the real and the really made-up is that it appears to be where most of us spend most of our time as epistemically correct, socially created, and occasionally creative beings. We dissimulate (Taussig 1993: xviii).

The granting of autonomy to the Ladakh region of Jammu and Kashmir (J&K) in September 1995 was warmly welcomed by politicians from the main political parties in New Delhi. Prime Minister Narasimha Rao telegraphed his congratulations to Ladakh's leaders, and the Indian national press reported the event in glowing terms. Already in the 1930s political leaders from Ladakh had been demanding special administrative arrangements, resources, and policies in recognition of the 'distinct identity' of the region (Bray 1991; van Beek 1998b; van Beek and Bertelsen 1997). At last everyone agreed, it seems, that the recognition of Ladakhis' demands was timely, necessary, and just. At the swearing in of the newly elected members of the 'Ladakh Autonomous Hill Development Council, Leh' (LAHDC),[1] Governor Krishna Rao, local politicians, religious leaders, and representatives of 'social' organisations such as the Ladakh Buddhist Association and the Muslim Anjumans,[2] were gathered on Leh's pologround to celebrate this moment of recognition of Ladakh's 'identity'.

---

1. Autonomous Councils were offered to both Leh and Kargil district, but the latter declined the offer for the time being. Kargil's population feels vulnerable because of the district's greater dependence and proximity to the Kashmir valley, and it was feared that accepting regional autonomy might have been read as lack of support for the militants there (van Beek 1996). Since 1997, Pakistani troops have repeatedly shelled Kargil town, and in the spring of 1999 a major incursion across the Line of Control (LoC) forced tens of thousands of people to flee to safer places. These events, too, were interpreted by some as 'punishment' for lack of support for militant separatists. See *Himal* (May 1998) for a series of articles on the problems of the populations on both sides of the LoC.

The Ladakh region comprises two districts, called Kargil and Leh after their respective capitals. The region covers the northern and eastern parts of J&K state, bordering on Baltistan (administered by Pakistan) and Tibet (under China's rule). Kargil district has a predominantly Muslim population, while Leh is inhabited almost exclusively by Buddhists. The total population of the region, estimated at more than 200,000, is almost equally divided between the two 'communities'.[3] A 'cold desert'(Bhasin 1992) on the western edge of the Tibetan plateau between the Himalaya and Karakoram ranges, the economy of the region is based on subsistence agriculture and animal husbandry. State and army employment, provision of local produce and labour, and tourism, constitute the main sources of monetary income.

There is little agreement among the celebrants who gathered on Leh's polo ground to inaugurate the council, among academics or 'ordinary' Ladakhis, as to exactly *what* Ladakh's identity is, or ought to be. Yet references to such an identity are made when Ladakh is represented in words or images, in political negotiations, or in marketing Ladakh as a tourist destination or worthy recipient of development aid (van Beek 1998a). The question arises as to *how* we should understand the fact that people can talk about and celebrate Ladakhi identity in this manner as if 'it' *is* in fact unproblematic and matter-of-fact like. Many of the actors gathered on the polo ground were quite aware of their disagreement about what Ladakhi identity is. Moreover, as we shall see, *Ladakhi* identity is officially impossible, and Ladakhis' own social experience 'falsifies' the simple categorisations that are in official use.

2. There are two main Muslim organisations in Leh. The Anjuman-e Mu'in-e Islam is the main Sunni social organisation. The Anjuman-e Imamia is its Shia counterpart. There is also, in political contexts, a Ladakh Muslim Association (See e.g. Pinault, in press). However, this is merely an ad hoc body without formal membership, leadership, or constitution, and presently defunct. The main Buddhist organisation is the Ladakh Buddhist Association (LBA). Other prominent Buddhist social organisations are the All-Ladakh Gonpa Association and the Lamdon Social Welfare Organisation. In addition, many monasteries have established welfare associations.

3. Population figures are estimated on the basis of extrapolation from decennial growth rates at the time of the last regular census held in 1981 and population figures form a 'mini census' conducted in 1987 in connection with the granting of Scheduled Tribe status to the majority of Ladakh's population (discussed below). The report from this special census remains classified.

The fetishism of identities

As I have argued elsewhere (1996; 1997b), in analysing the discourse of identity in politics in the Ladakh region, acceptance of the terms of the contestation as representative of 'real' identities in Ladakh would mean abandoning analysis precisely at that point where it should begin. This would produce a tautological reasoning where what we observe and are presented with is treated as in fact objective and representative.

While most anthropologists are highly sceptical towards the straightforward primordialist reasoning still dominant in mainstream political science, there are fewer who will interrogate the notion of identity per se. Concrete, 'empirical' identities may be socially constructed, but the existence of a set of collectivities that are more meaningful and stable than other collectivities at a certain moment in world-historical time-space is assumed, and explained by reference to the 'cultures' and 'systems of meanings' that are tautologically imputed to these groups. The identity of the group explains the group's identity.[4] Identity is reified and made to stand for itself, as something that explains, the key to social order, rather than something which needs analysis, contextualisation and explanation. In this culturalist avatar of biological essentialism, 'identity' is fetishised, groups appear to exist 'naturally' and singularly.[5] This notion, in public use as well as in much academic discourse, serves to obscure the constitution of identities and the ongoing play of identifications and representations.

On the other hand, a dismissal of the idiom of politics — identity, community, religion — as merely epiphenomenal means abandoning the analysis of the *form* in which demands are made, the often bloody reality and apparent efficacy of identity politics. While the form of Ladakh's movement for regional autonomy between 1989 and 1993 was, indeed, what in South Asia is called 'communal', this characterisation not only fails to capture the substance of the movement, but also the very causes that gave rise to it.[6] The

---

4. James Tully (1995: 199), quoting Wittgenstein's *Philosophical Investigations*, writes: 'His interlocutor insists, surely, "a thing is identical with itself". Wittgenstein replies, there "is no finer example of a useless proposition, which yet is connected with a certain play of the imagination. It is as if in imagination we put a thing into its own shape and saw that it fitted"'.

5. The concept of 'community', perhaps even more so than identity, remains undertheorised. See e.g. Connolly (1991) and Holmes (1993: 176 ff).

6. 'Communalism' in the South Asian context refers to religious 'community' partisanship. For a thorough conceptual and historical discussion of communalism, see Pandey (1990, especially chapter 1).

demand for autonomy, to put it briefly, is rooted in the perceived discrimination of the region in the allocation of resources by the state government
of Jammu and Kashmir. Demands reflect this economic and political complex
of causes fuelled by fundamental changes in local livelihoods and expanding
state intervention. The communal form or idiom of the movement — the
'language of contention' (Roseberry 1996) — is above all a consequence of the
reading by sections of Leh's political elite of the Indian political system *in
practice*. There is a strong local belief that communalism — a term that in
South Asia refers to the politics and practices of sectarianism and religious
community exclusivism — dominates the political process, in spite of the fact
that such bias is officially denied and denounced.

In the following, I will suggest that we need to distinguish between the
everyday conception and use of concepts such as 'identity' as necessary
fictions in the context of contestations over access to and allocation of
(cultural, political, economic, symbolic) resources, and the ultimate impossibility, or lack of *fit*, between such concepts and the multiplicity and fluidity
of practices of social identification. Many recognise the 'fact' that any specific
'identity' is a fiction and cannot correspond with the totality of the *social* that
supposedly represents.[7] Yet this fictitiousness is forgotten, or ignored, like
a public secret (Taussig 1993).[8] We all live in a 'realm of appearance and
artifice' (Bewes 1997: 112), muddling through with necessarily limited understandings of our 'real conditions', understandings which are in turn structured through relations of power and by (culturally coded) notions about
reality.

Since the circumscription (e.g. by bureaucrats, scientists, or activists) of any
single 'identity' must necessarily conflict with people's lived experience of
multiple and relatively fluid identifications, it is unlikely that any such
singular 'identity' is simply, naturally, or consistently accepted by social
actors.[9] And because people generally are very well capable of distinguishing

---

7. It is worth remembering the distinction between *vertreten* and *darstellen* that is
   embedded in the concept. See e.g. Spivak (1988).
8. The importance of memory and forgetting as active processes is discussed elegantly in
   Anderson (1991; 1993) and in the recent collection edited by Gillis (1996).
9. At the same time, stereotypes, e.g. about 'ethnic' groups, often persist in the face of
   experiences and 'facts' that would appear to debunk them. For Žižek (1992: 49) this is
   'proof' that an ideology is really succeeding. Although approaching ideology from a
   different angle, Etienne Balibar similarly sees the impossibility of dispelling racist ideas
   through information as a consequence of the fact that racism is '*effective* thinking upon
   an *illusory* object' (Balibar and Wallerstein 1991: 221 emphasis in the original). It is this

between the appropriate contexts for specific identifications, the acceptance *in specific contexts* of particular 'necessary fictions' such as a specific articulation of Ladakhi 'identity' does not necessarily cause anxiety or insecurity in individuals about their own 'identity'.

The question arises how we should understand what appears to be the disappearance of diversity, fluidity and multiplicity from conceptions of identity. Surely no system of classification, no matter how hegemonic or violently instituted, can erase social experience altogether.[10] Just because singular or monochromatic social order is bureaucratically applied, politically claimed, and scientifically imagined and underwritten, does not make it so in the entirety of social existence and experience. The will to order, in short, does not *fully* determine social reality. The question, then, is how social actors *practically* deal with this real ambiguity and instability that forever flies in the face of their orderings. As Timothy Bewes (1997: 59) puts it succinctly: 'The business of humanity is precisely one of compromise, "inauthenticity" and fabrication.' Ongoing processes of reconciliation of the impossible — dissimulations — are, then, the substance of culture.

Official identities, social identifications

As Herzfeld (1992: 108) notes, 'cultural identity is the material of national rhetoric, social variation that of everyday experience'. Our everyday identifications, in other words, are creative and multiple, drawing on a range of repertoires depending on what we think the social situation might require. Different social situations, then, elicit or require different forms of identification. What makes agreement and everyday use of 'identity' possible is precisely the lack of definition of what exactly Ladakhi identity *is*, and that it is in those instances when unambiguous, singular, and bounded identities are expected or demanded, that the desire for semantic purity makes the irreducibility of practices of social identification appear as problematic and even pathological. This in turn may then be used as a justification for restoration of a purportedly 'natural' or 'traditional' order.[11]

---

misrecognition of the constructs of the mind — and its real effect that 'whoever classifies ... causes to exist in practice that illusion that is collectivity based on the similitude of its members' (ibid. 221) — that makes identity fetishism so pernicious.

10. Totalitarian ideology may seek such a total 'hold' over people, where subjects 'no longer feel any contradiction between it and reality' (Žižek 1992: 49). It is this *desire* to erase the 'traces of its own impossibility' that is typical of ideology.

11. See e.g. the discussions by Billig (1995) and Herzfeld (1992; 1996).

The impossibility of grounding national identity in essences of blood, language or territory was already recognised by Renan (1992 [1887]), as was the need to forget — and remembering to forget, as Anderson (1991: 200) reminds us. It was, according to him, the active willingness of individuals to identify with the impossible idea of the nation, that made the nation exist. To engage in deconstruction of certain identities, therefore, is a rather pointless exercise if the aim is to show their lack of authenticity or fit with social practice. All social identities, all communities can be subjected to such an exercise. Rather, as Anderson exhorts us, we should investigate the ways in which communities are imagined, the conditions and processes that make their existence appear *as if* they were independent of ongoing production, dissimulation, and representation. Dissimulation, then, is not necessarily duplicitous or disingenuous, but the very substance of social identification.

While the 'violence' of imposing singular identities on people is widely recognised today by social theorists, political and bureaucratic practice — rooted in and constitutive of a particular global ordering — requires a relatively stable singular order in order to fulfil promises of political representation and proper management. Liberal democracy, citizenship, and the discourse of rights, practically require that demands or claims be justified through reference to some form of collective identity.[12] Hence, we see a gradual convergence, through the mutually conditioning, reflexive processes of identification and classification of diverse social actors, of the imagined order with the order of practice. Social reality, at least in a rhetorical and performative sense, asymptotically tends towards compliance with the desired grammar of identities constructed by academics, bureaucrats, political leaders, and 'ordinary' people. The world, through the constitution of an ever finer matrix of sub-national, minority, or indigenous peoples, becomes gradually more compliant with the 'universal code of particularity', and the metaphorical quality of conceptions of 'identity' is gradually forgotten or ignored. Yet the appearance of stability of 'identities' is necessarily precarious and temporary. 'The moment of the 'final' suture never arrives' (Laclau and Mouffe 1985: 86).

12. This point, of course, is central to the argument for what Spivak calls 'strategic essentialism', and a common consideration in political movements of 'indigenous peoples' (see e.g. Assies 1994; Dyck 1985; Stavenhagen 1994).

Identifying Ladakhis

The justifications of demands offered by Ladakhi political activists in terms of Ladakhi 'identity' are to be understood first of all in the context of the normative frame of identification offered by the state.[13] The rise and prevalence of the politics of identity, and identity discourse, testifies above all to the hegemony of modern ideas and institutions such as nation and state (Handler 1994: 38).[14] Despite premature rumours of the death of the nation-state and the end of history, the contemporary world continues to be organised politically and administratively through the states system.[15] This system is characterised by what Michael Billig calls a 'universal code of particularity' that *constitutes* national identity as a 'form of life', a code that assumes an 'identity of identities' (Billig 1995: 73). Yet, this code, enshrined for example in international law and the United Nations charter, presents itself as merely *recognising* the reality of a world of peoples and nations and seeks to give each a proper home, i.e. a state. More appropriately, this code must be understood as *constitutive* of the 'natural' order it seeks to represent.

The preamble to the Constitution of the State of Jammu and Kashmir states its project and basis of legitimacy unambiguously:[16]

We the people of Jammu and Kashmir, having solemnly resolved [...] to secure to ourselves [...] Justice, social, economic and political; Liberty of thought, expression, belief, faith and worship; Equality of status and of opportunity, and to promote among us all: fraternity, assuming the dignity of the individual and the unity of the Nation (Jammu and Kashmir 1986: 314).

13. This is not to suggest that scientists and bureaucrats unilaterally construct representations of Ladakhi identity/-ies out of thin air. They also draw on local practices, and local actors are implicated in the same process of production of representations of singular identities.

14. 'Realist' international relations theorists on the other hand see the rise of identity politics as an expression of the vitality of ethnic identities at a world-historical time of the birth of a new order. See e.g. Horowitz (1985); Jalali (1992-93); Moynihan (1993). While such positions may be regarded as hopelessly inadequate and outdated by anthropologists, it is worth recognising that this classical perspective continues to predominate among policy-makers and politicians, if not among the general public.

15. A useful overview of the debate is offered by Mann (1996).

16. The State of Jammu and Kashmir has a special status within the Indian Union, specified in Article 370 of the Constitution. It is the only state with a separate constitution. All laws passed by the Central Government and affecting the State need to be ratified separately by the J&K State Assembly, as happened in October 1997 with the Ladakh Autonomous Hill Development Council Act.

This is a promise against which government's performance and indeed legiti-macy can be measured. In order to fulfil its obligations in this connection, the state arrogates itself the right to tax, and to allocate and administer the resources at its disposal according to the plans its expert committees formulate. In this connection, the state relies on its officials and experts to collect the facts about the region that it requires in order to do its job properly and efficiently. Governmentality demands unambiguous, 'classified' information; the fluidity and ambiguity of identifications not only become 'embarrassing', as Herzfeld (1987: 27) suggests, but intolerable. The Indian nation may be fragmented and define itself through 'unity in diversity', but these fragments should be stable, and they should be Indian.

Dedication to developmentalism, preferential treatment of minorities and other disadvantaged groups, and the primacy of bureaucratic procedure and 'rule-by-record' (Smith 1985), but also the dark realities of communalism, are central elements of the culture of the Indian state, as expressed in the Constitution and official publications. For the state, clear, unambiguous classification of Ladakh's population and the region as a whole are necessary in order to administer and develop the area. For Ladakh's political leaders, a distinct, unambiguously defined, singular Ladakhi 'identity' would serve to strengthen and justify the demands for autonomy, reservations (positive discrimination), and other benefits. Various actors, ranging from colonial and national Anthropological Survey of India social scientists (engaged in the encyclopaedic task of identifying and describing 'the people of India'), to Ladakhi politicians — and from local administrators and IAS officers to tourism operators — share an interest in finding a 'coherent' scheme of clas-sification and ignoring, or at least not focusing on, that which contradicts, defies, or escapes the taxonomic grid. Such official and scientific frames of classification are normative to the extent that benefits, rights, and resources are allocated to those who fit the frame and the grammar of identification that organises it.[17]

Representations of Ladakhi identity, whether official, bureaucratic, elite, or popular, rely on the expert visions, texts and images presented in the

17. This 'imperialism of categories' (Nandy 1990: 69) constitutes the essence of colonisation, as Comaroff and Comaroff suggest (1991: 19). However, drawing on Foucault, I would argue that it is an expression of 'governmentality', rather than of colonialism per se (Foucault 1991). I disagree with the Comaroffs, when they argue that this kind of process turns the colonised others into 'pliant objects and silenced subjects of our scripts and scenarios'. Rather, the colonised others are themselves actively involved in the process of 'conceptualising, inscribing and interacting'.

work of earlier administrators and scientists. Principal among these were the earliest encyclopaedic accounts of the region offered by British bureaucrats and scientists, whose formulations continue to be discernible in today's scholarly and official accounts. Especially the descriptions of Ladakh's population in Frederic Drew's *Jammu and Kashmir Territories* (1976 [1875]) and Cunningham's *Ladak* (1973) have had a major impact on the perceptions and representations of the people of the region.[18] Initially, there was little consistency in the use of terminology, *race*, *tribe* and *community* being used rather indiscriminately. A.S. Singh, the author of Ladakh's 'Code of Tribal Custom', reports that the information is based on 'a gathering fully representing the *tribes* concerned' (Singh 1912, emphasis added), but begins with a discussion of the *races* of Ladakh. His list includes Ladakhis, Changpas, Baltis, Dards, Mons and 'Miscellaneous Tribes', and is based mostly on Drew's work. Attempts at unambiguous classification such as this were always plagued with difficulty, given the ambiguous social reality they were supposed to capture and represent. As census operations in the State became more 'scientific', the embarrassing multiplicity of 'caste' names became intolerable. The 1911 census, which allowed self-identification, produced almost 6,000 'caste' and more than 28,000 'sub-caste' names (Census 1911). For the next census, in 1921, 'The enumerators were strictly warned against recording nicknames, family titles and septs, whose number in this State is legion'. In order to better prepare the staff, 'lists of the more important races, tribes and castes with their sub-castes had been prepared and circulated to the Census Officers well in advance of the primary enumeration, and this list proved to be of great value in the registration of caste...' (Census 1921: 146). Subsequently the list of possible choices was progressively limited until the recording of race/caste/class/community was discontinued in the spirit of national equality in 1947.[19]

In official descriptions ambiguity continued to reign until the confusion was officially ended in 1989 through the recognition of the eight Scheduled Tribes of Ladakh (van Beek 1997b). The resolution of ambiguity was only apparent, as people in Ladakh tried to figure out to which 'tribe' they were supposed to belong. Some of the names referred to regional identifications

---

18. They have also been appropriated as 'evidence' by Ladakhi political activists and their sympathisers to bolster their claims. See e.g. KRBMS (1935), and Buddhist memoranda of 1932 (Buddhists 1932) and 1949 (Ladakh Buddhist Association 1990 [1949]).

19. See van Beek (1997a) for a more detailed historical analysis of census classifications of Ladakh's population. Important discussions of the politics of enumeration in India include Appadurai (1993), Cohn (1991), Jones (1981), and Pedersen (1986).

(e.g. Balti, Changpa, Purigpa), others to occupational identifications (Mon, Beda). It is only the official Scheduled Tribe (ST) Certificate, which states the tribal identity of the holder, that fixes people's identities unambiguously. A lively trade in ST certificates developed because of the considerable benefits attached to ST 'identity', such as cheap loans, easier access to higher education, and government employment quota. Complaints inevitably followed, and the administration and local courts continue to wrestle with the problem of corrupt practices in the issuing of certificates and the settlement of disputed cases. As these examples illustrate, the proclamation of tribes and other 'racial', 'ethnic' or 'community' classifications failed to find a shared identity that could capture the identifications of people in Ladakh. But why not simply 'Ladakhis'?

A look at the communities identified by Drew, in the *Code of Tribal Custom* (Singh 1912), Ramsay's *Practical Dictionary* (1890), the Census, *Gazetteer* (1890 [1974]), and other official and scientific texts shows that religion is deployed as the effective organising principle. In these texts the designation Ladakhis is frequently reserved for Buddhists, while Balti and Beda are treated as exclusively Muslim. With slight modifications, this is the ethnographic and bureaucratic practice we find even today, as reflected in R.S. Mann's *The Ladakhi*, partly based on a field study carried out in 1970-71 and published by the Anthropological Survey of India. Mann recognises the existence of more 'ethnic groups', as he calls them, but maintains that Ladakhis are properly Buddhists (Mann 1986: 12). Also in the application of the ST classification since 1989, certain categories (e.g. Balti, Bot/Boto) were effectively 'filled' on the basis of religion.[20]

The preoccupation with religion as constituting a general and irreducible principle of classification derives from British (and Indian) preoccupations, rather than from social practice in Ladakh — at least in the sense of it being *the* fundamental principle of identification. This colonial influence is also illustrated by the gradual move from 'race' to (religious) 'community' in the census classifications applied in Ladakh, which in accordance with waxing British involvement reflected British imaginings of the imputed essence of Indian society: caste and religious community. Religion, in British imagination and political practice was the irreducible essence of communal identity,

---

20. In local parlance in Leh, the term Balti is used to refer to Shia muslims, also those from the region known as Purig. The existence of the formal 'tribal' identity of Purigpa is practically ignored in daily use in Leh, although that is the official designation for the vast majority of Shias from Kargil district.

as expressed in the South Asian usage of the term communalism.[21] It was inconceivable that people adhering to two different religions could form a single community. Ladakhis, therefore, had to be Buddhists, and Muslims had to be something else.

To ignore, downplay, or dismiss the Islamic element as 'foreign' was also in line with scholarly preoccupations with Ladakh as a surrogate for Tibet. Often referred to as 'Western' or 'Little' Tibet, Ladakh was regarded as a sufficient substitute for traditional Tibetan culture and religion as long as Tibet remained off-limits for Europeans. Scholarly publications, also recent ones, frequently reflect this 'tibetocentricity' and rarely adequate attention is given to Islam or 'muslim' contributions to what people in Ladakh themselves commonly regard as a hybrid culture.[22] While some local origin stories are variations of a familiar Tibetan myth, there are also examples of presumably indigenous, local stories in which first settlers are said to have come from different places. Aggarwal (1994), for example, recounts how people in the village of Achinathang refer to themselves as being from 'mixed strains of barley grain'.[23]

People in Ladakh, like people everywhere, identify with different social groups and shift 'identities' frequently and often unreflectedly depending on their own and others' readings and expectations of their situation. They are, unsurprisingly, embedded in a series of often overlapping and/or crosscutting webs of belonging, which may be based on age or gender, kinship or occupation, or other dimensions of social life. Buddhism, for example, can serve as a shared reference for about half the population, but more important for daily religious practice are the sub-sect and monastic affiliation of the household, or the personal links with specific teachers and deities who may belong to different traditions.[24] Households, arguably the most impor-

---

21. On the British perception of religious community in India, see e.g. Pandey (1990) and Inden (1990).

22. See Aggarwal (1994; 1997) for a discussion of this issue. More recently, anthropologists and sociologists working in Ladakh have begun to pay more attention to Islam. Examples include work of Dollfus (1995), Grist (1993; 1995; 1998), and Srinivas (1995; 1997).

23. Aggarwal (1994), Dollfus (1989), and Kaplanian (1991) offer discussions of local oral traditions regarding the settlement of the region. Little is known about the early history or population of the region prior to the tenth century.

24. Muslims similarly identify with different religious traditions, such as Sunni, Shia, and Nurbakshia. On Shias and Sunnis, see e.g. Pinault, 1999. Shias in the Suru valley of Kargil District follow different spiritual leaders known as Agas and there has been considerable conflict between different factions. See Grist (1998, especially chapter 3) for a discussion of this issue. There is no Muslim community in any simple sense, any

tant social units in Ladakh (Aggarwal 1994; Dollfus 1989; Phylactou 1989), are commonly connected by different labour sharing arrangements (such as *ra.res/ba.res*),[25] residential organisations (*bcu.tsho*), 'clan' affiliations (*pha. spun*),[26] and religious associations (for example *chos.spun*), but these networks are not commonly congruent.

In the course of their daily lives, then, people in Ladakh 'manage' a range of social 'identities', some of which may be contradictory or overlapping. Regional antagonisms,[27] 'traditional' hierarchy, new money and political affiliations all conspire against singular identifications across Ladakh, although especially when travelling outside the region, or interacting with outsiders, people do identify and are indeed identified as Ladakhi.[28] As socially skilled actors, people generally have a good sense for which social 'identity' is salient and appropriate in a certain situation. It is when situations are *not* clear, or when different orders clash in a certain setting, that problems of identification arise.

State and bureaucratic insistence on semantically pure categories constitute an important and growing source of situations where reconciliation, hiding, or forgetting of 'identities' is required, but this kind of problem is not unknown in the 'traditional' sphere. Proper seating order (*gral*) , for example,

more than there is a Buddhist 'community' in Ladakh. Yet, the principle of such a community is recognised e.g. through the Buddhist term *nang.pa* [insiders]. I have heard Muslim leaders use the term *qom* in this 'community' sense, explaining that on a certain political question they needed to consult their *qom*.

25. See Dollfus (1989, especially chapter 7) for a detailed discussion of *las.bes* and other relations of reciprocity and mutual aid in the village of Hemis Shugpacan in lower Ladakh (*gsham*).

26. A *pha spun* is a group of households that help one another with arrangements surrounding birth, marriage, and death. They are commonly identified through the worship of a specific deity or *pha lha*. In principle the name suggests a patrilineal 'clan', but this is certainly not always the case in practice. Rather, membership is relatively open to newcomers. The practices and principles of *pha spun* vary considerably across Ladakh (and across time, no doubt). For discussions, see e.g. Brauen (1980); Dollfus (1989); Gutschow (1995); and Phylactou (1989).

27. Significant antagonisms exist for example between Leh and the regions of Sham and Changthang. In Leh extensive repertoires of 'ethnic' jokes exist that poke fun at the greed of Sham's traders, or the backwardness of Changpa nomads. These days, the rivalry and suspicions are expressed particularly clearly during election campaigns.

28. The recognition and significance of regional provenance is illustrated by the fact that e.g. the large monastery of Tashilhunpo in Shigatse in Tibet had a separate 'hostel' (*khang.tshang*) for monks from Ladakh.

is a crucial element at any gathering.[29] The seating of guests requires an assessment on the part of the hosts of the relative status of each visitor or guest. However, there are different systems of ranking, and the accommodation of these different systems in a given social situation can cause headaches, since mistakes can have serious consequences.[30] In principle, monks and other religious leaders are seated highest, and according to their rank. Nobility is similarly seated according to rank, with the royal lineage at the head. Age, gender, economic standing, social respectability, and 'caste' (in the case of stigmatised groups such as *Mon* and *Beda*) may all go into the deliberation. But how should one weigh the relative importance of these rankings when they need to be accommodated at the same event? Where does one seat the headmaster with respect to the local nobility? What about army officers, local politicians, formally higher status nobles, and technically always superior incarnate lamas (*sprul.sku*)? Since a final, formal calculation of rank and place is not possible, the social viability of any such arrangement depends on the willingness of guests and hosts to accept the assessment — usually arrived at after considerable discussions among the hosts and their friends and helpers. They must agree to suspend the argument at some point, as final, objective criteria — even those supplied by 'tradition' — and social practice cannot be made to agree without such dissimulation.

The management of these incommensurable orders at the local level relies, then, on a degree of dissimulation and active willingness on the part of those involved in accepting a measure of inconsistency. When we shift analysis to the level of collective 'identity' at the regional and national level — where stakes are higher in important respects — the impossibility of matching singular semantic orders and multiple social practices becomes more pronounced and still more open to contestation.

29. Aggarwal (1994) reports a case where an entire group of households was put under a 'social boycott' (*me.len chu.len chad.pa*) because at a wedding hosted by this (low status) group, bride and groom and their relatives were deemed by the invited (higher status) villagers, to have been seated too high. The conflict endured for months.
30. The minutes of meetings of the Young Men's Buddhist Association (which cover the 1938-1952 period, albeit with significant gaps) show how a considerable part of the organisation's energy was devoted to arbitrate in cases of disputes over alleged insults by inappropriate seatings at social events.

The clash of communities?

Like elsewhere in the subcontinent, religious community became the basis of political representation in Kashmir's Praja Sabha, the popularly elected Assembly established in 1934.[31] Ladakhi political activists, educated and assisted by neo-Buddhist Kashmiris and other outsiders, learned to formulate their demands in terms of religious community.[32] Consequently, regardless of whether unambiguous communities on the basis of religion existed on the ground, religious identity became a central theme in political strategies of Ladakhis, most clearly and violently during the agitation of 1989-92. This campaign to 'Free Ladakh from Kashmir' was led by the Ladakh Buddhist Association (LBA) and involved a three-year social boycott of Muslims, banning all types of interaction between the 'communities'.[33] As Buddhist political leaders later indicated, their choice for a communal strategy was a conscious one, since — as one of them put it — 'we are living in a system that is communal'. The 'playing of the communal card', LBA leaders reasoned, would ensure them the attention of the central government, especially given the simultaneously escalating 'Muslim' insurgency in the Kashmir Valley. The campaign involved a strong emphasis on Buddhism as *the* authentic, shared identity and culture of Ladakh, and a social boycott was imposed on Muslims. Young men adopted the earrings once worn by Buddhist nobles, the Tibetan script suddenly appeared on the signs of shops not owned by Muslims to make it easier to know where one could do business, and on religious holidays loudspeakers on the main temple in Leh rang with the tape-recorded recitations of monks.[34] Many observers, including academics, were quick to accept the agitators' claim that the agitation was a spontaneous uprising of the Buddhist Ladakhis against the discriminatory policies of the Muslim dominated State government. Close analysis of the his-

31. Kooiman (1995) is overstating the case when he suggests that separate electorates were not a feature of the political system in the 'Princely States'.
32. For a detailed discussion of the role of neo-Buddhists, see Bertelsen (1997).
33. See van Beek (1996) for a comprehensive discussion of this process.
34. In 1995 this practice escalated into a competition between the muezzin of the Leh Sunni mosque and the taped monks of the Chokhang, just across the street from one another. Whenever the Muslims were called to prayer, the sound of the monks rang out as well. As a Buddhist activist joked, 'Now Buddhists are also called to prayer five times a day'.

Ladakhi Buddhist anti-Muslim Protest

tory and actual practices of the agitation, however, shows that such easy domestication is problematic.[35]

The demand for autonomy had been raised repeatedly, at least since the 1930s, and generally *not* in religious partisan ways, but through all-Ladakh idioms. For example, memoranda submitted to State and Central governments since the 1960s generally demanded 'declaration of the entire population of Ladakh as Scheduled Tribe', while the All-Ladakh Action Committee that spearheaded this movement for more than a decade comprised both Muslims and Buddhists from Kargil and Leh. It was also in this all-Ladakh context that the more recent articulations of the demand for regional autonomy were voiced in the early 1980s. A 'Memorandum submitted to the Hon'ble Minister of State for Home Affairs, Govt. of India on his visit to Leh on Feb. 7, 1982, on behalf of the people of Ladakh through Ladakh Action Committee, Leh' begins:

We regret to submit that with the continuous subjugative and maligned attitude of Jammu and Kashmir Govt. Ladakhies have so far been neglected in every sphere of developmental fields. Ladakhies remained economically, educationally and politically backward as were many many years back. [...] Their [a State cabinet delegation, MvB] visit was followed by a maligned conspiracy to wage a communal riot which fortunately was a unknown thing to Ladakhis and failed in totality and Ladakhies maintained their age old fraternity and communal harmony as usual. (Text as in original)

Similarly, 'broadlines' for regional autonomy drafted by the Ladakh Action Committee in 1982 demand autonomy for the entire Ladakh region, and an accompanying 'background note' deplores that 'by bifurcation of Ladakh into two districts of Leh and Kargil, the name of Ladakh has been wiped off from history and even geography. As a compensation for this emotional loss, the

35. As I have argued elsewhere, the representation of Ladakhi demands for autonomy in the course of the agitation involved a domestication of Ladakhi identity in two senses. First, the multiplicity of identifications in Ladakhi social practice was 'tamed' through its representation as a singular, coherent, and unambiguously bounded Buddhist identity. Secondly, representations of Ladakhi identity were 'Indianised' by the adoption of the communalist idiom that is so central to Indian politics. See van Beek (in press) for more detail.

people of Ladakh demanded divisional status for Ladakh with headquarters at Leh'.[36]

The Buddhist 'community' is deeply divided along class, regional, political ideological, and sectarian lines. Similarly, it is impossible to identify a homogeneous Muslim community in the complex social and political realities on the ground. Not only is there a significant division between Shias and Sunnis, but also political and class affiliations fragment the 'community'. In the initial stages of the agitation, the LBA sought to exploit these divisions by inviting Shias to join the 'Ladakh People's Movement for Union Territory Status' and targeting the Sunnis as foreign (Kashmiri) elements.[37]

The mobilisation of Buddhists and Muslims in the course of the agitation was a difficult and long process, and could never be maintained except for short periods and through the use of incentives, including threats and actual physical punishment.[38] Experiences during my repeated and prolonged stays in Ladakh during the early agitation period in June-October 1989 and subsequent years, suggest that there was no enduring mobilisation of 'the Buddhist community' in any meaningful sense of the term. People did show up to demonstrate, sometimes in large numbers, but they did so for a variety of reasons, such as to avoid sanctions like fines or beatings, to have a day on the town and visit relatives, or also because they strongly supported the LBA cause. The unity of Ladakh's Buddhists and of the Muslims, then, existed mostly as claims and representations, and the identity this unity supposedly reflected and constituted was of that elusive character in between the real and the really made-up. The fragmentation and recombination of different

36. These quotes are taken from an undated document entitled 'Regional Autonomy for Ladakh within the Framework of the Constitution of Jammu and Kashmir State. Broadlines for Regional Autonomy' and an undated 'Background note regarding events leading to the recent agitation in Ladakh' by Congress MP, P. Namgyal. Both are most likely from January or February 1982.

37. As mentioned in note 1, the predicament of the Shia population of Kargil District illustrates the consequences of these identifications. Caught between Buddhist radicals and the insurgents in the Kashmir Valley, their identity is reduced to Muslim. When refugees from Kargil and Dras sought refuge in Leh in the wake of the outbreak of large-scale fighting in the spring of 1999, the Youth Wing of the LBA issued a statement casting doubt on the loyalty of the Muslim refugees and demanding their ouster from Leh. Later, the LBA, Muslim associations, and other political and social organisations met and promised to maintain harmony and to defend Ladakh against all intruders.

38. A more elaborate discussion can be found in van Beek and Bertelsen (1997) and Bray (1991).

sections of the population in the wake of the creation of the Hill Council illustrates these unstabilities.[39]

Representing Ladakhi 'identity'

Just as subordinates are not much deceived by their own performance there is, of course, no more reason for social scientists and historians to take that performance as, necessarily, one given in good faith (Scott 1990: 90).

The communal division of society in the context of the Ladakh Buddhist Association campaign, although created with sticks as well as carrots, and heavily policed and sanctioned, constitutes, then, an important set of identifications in official and public discourse in Ladakh. Yet this simple communal, binary reading of Ladakh as populated by two communities, cannot be recognised officially. As noted earlier, communalism is publicly deplored, regarded as the source of all evil and a most serious threat to the survival of the nation. Ladakh's Buddhist 'identity', therefore, could not be officially recognised, and certainly could not be made the basis for political representation and empowerment. So, towards the end of his address to the first meeting of the Ladakh Autonomous Hill Development Council, Leh, the Governor of Jammu and Kashmir finally acknowledged the existence of Islam, and explicitly stated that 'Our country is a tapestry of different cultures, customs and traditions. ... This land [Ladakh] has been blessed by the confluence of two of the greatest religions of the world. May this glorious intermingling of cultures be strengthened'.[40]

In the contestation over the allocation of political, economic, and other resources, state actors, academics, and local activists in Ladakh represent their demands and justifications in terms of the hegemonic discourse of the Indian state. Since difference — cultural, economic, climatic — warrants special attention, measures, and privileges, the art of representation consists in finding a way of balancing the irreducible complexity and multiplicity, the tensions and contradictions of local identifications and practices of belonging, with the expectations and demands for unambiguous singular collective identity of the state and the academics and other experts it relies on. The stability or persistence of certain 'identities' — for example of 'religious identity' through the erasure of Muslims from many academic, official, and

---

39. For a discussion of post-Hill Council developments, see van Beek (1999).

40. Earlier in his speech, he refers only to Buddhism as Ladakh's 'unique cultural heritage' and even quotes the Buddha.

popular understandings of Ladakhi identity — is inherently unstable in that it is premised on an acceptance of a representation of Ladakhiness that is convincing not by virtue of its 'reality' or 'deep rootedness' in Ladakhi culture, but by its correspondence with the expected (cultural) forms of singular identities that are characteristic of the hegemonic discourse of identity and difference in its Indian form.

As argued earlier, several different logics of identification operate in social and political practice in Ladakh. The irreducible multiplicity of everyday social identifications has been domesticated officially through the recognition of eight 'tribes'. In addition, there is the communalist idiom and political practice that permeates the Indian polity and some levels of Ladakhi social and political practice. The composition and structure of the Hill Council reflect the simultaneous and contradictory operation of several of these principles. First, people are elected to represent different constituencies, which are geographically defined. In drawing the boundaries of constituencies, religious, political ideological, and economic considerations have all played a role in order to prevent domination by the urban centres and to ensure representation of at least some Muslims. In addition, the Governor appoints four members to represent 'principal minorities', i.e. Muslims, women, and a representative for 'backward classes'. Hence, officially, Ladakh's unique conditions and characteristics, particularly climate and geography, are referred to in the 'Reasons for Enactment' accompanying the Ladakh Autonomous Hill Development Council Act. The process towards achievement of this recognition of Ladakh's autonomy and unique identity, however, was driven by a communalist strategy arguing on the basis of religious 'identity', and communal identifications are recognised and to some extent enshrined in the implementation of the Act. The political process since the (official) abandonment of the communal strategy by the LBA leadership in 1992, as well as a close analysis of the historical antecedents of the movement, show that class, regional, and sectarian 'identities' have had and continue to have a significant influence. In daily social interactions, people continue to shift, claim, contest, and deny specific 'identities', whose 'origins', salience, 'reality' and so forth cannot be easily settled, fixed, or deconstructed. Meanwhile, almost all Ladakhis carry a card that identifies them unambiguously as 'a Balti', 'a Bot/Boto', 'a Changpa', ...

Conclusion

The 'unique identity' that was celebrated on the Polo ground and which is referred to time and time again in the rhetoric of representation in academic, bureaucratic, and political texts, is not an 'identity' in any formal sense at all. It does not constitute a homogeneous, singular, unambiguously defined and bounded 'entity'. In fact, outside these representations, in other spheres of social and cultural practice, there is no unity at all, as illustrated also by the rapid fragmentation of the precarious unity displayed at the first meeting of the Hill Council. Ladakhi 'identity' is not just or really Buddhist, nor is it just or really a series of tribal communities. Its ambiguity, multiplicity, and fluidity is irreducible. Yet, these communal and tribal identities are necessary 'fictions'. It is only through the imagining of such order, its 'proper' identification and representation, that the state can recognise its existence and empower it, and manage it. Therefore, in spite of the contradictions between such singular notions and their own everyday experiences of difference, people in Ladakh, not only the political elite, can 'live' with such a fiction, as long as it is allowed a measure of incompleteness and openness, and as long as 'membership' is not circumscribed in too exclusive a fashion or associated with too far-reaching implications in terms of livelihoods and social practice. In other words, as long as such official identities can be treated much like other social 'identities', there is no question of anxiety or confusion: even the tribal identities can therefore be accepted and put into use. They have their proper place and context.

As long as official discourse of 'identity' in practice and implications resembles in its tolerance of ambiguity, difference and even paradox, the everyday creative identifications that characterise the social reality it purports to merely represent, such 'category mistakes' do not interfere with the inhabitability of the social orders people construct. It is precisely the ambiguity of local practices of identification that makes it possible for people to imagine their shared identity ('Ladakhi') in an unproblematic, even unreflected fashion. It is the lack of narrowly defined characteristics and criteria of proper Ladakhiness that makes Ladakhiness possible in social practice: 'it' can exist, because it remains relatively undefined, undemarcated in any rigid sense, allowed to exist somewhere between the real and the really made-up.

It is this 'everyday' reality of the irreducibility of difference — an appreciation that does not mistake the metaphors of 'identity' for the 'reality' it symbolises — that is sought to be banished from the rationalised, objectified, systematicity demanded by science, bureaucracy, law, and the principles of liberal representative democracy. The positing of categorical purity makes everyday practices of social identification intolerable and causes Ladakhi 'identity' to appear like a cynical, inauthentic construct. It is only through the acceptance of the imperfection of the match between (singular, stable, homogenous) imputed 'identity' and (multiple, fluid, heterogeneous) social practices of identification, that social life — indeed social 'groups' — are made possible.

For a brief moment, then, the Governor, the President, Parliament, and people in Ladakh together created and enabled the temporary semblance of stability that is required for an 'identity' to be identified and celebrated. It could only be imagined in such a way, differently for different people. Identity of imagining is not necessary, just a willingness to imagine identity. The domesticated, non-communal but partly religiously defined, unified but fragmented, notion of Ladakhi 'identity' is, in other words, real yet unreal, a fiction with a material presence. The currency of this notion, and the fact that it serves as the basis of so much concrete action, legitimises and justifies allocations, claims and demands, relies on its ambiguity which needs, however, to be forgotten now and then — at least officially. We identify, therefore we dissimulate.

Acknowledgement

This contribution is based on research made possible in part through a Jennings Randolph Peace Scholar Award from the United States Institute of Peace. Supplementary support for fieldwork in Ladakh in 1993-95 was granted by the Peace Studies Program, International Political Economy Program, and South Asia Program, all at Cornell University. The ideas and material upon which this argument is based have been developed in the course of research and professional activities in Ladakh since 1985. I gratefully acknowledge the collaboration, support and encouragement I have received from numerous people in Ladakh. I thank the organisers and other participants of the 'Multiplex Identities as Cultural Resources' workshop in Mook, especially Willy Jansen who provided insightful comments on the original presentation. Henk Driessen and Ton Otto also offered valuable comments and editorial suggestions. Final responsibility for what is presented in this contribution is, of course, solely mine.

Bibliography

Aggarwal, R. 1994. From Mixed Strains of Barley Grain: Person and Place in a Ladakhi Village. Ph.D. Dissertation, Indiana University, Bloomington.

Aggarwal, R. 1997. 'From Utopia to Heterotopia: Towards an Anthropology of Ladakh'. In: H. Osmaston and Nawang Tsering (eds.), *Recent Research on Ladakh 6. Proceedings of the Sixth International Colloquia on Ladakh. Leh, 1993*. Bristol: Bristol University, 21-28.

Anderson, B. 1991. *Imagined Communities: Reflections on the Origin and Spread of Nationalism*. London: Verso.

Anderson, B. 1993. 'Replica, Aura, and Late Nationalist Imaginings'. In: *Qui Parle?* 7(1), 1-21.

Appadurai, A. 1993. 'Number in the Colonial Imagination'. In: C. Breckenridge and P.T. van der Veer (eds.), *Orientalism and the Postcolonial Predicament*. Philadelphia: University of Pennsylvania Press, 314-39.

Assies, W.J. 1994. 'Self-Determination and the New Partnership: The Politics of Indigenous Peoples and States'. In: W.J. Assies and A.J. Hoekema (eds.), *Indigenous Peoples' Experiments with Self-Government*. Amsterdam: IWGIA, 31-71.

Balibar, E. and I. Wallerstein 1991. *Race, Nation, Class; Ambiguous Identities*. London: Verso.

Beek, M. van 1996. Identity Fetishism and the Art of Representation: the Long Struggle for Regional Autonomy in Ladakh. Ph.D. dissertation, Cornell University, Ithaca, N.Y.

Beek, M. van 1997a. 'Contested Classifications of People in Ladakh: an Analysis of the Census of Kashmir, 1873-1941'. In: H. Krasser, M.T. Much, E. Steinkellner and H. Tauscher (eds.), *Tibetan Studies. Proceedings of the Seventh Seminar of the International Association for Tibetan Studies, Graz 1995*. Graz, 35-49.

Beek, M. van 1997b. 'The Importance of Being Tribal, or: the Impossibility of Being Ladakhis'. In: T. Dodin and H. Räther (eds.), *Recent Research on Ladakh 7. Proceedings of the Seventh Colloquium of the International Association for Ladakh Studies held at Bonn/St. Augustin, 12-15 June 1995*. Ulm: Universität Ulm, 21-41.

Beek, M. van, and K. Brix Bertelsen 1997. 'No Present without Past: the 1989 Agitation in Ladakh'. In: T. Dodin and H. Räther (eds.), *Recent Research on Ladakh 7. Proceedings of the Seventh Colloquium of the International Association for Ladakh Studies held at Bonn/St. Augustin, 12-15 June 1995*. Ulm: Universität Ulm, 43-65.

Beek, M. van 1998a. 'Prisoners of Shangri-La'. In: *Himal* 11(9), 44.

Beek, M. van 1998b. 'True Patriots: Justifying Autonomy for Ladakh'. In: *Himalayan Research Bulletin* 18(1), 35-45.

Beek, M. van 1999. 'Hill Councils, Development, and Democracy: Assumptions and Experiences from Ladakh'. In: *Alternatives* 24(4), 435-59.

Beek, M. van (in press). 'The Art of Representation: Domesticating Ladakhi Identity'. In: C. Jest and P. Dollfus (eds.), *Identities in the Himalayas*. Paris: CNRS.

Bertelsen, K. Brix 1997. 'Protestant Buddhism and Social Identification in Ladakh'. In: *Archives de Sciences sociales des Religions* 99 (juillet-septembre), 129-51.

Bewes, T. 1997. *Cynicism and Postmodernity*. London: Verso.

Bhasin, M.K. 1992. *Cold Desert: Ladakh. Ecology and Development*. Delhi: Kamla-Raj Enterprises.

Billig, M. 1995. *Banal Nationalism*. London: Sage Publications.

Brauen, M. 1980. 'The Pha Spun of Ladakh'. In: M. Aris and A.S. Suu Kyi (eds.), *Tibetan Studies in Honour of Hugh Richardson*. Warminster: Aris & Phillips.

Bray, J. 1991. 'Ladakhi History and Indian Nationhood'. In: *South Asia Research* 11(2), 115-33.

Buddhists, Representatives of Kashmir 1932. Memorandum of the Kashmir Buddhists. *The Mahabodhi* 40(3), 127-31.

Census of India 1911. Vol. XX, Kashmir. Lucknow: Newul Kishore Press, 1912.

Census of India 1921. Vol. XXII, Kashmir. Lahore: Mufid-I-Am Press, 1923.

Cohn, B.S. 1991. 'The Census, Social Structure, and Objectification in South Asia'. In: B.S. Cohn (ed.), *An Anthropologist Among the Historians and Other Essays*. New Delhi: Oxford University Press.

Comaroff, J., and J. Comaroff 1991. *Of Revelation and Revolution: Christianity, Colonialism, and Consciousness in South Africa*. Chicago: Chicago University Press.

Connolly, W.E. 1991. *Identity/Difference: Democratic Negotiations of Political Paradox*. Ithaca: Cornell University Press.

Cunningham, A. 1973. *Ladak, Physical, Statistical and Historical*. Delhi: Sagar Publications.

Dollfus, P. 1989. *Lieu de neige et de genévriers: Organisation sociale et religieuse des communautés bouddhistes du Ladakh*. Paris: Centre National de la Recherche Scientifique.

Dollfus, P. 1995. 'The History of Muslims in Central Ladakh'. In: *The Tibet Journal* 20(3), 35-58.

Drew, F. 1976 (1875). *The Jummoo and Kashmir Territories*. New Delhi: Cosmo Publications.

Dyck, N. (ed.), 1985. *Indigenous Peoples and the Nation-State: Fourth World Politics in Canada, Australia and Norway*. St. John's: ISER.

Foucault, M. 1991. 'Governmentality'. In: G. Burchell, C. Gordon and P. Miller (eds.), *The Foucault Effect: Studies in Governmentality*. London: Harvester Wheatsheaf, 87-104.

Gillis, J.R. 1996. *Commemorations: The Politics of National Identity*. Princeton: Princeton University Press.

Grist, N. 1993. 'Muslim Kinship and Marriage in Ladakh'. In: C. Ramble and M. Brauen (eds.), *Anthropology of Tibet and the Himalaya*. Zürich: Ethnological Museum of the University of Zürich, 80-92.

Grist, N. 1995. 'Muslims in Western Ladakh'. In: *The Tibet Journal* 20(3), 59-70.

Grist, N. 1998. Local Politics in the Suru Valley of Northern India. Ph.D. thesis, Goldsmiths College, University of London, London.

Gutschow, K. 1995. 'Kinship in Zanskar: Idiom and Practice'. In: H. Osmaston and P. Denwood (eds.), *Recent Research on Ladakh 4 & 5. Proceedings of the Fourth and Fifth Colloquia of the International Association for Ladakh Studies, Bristol 1989 and London 1992*. London: SOAS, 337-47.

Handler, R. 1994. 'Is "Identity" a Useful Cross-Cultural Concept?'. In: J.R. Gillis (ed.), *Commemorations: The Politics of National Identity*. Princeton, N.J.: Princeton University Press, 27-40.

Herzfeld, M. 1987. *Anthropology Through the Looking Glass.* Cambridge: Cambridge University Press.

Herzfeld, M. 1992. *The Social Production of Indifference: Exploring the Symbolic Roots of Western Bureaucracy.* Chicago: University of Chicago Press.

Herzfeld, M. 1996. *Cultural Intimacy: Social Poetics in the Nation-state.* London: Routledge.

Holmes, S. 1993. *The Anatomy of Antiliberalism.* Cambridge, Mass.: Harvard University Press.

Horowitz, D.L. 1985. *Ethnic Groups in Conflict.* Berkeley: University of California Press.

Inden, R. 1990. *Imagining India.* Cambridge, Mass. and Oxford: Basil Blackwell.

Jalali, R., and S.M. Lipset 1992-1993. 'Racial and Ethnic Conflicts: A Global Perspective'. In: *Political Science Quarterly* 107(4), 585-606.

Jammu and Kashmir, Government of. 1974. *Gazetteer of Kashmir and Ladak.* Reprint of the 1890 edition. Delhi: Vikas Publications.

Jammu and Kashmir, Government of 1986. *Jammu and Kashmir State: Ladakh Region.* Srinagar.

Jones, K.W. 1981. 'Religious Identity and the Indian Census'. In: N.G. Barrier (ed.), *The Census in British India: New Perspectives.* New Delhi: Manohar, 73-101.

Kaplanian, P. 1991. 'Mythes et légendes sur les origines du peuplement du Ladakh'. In: E. Steinkellner (ed.), *Tibetan History and Language. Studies Dedicated to Uray Géza on his Seventieth Birthday.* Wien: Arbeitskreis für tibetische und buddhistische Studien, Universität Wien.

Kooiman, D. 1995. 'Communalism and Indian Princely States: A Comparison with British India'. In: *Economic and Political Weekly*, 2123-2133.

KRBMS 1935. *Triennial Report of the Kashmir Raj Bodhi Maha Sabha.* Srinagar: Kashmir Raj Bodhi Maha Sabha.

Laclau, E., and C. Mouffe 1985. *Hegemony and Socialist Strategy; Towards a Radical Democratic Politics.* London: Verso.

Ladakh Buddhist Association 1990 (1949). 'Memorandum submitted to the PM in 1949 by Chhewang Rigzin, President Buddhist Association of Ladakh on behalf of the People of Ladakh'. In: *Hindu World*, 30-33.

Mann, M. 1996. 'Nation-states in Europe and Other Continents: Diversifying, Developing, Not Dying'. In: G. Balakrishnan (ed.), *Mapping the Nation.* London: Verso, 295-316.

Mann, R.S. 1986. *The Ladakhi: A Study in Ethnography and Change.* Calcutta: Anthropological Survey of India.

Moynihan, D.P. 1993. *Pandaemonium: Ethnicity in International Politics.* New York: Oxford University Press.

Nandy, A. 1990. 'The Politics of Secularism and the Recovery of Religious Tolerance'. In: V. Das (ed.), *Communities, Riots and Survivors in South Asia.* Delhi: Oxford University Press, 69-93.

Pandey, G. 1990. *The Colonial Construction of Communalism in Colonial North India*. Delhi: Oxford University Press.

Pedersen, P. 1986. 'Khatri: Vaishya, or Kshatriya? An Essay in Colonial Administration and Cultural Identity'. In: *Folk* 28, 19-31.

Phylactou, M. 1989. Household Organisation and Marriage in Ladakh, Indian Himalaya. Ph.D. thesis, University of London, London.

Pinault, D. 1999. 'Muslim-Buddhist Relations in a Ritual Context: An Analysis of the Muharram Procession in Leh Township, Ladakh'. In: M. van Beek, K.B. Bertelsen and P. Pedersen (eds.), *Ladakh: Culture, History, and Development between Himalaya and Karakoram*. Recent Research on Ladakh 8. Proceedings of the Eighth Colloquium of the International Association for Ladakh Studies held at Moesgaard, 6-8 June 1997. Aarhus: Aarhus University Press.

Ramsay, H. 1890. *Western Tibet: a Practical Dictionary of the Language and Customs of the Districts Included in the Ladakh Wazarat*. Lahore: W. Ball.

Renan, E. 1992 (1887). *Qu'est-ce qu'une nation? Et autres essaies politiques*. Paris: Presses Pocket.

Roseberry, W. 1996. 'Hegemony, Power, and Languages of Contention'. In: E.N. Wilmsen and P. McAllister (eds.), *The Politics of Difference: Ethnic Premises in a World of Power*. Chicago and London: University of Chicago Press, 71-84.

Scott, J.C. 1990. *Domination and the Arts of Resistance; Hidden Transcripts*. New Haven: Yale University Press.

Singh, T. 1912. *Code of Tribal Custom in the Ladakh Tahsil, Jammu and Kashmir State*. Allahabad: The Pioneer Press.

Smith, R.S. 1985. 'Rule-by-Records and Rule-by-Reports: Complementary Aspects of the British Imperial Rule of Law'. In: *Contributions to Indian Sociology* 19(1), 153-76.

Spivak, G.C. 1988. 'Can the Subaltern Speak?'. In: C. Nelson and L. Grossberg (eds.), *Marxism and the Interpretation of Culture*. Basingstoke: MacMillan Education, 271-313.

Srinivas, S. 1995. 'Conjunction, Parallelism and Cross-Cutting Ties Among the Muslims of Ladakh'. In: *The Tibet Journal* 20(3), 71-95.

Srinivas, S. 1997. 'The Household, Integration and Exchange: Buddhists and Muslims in the Nubra Valley'. In: H. Osmaston and Nawang Tsering (eds.), *Recent Research on Ladakh 6. Proceedings of the Sixth International Colloquium on Ladakh. Leh 1993*. Bristol: Bristol University, 251-80.

Stavenhagen, R. 1994. 'Indigenous Rights: Some Conceptual Problems'. In: W. Assies and A.J. Hoekema (eds.), *Indigenous Peoples' Experiments with Self-Government*. Amsterdam: IWGIA, 9-29.

Taussig, M. 1993. *Mimesis and Alterity: A Particular History of the Senses*. London: Routledge.

Tully, J. 1995. *Strange Multiplicity; Constitutionalism in an Age of Diversity*. Cambridge: Cambridge University Press.

Žižek, S. 1992. *The Sublime Object of Ideology*. London: Verso.

CHAPTER 8

'We are One but Still Different': Communality and Diversity in Aboriginal Australia

Ad Borsboom and Janneke Hulsker

Introduction

The first Aboriginal magazine produced by Aborigines was, not without reason, called *Identity*. It was published between 1971 and 1982 and presented articles on current developments in Aboriginal issues and Aboriginal history to its readers. It also offered Aborigines the opportunity to publish short stories, biographies and present other forms of artwork. As the title implied, the magazine's continuing preoccupation was '... the clearer articulation of Aboriginality in all its dimensions' (Howie-Willis 1994: 492). The term *Aboriginality* gained currency in the seventies and eighties and has become a key-concept in the construction of Aboriginal identity ever since, or more aptly, of Aboriginal identities by Aboriginal people themselves. It was applied at once to an overall Aboriginal identity that united Aborigines from all parts of Australia on the basis of common cultural characteristics (clan, language, and place) and historical ones (the shared experience of being invaded, displaced, and oppressed). At the same time the concept offered ample room for differentiation on the basis of regional, local and even individual identities, one of the striking features in Aboriginal Australia before colonisation. The concept is comparable with similar concepts elsewhere as for example Maddock (1991: 10), Linnekin (1990: 145-74) and M. Tonkinson (1990: 191-237) demonstrate. Maddock (ibid.) points out that in Australia, Canada and New Zealand, identity has been more expressly conceived from the common use of terms such as *Aboriginality* and *Maoritanga*. He also refers to Tatz (1982: 13) who suggested an analogy with the term *Jewishness*, understood as an essence or totality inhering in or consisting of the collected thoughts, sentiments and efforts of Jewish people. Jewishness, in this view, transcends the differences among Jewish people and cannot be reduced to a single feature, however important it may be, such as the Jewish religion. The same applies to the term Aboriginality which also consists of collected thoughts, sentiments and efforts of Australian Aboriginal people and equally cannot be reduced to single features, such as 'traditional' Aboriginal religion.

The term Aboriginality was also used in opposition to the identification labels applied by white Australia until at least the seventies. Such labels divided Aborigines on the basis of racial premises and were applied in the public arena to separate the various Aboriginal categories in an essentialist way, with severe consequences for the lives of those to whom the categories referred. We are referring to terms such as 'full-blood', 'half-caste', 'quarter-caste', 'octoroon', labels which in the words of Aboriginal activists are derived from Social Darwinism and are particularly abhorrent and insulting to Aborigines. As Aboriginal author Fesl argues: 'This classification divides us into groups on the basis of guessed-at proportions of European blood (with the implication that) the more white blood, the more intelligent the child.' (1994: 491). These racial labels, for almost two hundred years used in the public domain and the basis for the institutionalisation of all Aboriginal people, separate Aborigines in mutually exclusive categories.

The concept of Aboriginality, which very well fits in Ortner's definition of 'summarising symbol' (1973: 1340), puts all the emphasis on inclusion and fluidity of Aboriginal identities. The label expresses the broad spectrum of Aboriginal ways and circumstances, which overlap and therefore cannot be separated in bounded, exclusive categories. Aboriginality both unifies the great variety of Aboriginal identities on a national level on the basis of generally shared cultural traits and shared historical experiences, and differentiates on regional and local levels on the basis of these very same cultural characteristics and historical processes. Starting from this concept the popular dichotomy 'real' Aborigines (meaning 'full-blood'), versus others who, by implication, are not 'real' Aborigines because of their skin, becomes a misnomer. It implies a contrast between those 'real Aborigines' in the bush which still have their 'authentic' ('static') cultural tradition and those whose lifestyles differ from that 'tradition' thus calling into question the Aboriginality of the great majority of people of Aboriginal descent (see also R. Tonkinson 1998: 295). Instead Aborigines have demonstrated many times, but particularly in questions of landrights, how to combine political skill in the Australian political process, together with a growing pan-Aboriginal identity, which is raising traditional Aboriginal culture to totally new levels of consciousness (R.M. Berndt 1977, and Borsboom and Dagmar 1984: 50-53). Keen (1988) concludes that many of the papers in his book on Aboriginal cultures in 'settled Australia' speak of continuities among elements of the culture of Aboriginal people in urban areas and of people more remote from the area of dense European settlement, implying the reproduction of some cultural forms from the pre-colonial era such as language and style, kin and household, economic processes, government and beliefs.

From the late 1960s on, urban Aboriginal movements joined forces with traditionally oriented groups in Arnhem Land and elsewhere in 'outback' Australia and supported the latter's claim for territorial and cultural autonomy. By joining forces with traditionally oriented Aborigines the larger Aboriginal movement became imbued with very strong Aboriginal meanings and values, derived from indigenous concepts such as the Dreamtime, the Land and the Law. Traditional Aboriginal concepts and values were increasingly used as rallying-points in the political confrontation with European Australians (cf. Borsboom and Dagmar, ibid.).

'Aboriginality', writes M. Tonkinson, 'is a tool of contemporary Aboriginal political struggle' (1990: 192). The term asserts that Aborigines share a common cultural heritage as well as a history of oppression by white society. 'The identification of common cultural themes and the maintenance of traditions — or their revival (and invention) where they are moribund or absent — are all part of the process' (ibid.). This creative process, the construction of a common culture, is what R. Tonkinson calls 'nation building' in Aboriginal Australia. 'The challenge for Aboriginal-nation builders has been to overcome problems of distance and cultural diversity, and to present a unified front and a positive self-image' (1998: 293).

Yet, at the same time the emergence of this form of pan-Aboriginality is accompanied by 'new affirmations of singular regional and local identities, which are only partly defined by traditional traits, Glowczewski notes (1998: 335). 'It is', she continues, 'as if pan-Aboriginality itself was creating the emergence of those identity singularities, as if the process of anthropological and social heterogenisation was part and parcel of the creation of political uniformity' (ibid.).

Our aim here is, first, to analyse the process of identity constructions in two completely different cultural environments: the Arnhem Land bush in northern Australia and urban Sydney in the southeast. Secondly, to show how in that process the multiple interpretations of Aboriginality — a constant oscillation between 'oneness' and 'distinctiveness' or between unification and differentiation — are at work. Although the history of European intrusion and its far-reaching consequences for the way people organise their daily lives in both environments could not be more different within Aboriginal Australia, we consider both situations as part of a continuum of present day Aboriginal domains, albeit at both ends of this continuum.

The Arnhem Land example

At an important ritual in central Arnhem Land in the early eighties, with participants from all over the region, an Aboriginal man called Ray tried to explain to one of us why, at one moment, he emphasised Aboriginal unity and at the very next asked attention for his clan background to distinguish himself from others present at that large ceremonial gathering. He used the phrase we choose in the title of this chapter: *we are one but still different*.[1] Oneness was politically relevant during that ceremony in which a great number of clans from all over Arnhem Land, northern Australia, celebrated their collective cultural heroes: two ancestral women — Sisters — who were equally important to all those present. Celebrating a communal Aboriginal background was relevant in the context of the political situation of that time, when the western world put a lot of pressure on the Aboriginal societies in Arnhem Land. Land rights, mining, competition with white agencies over political power, struggle for their own distinctive identity, control over resources; these are just a few of the major issues Aborigines have been concerned with during the last twenty-five years. By celebrating the Dreamtime exploits of these two women, all those present — despite their different clan backgrounds — were able to confess their common Aboriginal identity.

Yet, during certain stages of that particular ceremony, it appeared to be of great relevance to Ray to also distinguish between this common Aboriginal background on the one hand and his specific clan affiliations on the other. The right to sing, dance and paint certain themes within this elaborated ceremony and the right of control over corresponding sites and tracks of land within Arnhem Land are intrinsically connected. Therefore, depending on the context, it is equally important to articulate distinctiveness instead of oneness. Ray's statement, *one but still different*, in relation to the various stages of that ceremony was an apt characterisation of that phenomenon.

In this section on Arnhem Land we first explain how the Aboriginal notion of 'the Dreaming' provides the blueprint for Aboriginal identity constructions, and then turn to the importance of life-cycle rituals in that process. Finally we discuss the question why this constant switching between communality and particularism, or between collectivism and atomism, as it also has been called (Sutton 1995: 1), is not inconsistent but inherent in the very nature of Aboriginal cosmology.

---

1. Cf. also Glowczewski 1998, who chose a similar title for her contribution on aspects of Aboriginality.

The Dreaming

The most fundamental concept in Aboriginal religion is the Dreaming. Stanner (1966: 26-27) characterised 'the Dreaming' as ...'that which comprehends everything and is adequate to everything. It is the total reference of which anything else is a *relatum*. The Dreaming is, as Charlesworth (1984: 9-10) explains, a plurivocal term with a number of distinct, though connected meanings. First, the term refers to a narrative mythical account of the foundation and shaping of the world by ancestor heroes who themselves are uncreated and eternal. That period is often called 'the Dreamtime'. Second, it refers to the embodiment of the spiritual power of these ancestors in the land, in certain sites and in all species (including humans) so that this spiritual power is available to the people today. Third, the concept denotes what Aborigines call 'the Law': moral and social codes transmitted through religious practices of songs, dance, paintings and narratives. Fourth, it refers to the personal relation an Aborigine has with a specific site and spiritual being by virtue of his spirit-conception and of his membership of a clan. Thus an Aborigine may call a certain fish his personal 'dreaming' because his spirit was conceived at a water hole and connected with a mythical being of which that particular species of fish is the visible transformation.

So the concept 'the Dreaming' may refer to a sacred period; to ancestral heroes of that period whose embodiment in the land, natural species and humans makes their power relevant for the here and now; to sets of rules and behaviour comparable with the Indonesian concept 'adat' and to a person's personal spiritual origin and clan background.

It is this all-encompassing character of the concept 'the Dreaming' which provides Aborigines with a collective Aboriginal identity. Even in urban situations, where Aborigines acknowledge that they have lost most of the way of life connected with the Dreaming the concept plays an important role in the construction of an Aboriginal identity, usually referred to as 'Aboriginality (see our Sydney example and concluding section). In these urban settings the concept is much more vague than in Arnhem Land, and is usually explained in more general, unspecified terms: a spiritual connection with Mother Earth and natural species, community spirit and a caring attitude. It is not surprising that these elements are also used to position one's self against perceived western identities which in the eyes of many urban Aborigines have materialism, exploitation, individuality and egoism as their main features.

The Dreaming in the Arnhem Land situation is a much more 'lived in' reality and still very relevant to the daily life of its people. The term 'lived in' is used here in the sense that it '... assumes an aspect of naturalness to the participants', as Otto (1993: 8) explains this term in another context. The ancestral heroes and their spiritual power are real, the sacred sites they left behind are actual places in the landscape, often transformations of these beings; the designs on paintings are seen as 'footsteps' (lit.) of these beings, the Law is the point of reference for moral and social behaviour, and religious expressions of narratives, songs, dances and paintings are there to communicate with 'the Dreaming' and to experience its overwhelming power. In Geertz' terminology (1973) it is the model of — and model for — reality, and therefore the source from which a collective Aboriginal identity originates, despite differences in languages, social structure, kinship and religious forms of expression. The ancestral heroes such as the two Sisters mentioned above function as symbols of that unity. They are, what Maddock (1972: 105-17) calls 'Transcendental Powers': a class of world-creative powers who stand in the same relation to all people and therefore called transcendental as opposed to another class of world creative powers, the totemic beings who are parochial in character. We turn to these beings later. They connect many different Aboriginal groups and provide them with a common Aboriginal background. The two women came with the first sunset and travelled, roughly from east to west, with a great number of species in their wake that became the founders of the many clans in Arnhem Land. Transcendental powers, such as these two women, provide Aborigines over a wide area with a shared human identity, because all Aborigines, whatever differences in language, marriage system and ritual practices there are, relate to them.

Ray, when explaining that they all were one but still different, had many options to choose from in order to stipulate some of these differences. We now turn to these differences and try to explain why the same Dreaming-ideology also accounts for a number of specified identities, varying from large group formations to an individual identity. In ceremonial gatherings like those devoted to the two mythological women, it was relevant for him to distinguish between the cluster of Wild Honey clans to which he belonged, founded by a mythological being called Djareware, and clusters of other clans which were created by other mythological beings. The Wild Honey people presented in songs, dances and paintings their own section of the creation story, thus laying exclusive claims on specific knowledge and particular areas of land. The emphasis then was not on an all-encompassing Aboriginal — if not human — identity, but on regional identities within Arnhem Land, based on mythical founders of a number of clans who in their turn were linked to the transcendental class of world creative powers.

Djareware is such a being of regional importance and may in Maddock's terminology (ibid.) be called a totemic being because he is associated with particular clans to the exclusion of others. He too came with the first sunset but soon took a route of his own and founded two clans to the east before he entered the clan estate of our guide. He gave that part of the country its present shape and also left other totemic beings behind such as bees, stringy bark trees, flowers and honey-birds — beings which became the prototypes of the natural species of the same name. He also left his spiritual power — his essence — behind from which all living beings of that clan would emerge. He then continued his creative journey to the northeast where he founded a fourth Wild Honey clan. Compared with the route of the two women, which may extend indefinitely as the horizon of Aborigines broadens, Djareware's route is limited. Seen from Ray's perspective it stretches from two-named clan estates respectively some fifty and thirty kilometres to the east, to a place about forty kilometres to the northwest.

A further specification in identity construction takes place within such a chain of clans; Wild Honey clans in our example. Ray belonged to the Wild Honey Clan of the Djinang speaking people and he and his fellow clan members identified themselves in this context as Wurgigandjar: *people of the blossoming stringy bark flower*, the flower from which the bees collected nectar. This name applies only to them and not to the three other Wild Honey clans. How this further differentiation is symbolically expressed becomes again obvious in the context of religious ceremonies.

When Wurgigandjar people performed a particular clan ritual, which cele-brated the Dreamtime exploits of Djareware, representatives of other Wild Honey clans used to attend. Especially members from the Wild Honey clans from the east, where Djareware was first, were important. They had a say over the large ceremonial pole, which represented Djareware and other objects for that ritual. The Wurgigandjar people could only proceed with their preparations after their guests from the east had approved of these ceremonial paraphernalia. During those gatherings the eastern Wild Honey people would sing Djareware songs, in combination with totemic beings which were particular to their own clan country. Wurgigandjar people would also sing Djareware songs, but only in combination with species specific to their clan estate (see Borsboom 1978a and 1998). Thus clan identities within clusters of clans found their symbolic expression in this religious context.

The combination of Djareware songs with — for each clan — a different set of totemic beings, emphasises the rights and responsibilities for one's own clan estate. For example, the species sung by Wurgigandjar people in combination with Djareware related to specific sacred sites exclusive to their

clan land. The same applies to the other Wild Honey clansmen, who in each
case sing Djareware with a set of totemic beings exclusive to their clan and
clan estate. But because of the commonly shared ancestral being Djareware,
each clan has also a certain say in matters of land rights over all the sites and
tracks of land created by their founder. So at this regional level of group
formation Ray may again rightfully say *we are one but still different*. *One* when
he includes all Wild Honey people who originate from Djareware, *different*
when he refers to the specific set of totemic beings — symbolised in songs,
dances and paintings — which Djareware left behind in his own clan estate.

From here further differentiation is often relevant, depending on what
level of social formation one acts. Within the Wurgigandjar clan a distinction
is made between 'people from the top' and 'people from the bottom', phrases
which refer to families who belong to the higher and dry parts of the clan
estate and those to the lower and wet areas. Actually Ray would say 'I am
nongere (literally meaning 'ankle', e.g. the lower part of the country) and they
are *guragngere*' ('neck', e.g. the higher part of the country). The two different
identities on that level played a role in the daily affairs of the Wurgigandjar
and their relatives. Once, another Aboriginal man, also from the *nongere*
section, criticised his fellow clan members from the *guragngere* section for not
burning the country at the appropriate time. He considered that to be a
serious neglect but could not do much because the others would be angry
had he decided to act on his own account. In our society it could be compared to cleaning our brother's house — if in a mess — without asking him
first. This criticism extended to other kinds of behaviour, for example, that
some of the *guragngere* men were absent for too long, spent too much time
in places like Darwin and could therefore not be present at important
religious performances. Such signs of animosity occasionally popped up and
illustrated the strain and competition for prestige existing between members
of the same clan. A man of the *guragngere* section once told others that
nongere men gave one of us the wrong information about a certain ritual,
actually meaning that he did not agree with their interpretation of the
meaning of some ritual objects.

Here again, as in the previously analysed situations, the difference
between both sections became manifest in the symbolism of religious activities. For example, a ceremonial pole made by one group would be slightly
shorter than that of the other, notwithstanding the fact that in both cases the
pole represented Djareware, the bees and the blossom. Also a slightly different pitch in some of the songs, only noticed by trained ears, were signs of
subtle distinctions. One may conclude that the smaller the level of group
formation, the more subtle the symbols as markers of inclusion and ex-

clusion. Here the term 'diacritics' is applicable: claimed points of difference between groups, '... insofar as these are recognised and emphasised by members of the group concerned' (Watson 1990: 22). It mostly refers to small differences, which are hardly recognised by outsiders but are of great symbolic importance to the people involved. Also at this level the phrase *we are one (Wurgigandjar) but still different (nongere or guragngere)* has lost nothing of its strength.

And then, finally, some of our guides and mentors would in yet another context find it relevant to emphasise their own unique personal identity within either the *nongere* or *guragngere* lineage, an identity based on the place where the individual's spiritual conception took place. They would then refer to their Aboriginal names, which related to a particular site, or a totemic being connected with such a site. Thus a man from the *guragngere* section, whose part of the country was abundant with nectar, honey and flowering stringy bark trees, might identify himself with the bees, because their Dreamtime appearances are connected with his section of the country and with specific places therein. Perhaps early in pregnancy his mother (or her husband) had a dream about an exceptionally large beehive with a great many bees, and concluded that this was a message from the other side to explain the spiritual origin of their future child: the totemic bees — one of the manifestations of Djareware — from which the actual bees were the visible, material transformations. This spiritual background distinguishes him from others within the lineage, whose spirits may originate from other beings connected with Djareware, such as a honey-bird, stringy bark trees or stringy-bark flowers in blossom. Although we have not actually heard that expression, the person in question might have said in that context *we (guragngere) are one but I am still different*.

To summarise the above: on the basis of the notion the Dreaming and its complicated content, an Aboriginal person has a number of identities to choose from in any given context. This can be done without being inconsistent or having to adjust to different personalities all the time. Each level of identity construction is connected to the next one, because the notion of the Dreaming comprehends everything and is, to quote Stanner once more, adequate to everything. 'It is the total reference of which anything else is a relatum' (1966: 26-27). The cosmological wholeness is symbolised by the transcendental powers. From them all kinds of other species originated, some of whom became the founders of specific clans, their estates, and a number of other species connected with them. From these latter the spirit-children emerged which give name and identity to persons. Spirit child, totemic being, founder of clan(s), transcendental beings, they are related to one another in the same way as the various identities of Aborigines, which are articulated through them.

Age-grading

Religion, writes Geertz, is sociologically interesting not because, as vulgar positivism would have it, it describes the social order, '... but because, like environment, political power, wealth, jural obligation, personal affection, and a sense of beauty, it shapes it' (1973: 119). Notions about the Dreaming shape Aboriginal perceptions about the natural and social order, or, to put it differently, about the way people relate to nature and to one another. In Aboriginal thought relation to other persons and groups is mediated through totemic beings which represent natural species and phenomena. Creation of the world through a process of ever-ongoing differentiations among the world creative powers serves as a model for similar processes in the human world and simultaneously is a justification and legitimation of that process.

The main function of the ritual is, Geertz asserts (1973: 112), to convince people that 'religious conceptions are veridical and that religious directives are sound and somehow generated'. In a ritual, the world as lived and the world as imagined, fuses under the agency of a single set of symbolic forms (ibid.). It is from this perspective that the importance of life-cycle rituals in Aboriginal society must be seen. From birth to long after death, each person is subjected to a series of rituals, with persuasive authority, which shape his or her personality, perception of the natural and human world, and relations to others. Warner called this process 'age grading' (1937), a term which still is valid to characterise this process, although his conclusions that it only concerns men, is not valid at all. The age grading divides life in a number of stages, marked by the rites de passage: elaborate rituals set off birth, childhood, puberty, maturity and death. In this section we want to demonstrate how age-grading imprints on each person the variety of identities discussed above in such a way that every newly-added identity is in concordance with the former so as to maintain continuity in one's personality.

We put the emphasis here on the conception of the person as a cultural category. Morris (1994: 11) defines the notion of the person as a cultural category as a '... conception articulated specifically in the cultural representation of a specific community'. He continues by stating that as a cultural category the person is often clearly expressed in the ritual context, and it often has an ideological function. It is this ritual context which defines and shapes the various Aboriginal identities. In the following we take an imaginary male person[2] from the *guragngere* section of the Wurgigandjar Wild Honey clan as an example.

The age-grading system starts soon after birth, when the newly born baby receives his names. Although at that stage he is not yet aware of what happens, he will learn later when he is present at similar ceremonies of younger siblings. First a number of names are given, names, which refer to the spiritual identity of the individual. Early in pregnancy, the mother and her husband are aware that special dreams or exceptional occurrences might be signs that a spirit child is about to enter the womb to animate the foetus. The child's names are derived from a place, for example a particular beehive, and the species connected with it, for example bees. From now on his individual identity is definitely established. During the name giving ceremony the father and his brothers sing songs of the Dreamtime travels of Djareware and the totemic beings that travelled with him. As they belong to the *guragngere* section — the higher part of their clan estate — they emphasise their part of the clan's creation story. Therefore not only the personal but also the lineage identity is established at that ceremony.

At the age of five or six he usually gets a chance to participate in the first large clan ceremony called 'rite of diplomacy'. His clan relatives use this rite to establish contact with Aborigines from other areas, and in the present day even with Australian persons and institutions outside Arnhem Land (Borsboom 1978a and Wild 1986). Central to the ceremony is a large ritual pole, which represents the clan's founder, Djareware, together with bees, honey, birds and other elements connected with wild honey. During the preparations of this ritual, which takes several months, the young boy is instructed on Djareware's exploits: how he belongs to Djareware, how this ancestral hero designed the clan's country and left natural species behind everywhere, including the species from which his spirit originates. Here the young boy experiences that his personal identity is not only connected to his immediate family (*guragngere*), but also to the larger group of which this lineage is but one part, e.g. the clan. Now the emphasis is definitely on the clan as a whole and on this occasion the clan identity is added to the already established identities of lineage and individual.

The initiation rite at puberty is in some respects a break with previous

---

2. Women too are subjected to rites de passage, however a male researcher has little access to what is called 'women's business'. So the emphasis on males in this section is not so much yet another demonstration of male chauvinistic bias but a demonstration of people's gender-based limitations in gender-conscious societies like those of Australian Aborigines.

identities but in other respects a continuation thereof. In the personal realm it is definitely a break with the identity of child: he dies as a child to be reborn as a young man. From now on he also learns that gender identity becomes important in both the religious, social and economic affairs and that in many respects life is sexually bifurcated. In this sense there is no continuity with the previous stage: the transformation from child to young adult is abrupt, and so is the sudden division into the male and female realms of life. However, in relation to group formation, continuity remains despite the great abruptness in other fields. He loses nothing from his spiritual, lineage or clan identity, nor do his female siblings during their puberty rites. In fact, these identities are strengthened in the ritual. But also new insights are revealed, for example that Djareware not only created his own clan country but that of others as well, that his clan is part of larger aggregates and that there are important ritual and social relations between those clans. He experiences that a regional identity emerges on top of his personal and very local identity.

There also may be hints of the relation between Djareware and the Transcendental Beings. But in Aboriginal society knowledge is revealed in small portions and it may take years before he fully understands this. There is ample opportunity for this within the age-grading system. After initiation the young man will be a novice in the initiation rites of younger siblings and also participate in yearly seasonal rituals. In the years to come he will understand that reality exists of many layers and that each time another layer is pealed off.

The age-grading system is an ongoing process that continues until old age. When he has reached that stage he has not only learned from rituals to which he himself was subjected, but also from those organised for others. He sees new ceremonial objects that reveal new meanings or learns that already known objects have deeper meanings than previously thought. One of the most fundamental insights is that everything has an outside and an inside — or a material and a spiritual essence. All his adult life metaphors have been used to illuminate this: the relation of the outside, material world to the inside, spiritual world is as the flesh of a body to the bones, the latter being the foundation of the former; or as the bark of a tree to the inside, which carries the outside appearance; or as the public places to the sacred ones, the latter providing the energy and strength for the former, and so on (see also Keen 1994: 194, 252 and Morphy 1991: 78-99).

In the same way of reasoning he might come to the conclusion that the outside appearance of a line of bees flying to their nests — depicted in certain ceremonies as a beautiful long rope with white feathers — refers at a spiritual level to the sunbeams which lead to the sun, just like a line of bees to their nests. The sun, in turn, is seen as a transformation of the Two Sisters who came with the first sunrise and have become metaphors for the dry season (the Rainbow Snake with whom the two Sisters interacted is a symbol for the wet season). So now he understands that his very own personal identity is through a series of transformations, also connected with the grand scheme of things: the personal totemic beings (bees in our example) with founders of clans (such as Djareware), and finally with transcendental beings (the two ancestral women). Thus the Dreaming relates his personal, lineage, clan and regional identity with an all-encompassing Aboriginal identity. It is perhaps the most important message concealed in the symbolic capital of the age-grading system.

Discussion

As in many Polynesian creation myths (Gell 1995: 23) the creative epoch in Aboriginal thought occurred as a process of differentiation from a situation of immanence. First the cosmos was one and undifferentiated. Then came the transcendental beings such as the two Sisters who created the world as it is now: separating sky from earth, water from land, day from night and dry season from wet season, male from female. Their Dreamtime exploits were equally important to all people. From there the process of differentiation proceeded further. Out of these transcendental beings other ancestral beings emerged, which became the founders of specific natural species and groups of people connected with these species. Djareware is such a being. It created the Wild Honey clans to whom he allocated specific parts of Arnhem Land. Other beings did the same with other species and other clans. But the process of creation by differentiation went on: Djareware left other totemic beings behind in the estate of what became the Wurgigandjar clan and divided its country in two sections: a lower and a higher part which he allocated to the two lineages. Finally, he marked particular sites in both sections of the clan's land from which individual spirits-children could animate the foetus in women's bodies thereby establishing a person's exclusive personal identity. Gell's (ibid.) explanation for the Polynesians may equally apply to the epistemology of 'the Dreaming': what God (or the Transcendental Beings in the Aboriginal context) did was to articulate or differentiate the world into its basic components and qualities, but the substance of the newly articulated cosmos remains what it always was, nothing other than God himself. So God, or the Transcendental Beings, created the universe not *ex nihilo*, but as an ongoing process of differentiation out of a situation of immanence. But in the end the newly articulated differentiation on all levels, which became the model for differentiation in human society, appeared to be nothing more than a series of transformations of the Transcendental Beings themselves. Therefore the phrase *we are one but still different* is not just a casual remark of a creative person, but relates to one of the most basic elements in Aboriginal cosmology and world view.

Multiple variations of Aboriginal identification in Sydney

In Sydney the Aboriginal people live spread out over the metropolitan area, concentrated in the poorer suburbs near the city centre and at the fringe of the metropolitan area. The majority of the Sydney Aboriginal population comes from New South Wales, while a minority originates from places out of the state. Aboriginal residency in urban areas is a relatively recent phenomenon and started in the 1950s when a large number of Aboriginal people left the reserves in search of work (Rowley 1971, Smith and Biddle 1975). Others were brought to the cities as children under the assimilation policy (Gale and Brookman 1972: 87). This group is known as the stolen generations.[3] Hence the Sydney Aboriginal population appears to be rather heterogeneous. This does not hinder its members in identifying themselves as Aborigines, supporting the expression *We are one but still different*.

Being Aboriginal or identifying as such means different things in different situations. While the Arnhem Land case shows how people express their Aboriginality in terms of a cosmological framework, the following case from urban Australia shows that identifying as Aborigine in that context has a more political character. Just like the people in Arnhem Land, the people in Sydney articulate their distinctiveness as well as their oneness, depending upon the context in which they find themselves.

To illustrate how urban Aboriginal people express their distinctiveness, as well as their oneness, this part of the chapter will focus on a case which describes different ways of Aboriginal identification in Sydney.

3. From the early 1900s until the 1960s many Aboriginal children were taken away from their families under the assimilation policy to be raised in government institutions and church missions. These children are nowadays referred to as the stolen generations (Cummings 1990, National Inquiry into the Separation of Aboriginal and Torres Strait Islander Children from their Families [Australia] 1997).

An Aboriginal protest in Sydney

In August 1996 a demonstration was organised in Sydney's Hyde Park to protest against the proposed funding cuts in Aboriginal Affairs announced by the newly elected Liberal Government. It was organised to assemble people in Sydney who would join other Aboriginal and non-Aboriginal protesters in Canberra the following day.[4] On a lawn in the park a stage was built, decorated with Aboriginal and Torres Strait Islander flags and a banner with the text: 'Indigenous Resistance' and an illustration of a black fist. The audience consisted of a few hundred people, the majority of whom were Aboriginal. Some of them were covered in the Aboriginal colours: black, yellow and red. Others held Aboriginal flags or had subtly used the tricolour pattern in their clothing.

As part of the demonstration several performances took place on stage. At the beginning of each performance the participants paid respect to the Eora people, the original inhabitants of the Sydney area, for allowing them to perform on their land. Some of them also greeted the crowd in their own Aboriginal language. There were several bands, which performed that afternoon. One of them consisted of Torres Strait Islander, Pacific Islander and Aboriginal band members. The lead singer was an Aboriginal actress who sang about the Koori[5] heroine, Black Mary. There was also a rap group consisting of Aboriginal students from the Eora Centre[6] in Redfern, an inner Sydney suburb. They sounded like Afro-Americans when they sang about their lives as Kooris in the 'ghetto' of Redfern, known for its crimes, drugs, and police raids. Another performance was given by an Aboriginal writer, belonging to the stolen generations (the children who were taken away under the assimilation policy). She captured the audience by her storytelling under accompaniment of a didgeridoo player, and told everyone a local creation story about how the black snake became poisonous.

The performances were alternated by a range of Aboriginal political speakers working for different Aboriginal organisations in Sydney. They all

4. The national protest in Canberra made international headlines because an angry crowd managed to enter Parliament House by breaking through the glass walls and doors which separated the politicians from the protesters (*Sydney Morning Herald* 20/8/96).

5. The term *Koori* means *man* or *people* in many languages that were used in the southeastern part of Australia. Variations on the word *Koori*, such as: *coorie, kory, kuri, kooli* and *koole*, are found in many districts in New South Wales, Victoria and South Australia. In the lower Murray region in South Australia *Kuri* referred to a major dance cycle (Howie-Willis 1994: 559).

6. Aboriginal unit of TAFE (Technical and Further Education).

Aboriginal Protest Meeting in Sydney

made emotional speeches and some of them accused leading figures in Aboriginal politics of selling out their own people to white politicians. They said that Aboriginal people in Canberra cannot be trusted because they are *gubbahs*[7] and that it is time for other Aboriginal people to win their power back. They incited their audience to unite and undertake action. Rude words and name-calling were not shunned and the audience cheered and applauded after every speech.

After all the political heavyweights had spoken, an unknown young Aboriginal man entered the stage. He was dressed in a cloak with feathers and other ornaments and carried a staff. But before he had even said a word some people in the audience started joking about him. They hissed and did not seem to agree with what he was saying even though the message of his speech did not differ that much from his predecessors. One Aboriginal woman said to another woman: 'Who does he think he is?' The other woman

7. Aboriginal slang meaning *white men*, derived from the word *governor*.

answered: 'He must be a member of the Wannabee nation'.[8] They both started laughing.

'Indigenousness'

The above fragment of an Aboriginal protest demonstration gives an example of the complexity of relations between people who identify as Aboriginal. On the one hand, the speakers at the protest speak about indigenous resistance, inciting their Aboriginal audience to unite and undertake action against the federal government, while, on the other hand, both the speakers as well as the public make distinctions between Aboriginal communities and individuals on the basis of cultural differences as well as behaviour. During the protest some people are judged for their lack of 'Aboriginality'. In this section we will investigate how people emphasise both unity and diversity. The first is mainly based on specific historical correspondences such as a shared history of oppression, the second on cultural differences, like language.

At the protest the people seem to switch between the use of the term *Aboriginal* and *indigenous*. Both the banner, as well as the two different flags, illustrate the inclusion of other indigenous peoples who do not identify as Aboriginal. On stage this inclusion is confirmed by the pop group with Aboriginal, Torres Strait Islander and Pacific Islander band members. The question is: why are people who do not identify as Aboriginal actively involved in an Aboriginal protest? Apparently identifying as Aboriginal means identifying as an indigenous Australian. The identification as indigenous Australian places people in opposition to non-indigenous Australians, while at the same time it connects them with other indigenous peoples around the world who see themselves placed in opposition with other non-indigenous people.

The inclusion of other indigenous peoples in Aboriginal protest can however be an issue of discussion. We know of protests where Aboriginal people objected to the participation of Torres Strait Islander people because they were of the opinion that both peoples do not share the same experiences of oppression. They argued that Torres Strait Islander people were treated much better than Aboriginal people by the colonists on the basis of the cultural differences. When the colonists first encountered Torres Strait Islander people they were seen as horticulturalists as opposed to the

---

8. Wannabee is a fictitious name derived from the words *want to be*.

Aborigines who were considered to be primitive hunters. Some Aboriginal people also compared the treatment of Aboriginal and Torres Strait Islander people as one group, with the misguided perception that the groups who inhabited Australia in the past were one people. They regarded such treatment as another attempt by the authorities to control who belongs to whom.

Apart from the inclusion of other indigenous people, the illustration of a black fist on the banner refers to the inclusion of 'black' people around the world. This inclusion was especially popular in the late 1960s when Aboriginal people maintained regular contact with Black American movements, such as the Black Panthers (Burgmann 1993, Jennett 1980, Jones and Hill-Burnett 1982). The division that is made along the lines of 'black' versus 'white', however, differs substantially from the division indigenous versus non-indigenous. Although 'blacks' around the world share a history of oppression by 'whites' on the basis of racial differences, they do not necessarily share the basis upon which indigenous identification is founded, namely the claim that they were the original inhabitants of a specific area.

During fieldwork we noticed that on the occasions where urban Aboriginal people identify as indigenous Australian, the commonality they stress is the 'common experience of dispossession and racism, and "survival" as an identifiable people' (Hollinsworth 1992: 141). History divides the Australian population along the lines of the colonised and the colonists; the Aboriginal people and the 'white' or 'western' Australians. At the same time it unifies all Australian Aboriginal people on the basis of a shared contact history, resistance and survival. Although the contact histories of particular countries differ, colonial history does form a basis for indigenous peoples around the world to identify with one another.

Apart from the commonality on the basis of historical experience, there is also a resemblance between what different indigenous peoples perceive of as their heritage. In the case of the Australian Aborigines this heritage involves an ideological framework which determines how Aboriginal people should behave (Carter 1984: 127). Appropriate behaviour involves the use of specific languages and particular styles, like deportment and etiquette (Carter 1988, Schwab 1988). The ideological framework emphasises, amongst other things, the importance of kin-relations expressed in encouraging caring and sharing with family members; the importance of land which is seen as a means to obtain (economic) independence; and a world-view based upon the concept of the 'Dreamtime', entailing, for example, the ability to be in contact with the spiritual world. Each of these themes is loosely based on knowledge about the past and has been passed on as oral history. Another source of knowledge is to be found in remote areas, such as Arnhem Land, where indigenous cosmology, social structure and land still form a more or less coherent system.

Together, these themes are said to be part of an Aboriginal heritage connecting contemporary Aboriginal culture with that of their ancestors in the past. This connection serves as a legitimacy of their unique position as the first inhabitants of the Australian continent. For urban Aboriginal people it also serves as a connection between themselves and Aboriginal communities in remote areas where people maintain relatively tradition-oriented lifestyles. The emphasis on these particular themes as kin, land, and spirituality can serve to stress the opposition between indigenous people and their western counterparts. As Beckett points out, elements referring to a precolonial past or to Aboriginal cosmology as experienced by Aboriginal people from areas such as Arnhem Land 'only come alive in the course of political, social and cultural conflict' (1988: 212).

That people have made divisions along the lines of 'indigenousness' suggests that there is a purpose for doing so. On the occasion that people identify as indigenous they do this to demand an equal position in relation to the non-indigenous population. Indigenous people also want to derive exclusive rights — such as land rights — on the basis of the special status they attach to themselves (Maddock 1991, Peperkamp and Remie 1989, van der Vlist 1994). They base this status upon their unique position as original inhabitants of the area.

In Australia the Aboriginal people see that resources — political as well as economic — are not equally divided among Aboriginal and non-Aboriginal Australians. They want to change their subordinate position in society by trying to enforce such special rights in the form of land rights as well as monetary compensation for the confiscated land. Throughout Australian history Aboriginal people have united on particular occasions, on the basis of their shared subordinate position, in order to accomplish these goals (Goodall 1996, Lippmann 1991). Examples are the protests surrounding issues such as land rights, Aboriginal deaths in custody, and the stolen generations. Solidarity based on shared experiences of oppression serves as a means to bring about change and to dispute the unequal allocation of resources, for which the Australian authorities and the Australian public in general are held responsible. The same was happening at the Sydney demonstration where the protesters wanted to confront the federal government with their proposed funding cuts.

Identification as Koori

Apart from the regular use of the terms *Aboriginal* and *indigenous*, the speakers also refer to their identification as Koori. The contents of some of the performances reflect this regional form of identification by specifically using regional issues in their performances. One example is the rap group of Aboriginal students from the Eora Centre. They sing about their lives as Kooris in Redfern, their confrontations with the police and the specific places where they hang out. The same goes for the band that sings about the Koori heroine, Black Mary.[9] Being a regional historical figure she will be recognised much easier by people from the New South Wales region than people from, for example, Arnhem Land. Finally, the creation story as told by the poet has a regional origin, referring to species that live in the area from which the story originates.

In the late 1960s and early 1970s Aboriginal people increasingly replaced the term *Aboriginal* with regional Aboriginal names when referring to themselves. In New South Wales and Victoria people call themselves Koori. They also use this term to denote everything referring to people identifying as such. They speak for example about the Koori way, Koori organisations, Koori history, and use expressions such as Koori time. The name *Koori* has similar regional counterparts in the rest of Australia, like the Murri in Queensland, Nung(g)a in South Australia and Yolngu in the Northern Territory. These collective terms all originated from Aboriginal languages and can often be translated as people, friends or speech. Berndt and Berndt stress that these regional names are not tribal names but labels which are used 'to attempt to arrive at a general social identification in terms of Aboriginality ... as a result of alien impact, and of increasing estrangement from traditional Aboriginal ways' (1988: 35). Hence, it had the capacity to include Aboriginal people who had no knowledge about their traditional background or group affiliations.

As is the case with the identification of Aboriginal people on the basis of their shared history of oppression, the massive use of regional names also became more popular on the basis of particular needs. These needs concerned not so much the equal distribution of economic or political resources but the control over their own identity, as even this had been largely in the hands of the colonists. In the pre-colonial period Aboriginal people did not

9. Black Mary is an Aboriginal historical figure called Mary Ann from Wingham, northern New South Wales, who was legendary for her controversial relation with Captain Frederick Ward and their lives together as bush rangers (Janson 1996: 1).

perceive of themselves as one group (Tonkinson 1990: 191). It was only after the British set foot on shore in 1788 that the indigenous groups that populated the Australian continent were perceived of as *one people*: the Aborigines. From that moment onwards this perception was forced upon them by the colonial powers that controlled them (Attwood 1989).

When Aboriginal people increasingly started using regional names they no longer wanted to be labelled by others but to decide for themselves who they were and to whom they wanted to belong. Through choosing their own names the Aboriginal people were able to free themselves from the negative connotations and misconceptions surrounding the term *Aboriginal*. This made it possible to identify as people distinct from other indigenous people. After all, the term *Aboriginal* did not make such a distinction. It originally derived from the adjective to refer to anything that was native to a particular area (from the Latin *ab origine*). Through the use of regional names Aboriginal people were also 'asserting the distinctiveness of the many Aboriginal groups here before 1788, and reminding whites that the word "Aboriginal" and its meanings are not theirs' (Burgmann 1993: 37).

By referring to regional features of their Aboriginality the participants at the protest demonstrated that they identify as Koori. These regional features concern, for instance, regional historical events, regional heroes and mythological figures, but also the importance of specific places, plants and animals and the use of specific regional words, such as *gubbahs*. On the basis of their regional expressions it is safe to assume that an Aboriginal protest with the same goal would look quite different in another region of Australia because, there, the people would give their own regional interpretations of Aboriginality, reflecting, for example, their Nunga or Yolngu identity. Identifying as Koori enables the urban Aboriginal population of Sydney to unite; not on the basis of a label that was introduced by the colonists, but on a name they have chosen for themselves. At the same time the use of the term Koori recognises the cultural diversity amongst people who identify as Aborigine.

Nation affiliation

When listening to the political speakers, as well as the reactions of the audience at the different performances, most speakers introduced themselves as people from a particular nation by stating this specifically or by using their nation's language. In this way they legitimised their own Aboriginal identity towards the audience. The last speaker who was unknown to the audience and failed to introduce himself properly made his own identification as Aborigine open to suspicion. The joke about the Wannabee nation, referring to identification with local Aboriginal nations, showed that some people suspected him of pretending to be Aboriginal to take advantage of it. Apparently a nation affiliation is indispensable for someone to be accepted as Aboriginal. This can thus be regarded as another way of identifying as Aboriginal next to identification as Koori or as Indigenous Australian. In recent years Aboriginal people tend to fall back on pre-colonial notions of indigenous group affiliation, called 'nations', after the Native American adaptation of the term. These nations correspond with specific language groups, although in New South Wales there are not as many languages left as there are nations or language groups with which to identify.

Individual people identify with particular nations through their families of which the nations consist. Family name and place of birth is very important in providing the Aboriginal person with an accepted identity in interaction with other Aboriginal people (Barwick 1988, Eckermann 1973, Kendall 1994, Schwab 1988). Whenever Aboriginal people meet each other for the first time they ask: 'Who are you and where are you from?' When it concerns unknown people from the same region most people will recognise a family name and often know someone from that family, as in expressions such as: 'Oh, you're a Dickinson from Lismore!' A person is not considered a 'real' Aboriginal person according to many if he or she is not able or willing to give this information. This poses a serious problem for people from the stolen generations who have often lost all contact with their Aboriginal family and have difficulty establishing where they originate from, thus establishing their Aboriginal identity.

Local affiliations have always played a role but seem to have become more and more visible in the last decade. A possible explanation for this could be that over the years resources have become available to Aboriginal people that were not available before. In the past, Aboriginal identity was something that was better concealed, otherwise the consequences could be devastating (considering the way in which Aboriginal people were treated over the years). Nowadays land rights, monetary support, and specified jobs can be granted to people on the basis of their Aboriginality.[10] Hence, someone's Aboriginal identity is worth something. Apart from economic resources, political resources have become available as well. At the present time the

---

10. Although in public debate this can be grossly exaggerated. Extra subsidies are only available to organisations or projects to compensate the backward position of Aboriginal people in areas such as education, health and housing. The idea that people receive higher pensions or social security payments on the basis of their Aboriginality is a myth.

government employs a large number of Aboriginal people as liaison officers in government departments or in the federal employment scheme CDEP (Community Development Employment Projects). Sometimes this is sarcastically called 'the Aboriginal industry'. Others occupy political positions in Aboriginal organisations and act as representatives. Therefore it is not surprising that people in these positions are watched closely.

Acceptance on the basis of a nation affiliation is not always enough to be accepted by other Aboriginal people, especially when people are acting as representatives. For instance, at the protest leading political figures were accused of selling out their own people and acting as *gubbahs*. In the eyes of the speakers as well as the cheering audience, these people failed to live up to the expectations of their fellow-Aboriginal people. They failed to properly represent their people and were not acting in the appropriate 'Aboriginal way'. Thus being Aboriginal is not enough, people should also act accordingly.

Consider the case of a woman in Sydney who wanted to run in local elections as the Aboriginal candidate, which shows how Aboriginal people deal with unknown persons identifying as Aborigine. The woman in question stated that she was related to a well-known Aboriginal woman of a Wiradjuri family. But a number of Wiradjuri people who were related themselves to this Wiradjuri woman had never heard of the woman claiming to be related. When they confronted her and asked in what specific way she was related, the woman failed to give a credible explanation. This made the people even more suspicious and they started a petition in which they questioned her Aboriginality. People who knew that she was lying were asked to sign the petition.

This incident shows that there is a strict social control on anyone who claims to be Aboriginal. This can have serious consequences for persons who are not able to verify their Aboriginal identity on the basis of family name and place of birth, because according to Australian law a person is Aboriginal on the basis of descent, individual identification, and the recognition by the Aboriginal community. If people lose the recognition of the community they lose their Aboriginality and the specific rights based on their Aboriginality. So when it comes to legitimising one's personal identification as Aborigine, people do not look at Indigenous or Koori identity but at local nation affiliations and family connections to verify someone's personal claim to Aboriginal identity, thus preventing any possible misuse.

Discussion

The case of the Aboriginal protest in Sydney shows that identifying as Aborigine is a relational and situational process in which different forms of Aboriginal identification alternate. What can be seen here is that the speakers and musicians, as well as the Aboriginal people in the audience, participated in a complex process of displaying different interpretations of the concept of Aboriginality, as well as varying their own identification as Aborigine. The Sydney example shows that the different forms of Aboriginal identification each have their place in a particular context and provide people with the means to identify as Aborigines in different ways corresponding to different situations. As the identification on the basis of 'indigenousness' was mainly based on shared history, it provided the people at the protest with the opportunity to form a united front against the Australian government. Also, the identification as Koori proved to be useful in emphasising the cultural as well as historical differentiation between Australian Aboriginal people, thus taking control over what Aboriginality entails according to the Aboriginal protesters as opposed to the Australian authorities. Finally, the identification along the lines of nation affiliations offered the opportunity to legitimise the Aboriginality of the individual participants, ensuring that nobody was able to pretend to be Aboriginal in order to gain from it.

Conclusion

The cases presented here show how in two completely different cultural, political, historical and natural environments, people identify themselves as Aborigines. The conceptual tool, which unites Aboriginal people even at opposite ends of the spectrum of Aboriginal domains, is Aboriginality. The concept asserts that Aborigines share a common cultural heritage and a history of oppression by white society as well as an affirmation of singular regional and local identities, which also are — and always have been — an intrinsic part of Aboriginal ways of life. As such, the concept Aboriginality allows for a constant oscillation between 'oneness' and 'distinctiveness', a process which can be seen on two levels.

First, the process is at work *within* the two cases we analysed. Both Sydney and Arnhem Land Aborigines articulate unity or heterogeneity depending on the particular context and specific situations. The forms of identification differ but the underlying principles are similar. In Arnhem Land the common cultural heritage is based on the existence of Transcendental Powers, the articulation of differences on the existence of totemic beings closely connected to moieties, aggregations of clans, singular clans, lineages within clans and finally personal conception sites. Oneness and distinctiveness in the human world relate to the structuring of the cosmological order. In Sydney, Aboriginal unity is based on the shared history of oppression and displacement and on symbols such as the national Aboriginal flag and banners. Also themes like sharing among kin and empathy with the spiritual world, the land and the Dreamtime — albeit on a much more abstract level than in Arnhem Land — are seen as part of a common Aboriginal heritage. Distinctiveness in this urban setting is based on labels referring to nations, language groups and family names. Here, on the one hand, oneness and distinctiveness relate to a combination of shared history and an ideological framework based on indigenous Aboriginal concepts, and, on the other, to the structuring of the social world along labels like nations, languages and families.

The second level on which this process of unification and differentiation is at work can be seen *between* the two cases we discuss, situations as we said before, at the opposite ends of the Aboriginal spectrum. Aboriginality, as a tool of contemporary Aboriginal political struggle, is also an effort to construct a common Aboriginal culture, an effort to overcome problems of distance and cultural diversity in order to present a united front, and a positive self image (R. Tonkinson, 1998: 293). The 'lived-in' reality of the religious and social world of the Arnhem Landers inspires urban Aborigines in the articulation and construction of their ideological framework. The emphasis on a shared history of oppression and the struggle in the political arena, which originated mainly among urban Aborigines, sparked off irreversible changes in the field of landrights, social justice and cultural independence.

At the same time the conceptual framework of Aboriginality also accounts for differences between the various Aboriginal domains. The emergence of a pan-Aboriginal identity allows at the same time for singular regional and local identities and this process of social heterogenisation is, according to Glowczewski (1998: 335; see also our introduction), part and parcel of the creation of political uniformity.

The collected thoughts, sentiments and efforts which together give form and content to the umbrella concept of Aboriginality, enable Aborigines in all realms of today's Australia to articulate both their oneness and their distinctiveness. Therefore the expression *We are one but still different* gives voice to the most essential features of present day Aboriginal Australia.

Bibliography

Attwood, B. 1989. *The Making of the Aborigines*. Sydney: Allen & Unwin.

Barwick, D.E. 1988. 'Aborigines of Victoria'. In: I. Keen (ed.), *Being Black: Aboriginal Culture in Settled Australia*. Canberra: Aboriginal Studies Press, 27-32.

Beckett, S. 1988. 'The Past in the Present; The Present in the Past: Constructing a National Aboriginality'. In: S. Beckett (ed.), *Past and Present; The Construction of Aboriginality*. Canberra: Aboriginal Studies Press, 1-10.

Berndt, R. 1974. *Australian Aboriginal Religion, vol. I* . Leiden: Brill.

Berndt, R.M. 1977. *Aborigines and Change: Australia in the '70s*. Canberra: Australian Institute of Aboriginal Studies.

Berndt, R.M. and C.H. Berndt 1988. *The World of the First Australians: Aboriginal Traditional Life: Past and Present* (rev. ed.). Canberra: Aboriginal Studies Press.

Borsboom, A. 1978a. 'Dreaming Clusters among Marangu Clans'. In: L.R. Hiatt (ed.), *Australian Aboriginal Concepts*. Canberra: Australian Institute of Aboriginal Studies, 106-21

Borsboom, A. 1978b. *Maradjiri. A Modern Ritual Complex in Arnhem Land, North Australia*, (Ph.D. Thesis). Nijmegen: University of Nijmegen.

Borsboom, A. 1998. 'Knowing the Country. Mabo, Native Title and "Traditional Law" in Aboriginal Australia'. In: J. Wassmann (ed.), *Pacific Answers to Western Hegemony: Cultural Practices of Identity Construction*. Oxford: Berg, 311-35.

Borsboom, A. and H. Dagmar 1984. 'Cultural Politics: Two Case Studies of Australian Aboriginal Social Movements'. In: *Bijdragen tot de Taal-, Land- en Volkenkunde(BKI)* 140, 34-56.

Burgmann, V. 1993. *Power and Protest; Movements for Change in Australian Society*. Sydney: Allen & Unwin.

Carter, J. 1984. Aboriginality: The Affirmation of Cultural Identity in Settled Australia. (M.A. Thesis). Canberra: Australian National University.

Carter, J. 1988. 'Am I Too Black to Go With You?'. In: I. Keen (ed.), *Being Black: Aboriginal Culture in Settled Australia*. Canberra: Aboriginal Studies Press, 65-76.

Charlesworth, M. 1984. 'Introduction'. In: Charlesworth (et al.), *Religion in Aboriginal Australia. An Anthology*. St. Lucia: University of Queensland Press, 1-21.

Cummings, B. 1990. *Take This Child ... From Kahlin Compound to the Retta Dixon Children's Home*. Canberra: Aboriginal Studies Press.

Eckermann, A.K. 1973. 'Group Identity and Urban Aborigines'. In: D. Tugby (ed.), *Aboriginal Identity in Contemporary Australian Society*. Ryde, N.S.W.: Jacaranda Press, 27-41.

Fesl, E.D. 1994. 'Identity'. In: D. Horton (ed.), *The Encyclopaedia of Aboriginal Australia. Aboriginal and Torres Strait Islander History, Society and Culture*. Canberra: Aboriginal Studies Press, 491.

Gale, F. and A. Brookman 1972. *Urban Aborigines*. Canberra: Australian National University Press.

Geertz, C. 1973. 'Religion as a Cultural System'. In: *The Interpretation of Cultures*. New York: Basic Books, 87-126.

Gell, A. 1995. 'Closure and Multiplication: an Essay on Polynesian Cosmology and Ritual'. In: D. de Coppet and A. Iteanu (eds.), *Cosmos and society in Oceani*. Oxford: Berg, 21-57.

Goodall, H. 1996. *Invasion to Embassy: Land in Aboriginal Politics in New South Wales, 1770-1972*. St. Leonards, N.S.W.: Allen & Unwin in association with Blackbooks.

Glowczewski, B. 1998. '"All One But Different". Aboriginality: National Identity versus Local Diversification in Australia'. In: J. Wassmann (ed.), *Pacific Answers to Western Hegemony. Cultural Practices of Identity Construction*. Oxford: Berg, 335-55.

Hollinsworth, D. 1992. 'Discourses on Aboriginality and the Politics of Identity in Urban Australia'. In: *Oceania* 63(2), 137-55.

Howie-Willis, I. 1994. 'Identity'. In: D. Horton (ed.), *The Encyclopaedia of Aboriginal Australia. Aboriginal and Torres Strait Islander History, Society and Culture*. Canberra: Aboriginal Studies Press, 491-92.

Howie-Willis, I. 1994. 'Koori'. In: D. Horton (ed.), *The Encyclopaedia of Aboriginal Australia, Aboriginal and Torres Strait Islander History, Society and Culture*, Canberra: Aboriginal Studies Press, 559.

Janson, J. 1996. *Black Mary and Gunjies; Two Plays by Julie Janson*. Canberra: Aboriginal Studies Press.

Jennett, Ch. 1980. *Ethnic Politics. Aboriginal Black Power and Land Rights Movement of the 70s*. Australasian Political Studies Association Annual Conference 22nd.

Jones, J. and J. Hill-Burnett 1982. 'The Political Context of Ethnogenesis; An Australian Example'. In: M. Howard (ed.), *Aboriginal Power in Australian Society*. St. Lucia: University of Queensland Press, 214-46.

Keen, I. (ed.), 1988. *Being Black: Aboriginal Culture in Settled Australia*. Canberra: Aboriginal Studies Press.

Keen, I. 1994. *Knowledge and Secrecy in an Aboriginal Religion. Yolngu of North-East Arnhem Land*. Oxford: Claredon Press.

Kendall, C. 1994. 'The History: Present and Future Issues Affecting Aboriginal Adults Who Were Removed as Children'. In: *Aboriginal and Islander Health Worker Journal* 18(2), 18-19.

Linnekin, J. 1990. 'The Politics of Culture in the Pacific'. In: J. Linnekin and L. Poyer (eds.), *Cultural Identity and Ethnicity in the Pacific*. Honolulu: University of Hawaii Press, 149-75.

Lippmann, L. 1991. *Generations of Resistance; Aborigines Demand Justice*. Melbourne: Longman Cheshire.

Maddock, K.J. 1972. *The Australian Aborigines. A Portrait of Their Society*. London: Allan Lane, The Penguin Press.

Maddock, K.J. (ed.), 1991. *Identity, Land and Liberty: Studies in the Fourth World*. Nijmegen: University of Nijmegen, Instituut voor Culturele en Sociale Antropologie.

Morphy, H. 1991. *Ancestral Connections. Art and an Aboriginal System of Knowledge*. Chicago: The University of Chicago Press.

Morris, B. 1994. *Anthropology of the Self. The Individual in Cultural Perspective*. London: Pluto Press.

National Inquiry into the Separation of Aboriginal and Torres Strait Islander Children from their Families (Australia) 1997. *Bringing Them Home; Report of the National Inquiry into the Separation of Aboriginal and Torres Strait Islander Children from Their Families, April 1997 [Commissioner: Ronald Wilson]*. Sydney: Human Rights and Equal Opportunity Commission.

Ortner, S. 1973. 'On Key Symbols'. In: *American Anthropologist* 75, 1338-46.

Otto, T. 1993. 'Empty Tins for Lost Traditions? The West's Material and Intellectual Involvement in the Pacific'. In: T. Otto (ed.), *Pacific Island Trajectories*. Canberra: Australian National University, 1-29.

Peperkamp, G. and C.H.W. Remie (eds.), 1989. *The Struggle for Land World-wide*. Saarbrücken and Fort Lauderdale: Breitenbach.

Rowley, C.D. 1971. *Outcasts in White Australia: Aboriginal Policy and Practice, Volume II*. Canberra: Australian National University Press.

Schwab, J. 1988. 'Ambiguity, Style and Kinship in Adelaide Aboriginal Identity'. In: I. Keen (ed.), *Being Black: Aboriginal Culture in Settled Australia*. Canberra: Aboriginal Studies Press, 77-96.

Smith, H.M. and E.H. Biddle 1975. *Look Forward, Not Back; Aborigines in Metropolitan Brisbane 1965-1966*. Canberra: Australian National University Press.

Stanner, W.E.H. 1966. *On Aboriginal Religion*. The Oceania Monograph 11. Sydney: Sydney University Press.

Sutton, P. 1995. 'Atomism versus Collectivism: The Problem of Group Definition in Native Title Cases'. In: J. Fingleton and J. Finlayson (eds.), *Anthropology in the Native Title Era*. Canberra: Native Title Research Unit, Australian Institute of Aboriginal and Torres Strait Islander Studies, 1-11.

Tatz, C. 1982. *Aborigines & Uranium and Other Essays*. Richmond: Heinemann Educational.

Tonkinson, M.E. 1990. 'Is it in the Blood? Australian Aboriginal Identity'. In: J. Linnekin and L. Poyer (eds.), *Cultural Identity and Ethnicity in the Pacific*. Honolulu: Hawaii University Press: 191-219.

Tonkinson, R. 1998. 'National Identity: Australia after Mabo'. In: J. Wassmann (ed.), *Pacific Answers to Western Hegemony. Cultural Practices of Identity Construction*, Oxford: Berg, 287-311.

Vlist, van der L. (ed.), 1994. *Voices of the Earth: Indigenous Peoples, New Partners & the Right to Self-determination in Practice*. Utrecht: International Books and the Netherlands Centre for Indigenous Peoples.

Warner, W.L. 1937. *A Black Civilisation. A Social Study of an Australian Tribe*. New York: Harper Brothers Publishers.

Watson, J. 1990. 'Other People Do Other Things: Lamarckian Identities in Kainantu Subdistrict, Papua New Guinea'. In: J. Linnekin and L. Poyer (eds.), *Cultural Identity and Ethnicity in the Pacific*. Honolulu: University of Hawaii Press, 17-43.

Wild, A., 1986. *Rom. An Aboriginal Ritual of Diplomacy*. Canberra: Australian Institute of Aboriginal Studies.

CHAPTER 9

Cultural Resources of Elite Identity:
The Vicissitudes of the Polish Gentry[1]

Longina Jakubowska

Introduction

People in Poland who, in 1990, were in their sixties or older had lived in at least four distinctive social structures: in pre-communist society, under Stalinism, in post-Stalinist state socialism, and finally, in post-communism. These four social structures had different 'space structures' (cf. Bourdieu 1984) with strikingly different criteria for ascent in each system of stratification. It follows that one would have to possess quite different types of capital to be successful in the social hierarchy over time which would require learning how to dispose of devalued assets, acquiring those assets whose value had increased, and understanding how to convert old, now devalued assets into new, more valued power.

It appears that the gentry in Poland mastered the skill of capital conversion. Displaced and stripped of economic assets by the communist government, they survived the system which had attempted to destroy them. Moreover, they re-emerged in the post-communist era as a cohesive and, once more, significant group. In fact, the apparent complete break with the pre-war class structure in Poland was largely chimerical (Nagengast 1991) and the society remained guided by essentially the same driving principles, symbols, and modes of identification. Overt manifestations of radical departure from former values were superficial and made for the benefit of the ruling communist political elite. The split between private and public

1. This article is part of a larger project on the history of the gentry in communist and post-communist Poland. Research was conducted in 1994/95 and was made possible through a Fulbright Research Grant, and the support of the Univerity of the Pacific and the Polish Academy of Sciences. I would like to express my appreciation to Ton Otto, Henk Driessen, and Anton Blok for their comments on the earlier version of this paper.

domains was such a widely spread phenomenon that Polish sociological literature developed a special term for it. 'Social dimorphism' referred to compartmentalised behavior which meant that a variety of life styles, practices, and beliefs could function under the apparent social uniformity. In this two-dimensional social world the gentry constituted an elite parallel to the official power elite.

The identity of the gentry is grounded in an historically acquired privileged class position. Its strength depends on a fortuitous conjunction of several factors: powerful historical legends in combination with presumed biological endowment and messianic elements blended with a cherished nationalist ideology. They defined in the past the culture of the gentry as a class and as a nation. The claim to exclusivity of cultural heritage was a resource which enabled the gentry to flourish even in the environment controlled by a hostile regime. The potential for multiplicity of interpretations inherent in the concept of culture, allowed for multiplex identifications which gave a meaning to individual members of the gentry in the absence of other means to display status.

Capital inherent and inherited

While sharing many characteristics with its western counterparts, the Polish gentry, *szlachta*, is in numerous respects exceptional. Like other European nobilities, it originated in the practice of granting land in exchange for military service to the kings. Unlike them, it was able to convert these grants into inalienable hereditary possessions in both male and female lines. It gradually established hegemony forming a state which, in the course of the 16th century, became known as the 'republic of the gentry'.

The gentry's economic power was primarily based on a monopoly on landownership and a full jurisdiction over serfs. As a matter of fact, while serfdom was in decline west of the Elbe, it affirmed itself to the east of the river. Compulsory labour dues were systematically increased, so that by 1520, corvee labour of six days a week was allowed by law. This came at the opportune time of economic boom in western Europe. While population growth and price rises made Polish grain extremely profitable, in the long run the strategy of the gentry to direct the manorial system almost entirely towards production for export caused the decline of the cities and undermined the monetary economy. The nobility subsequently forced peasants to purchase necessities from manor stores rather than from urban merchants, which further contributed to the collapse of internal markets.

The gentry fortified its economic power by securing control over the political system. To start with, the ruler was reduced to the status of primus inter pares and after the Jagiellonian dynasty became extinct (1572), a new system of electoral monarchy was introduced. The most striking example of a gentry prerogative was the *nihil novi* decree (1505) which forbade the kings to legislate on matters concerning the gentry or to introduce reforms of any kind without its concurrence. Since 1652, unanimity was necessary for the passage of all new laws. Embodied in *liberum veto*, whereby a single member of the Parliament could invalidate the entire work of a given session, the decree served to strengthen the position of the gentry. Elected monarchs, kept chronically short of cash by the Parliament, were forced to use royal domains as collateral against loans from magnates and to purchase the gentry's loyalty through grants of crown lands and villages. Revenues from royal holdings became important sources of income for the upper nobility. The system of central governance was effectively paralysed, the kingship weak or contested, and the power of the gentry undisputed. All these factors made the Polish state vulnerable to the expansionist policies of its neighbours. At the end of the 18th century Poland disappeared except as a memory, a nationalist program, and a set of administrative subdivisions of the enlarged adjacent empires: Russia, Prussia, and Austria.

The extent of power and privilege that the Polish gentry won for itself encouraged the invention of a myth of separate origins which located its roots in an ancient Sarmatian tribe of warriors from the Black Sea Steppe who had resisted incorporation into the Roman Empire, conquered indigenous people, and became masters over the subservient masses. They were supposed to be of a different race, their Sarmatian identity embodied in distinct features, practices, dress, even weapons. The origin myth took on messianic overtones. Nobility bestowed upon by God, the gentry believed to be bound by a sacred covenant to defend the frontiers of Christianity. Against the history of conflicts with Orthodox Muscovy, Protestant Sweden, and even the Muslim Ottoman Empire, Sarmatian ideology fused with Catholicism. The coronation of Holy Mary as the Queen of Poland in the 17th century is perhaps the best illustration of how religious mysticism converged with national ambition.

What gave Sarmatian ideology much of its potency was the large size of the gentry. Themselves believing that they were as many as grains of sand in a sea, their number reached ten percent of the total population, far greater than the nobility in any other part of Europe.[2]

Although in the course of time the influence of the greater nobility grew at the expense of the lesser and the system grew more oligarchical, gentry ideology remained fiercely egalitarian. 'A gentryman upon his patch/is any magnate's match', the saying went. While the magnates maintained their own courts and private armies, the grandeur of which astonished western aristocrats, the poorest of the gentry could hardly make a living and some had no land at all. Yet the canon of equality was so absolute that *szlachta* resisted all attempts to introduce titles and orders. Perhaps because practice contradicted ideology, the political and social creed of Sarmatism asserted itself forcefully. It fostered the image of a nobleman-citizen who was active in public life, proud and independent in thoughts and actions, secure of his property and privileges, entrusted by God with a mission to defend Christianity, and yet firmly grounded on his rural estate amidst a large extended family. The gentry's ethos barely corresponded with reality but in masking the tremendous economic differentiation among them, it provided a convincing justification for the political unity of nobles. The idiom of brotherhood in particular had a special potency for asserting and naturalising class separateness; by drawing upon the (mythical) past it was not only able to posit a common origin but also to claim substantial identity in the present. Whether rich or poor, they were brothers with a religious mission and a sense of national destiny, which gave them moral conviction and political determination to resist central authority and maintain autonomy.

Foremost, all gentry shared the explicit understanding that the gentry constitutes a nation, that the state must be subservient to the gentry because it exists in order to serve them, and finally, that Poland is what the gentry embodies. In fact, the state was divided into clearly established classes: the gentry, who were the nation, and the peasants, who were the serfs and had no rights. 'The nation was Polish, the peasants were peasants' (Narkiewicz 1976: 9).

The patriotic discourse born during the Partitions (1794-1918) gave a new character to anticentralism, democracy, and freedom, which the gentry espoused. The nobility became viewed as the repository of state tradition and, indeed, played the leading role in resistance movements and insurrections. The great noble families, which often accepted aristocratic titles from foreign monarchs, were not always supportive of reforms or conspiracies. With kinship and other ties to noble houses elsewhere in Europe, they were not convinced of the virtues of nationalism nor did their immediate interest lie in changes to the economic and political structures. For the most part, the rebels were middle and lesser gentry who regarded them-

2. Tilly (1993) estimates that in western Europe in the same historical period there were on average 1-2 nobles per 100 in the population at large.

selves as the conscience, the directing force of the nation, bearing responsibility for its liberation and for preserving Polish culture. All insurrections
(1830, 1848, and 1863) failed, mostly due to the reluctance of their leaders to
appeal to peasants. Serfdom still intact, the latter had little motivation to join
what they perceived was a gentry cause.[3] The gentry rebels paid with their
lives, personal freedom, and property. Since land was at once material and
symbolic, the punishments appropriately included confiscation or compulsory sale of their estates. Failed attempts at securing sovereignty made the
gentry eventually realise that the group could no longer pretend to be the
only valid political and cultural representation of the nation.

As Poland became independent in 1918, the state was restructured in line
with democratic reforms sweeping Europe. The hegemonic power of the
gentry declined, but its privileged position did not completely erode.
Although the gentry, as a class, lost its entitlement to be the sole legislator,
many nobles came to occupy seats in the new Parliament and continued to
form the largely conservative power elite. The dispossessed or impoverished
gentry, whether due to political repressions or economic failure, were forced
to migrate to cities, enter professions, and join the growing ranks of intelligentsia. Although the society had become more differentiated, its fundamental structural duality remained intact and certain to influence personal
life trajectories. The gentry, both as individuals and as a social category,
continued to dominate intellectual, cultural, and bureaucratic domains setting
the standards against which all else should be measured.

It is against the background of this heritage that we must understand the
gentry's fate after the war, because although the circumstances of people's
lives changed radically, the cultural inscription which they had carried over
from the past connected their collective experiences with historical meanings.

The politics of World War II left Poland in the Soviet sphere of influence.
Since the Polish communist party had never a large following, the Soviet-
backed government installed in 1944 lacked popular legitimacy. In an effort
to obtain the support of the majority of the population, i.e. the peasants, it
immediately introduced a radical land reform as its first legislative and
administrative act. Large landed estates were nationalised and subsequently
turned over to landless and poor peasants or formed state agricultural farms.
A special ordinance called for an instantaneous removal of landowners from

---

3. Serfdom was gradually abolished in the course of the 19th century. In Prussia, the
   process started in 1807, in Austria in 1848, and in Russia in 1864. Emancipation of
   peasants dealt a severe blow to the manorial economy.

their expropriated estates because the lingering presence of the former masters was suspected to inhibit peasants from participation in land distribution. In what became its historical predicament, the landowners lost at once their land and their home. The reform thus effectively eliminated the gentry from the countryside — its historical stronghold, locus of power, sentiment, and identity. Again, they migrated to urban centres where, in the radically altered circumstances, they nonetheless still managed to form a parallel (although hidden) elite.

Instrumentality of skills and identifications

Cultural capital accumulated through centuries of advantage (prestige inherent in the name and the title, direct descent from persons of historical significance) endowed the gentry with an agency that even the communist regime could not deny. Nor could the regime dismiss the gentry's possible usefulness to the state in a variety of roles.

The country had suffered tremendous damage during the war and was in need of immediate rebuilding. The complete overhaul of its economic structure which the government intended was an equally urgent political imperative. Yet, the communist cadres were small. Moreover, they were politically compromised by their association with the Soviet Union, the descendant of an historic enemy and one of the occupying forces during the war. Education was the traditional privilege of the upper-classes. Polish society was, therefore, short of qualified labour, and even of people with general literacy and rudimentary skills, to carry out the project of rebuilding the country.[4] The reconstructing and the restructuring of the country's economy could not be accomplished without the participation of the educated class. Consequently the skills, which the gentry had acquired as part of their general class upbringing, became their most valuable asset. The gentry were simply indispensable in running the state regardless of its political system. The state could not function without them, nor could the gentry survive without the state.

After having lost most of their material possessions, the gentry needed a source of income on the one hand, and a place in society on the other. In general, with the exception of highly visible posts from which they were excluded for reasons of ideology and propaganda, the gentry were well positioned to find employment in a variety of capacities within the new

---

4. In 1939, approximately 20% of the population was illiterate.

system. Managerial positions in agriculture came closest to their former occupation as estate owners. The rhetoric of patriotism with its logic of duty and service to the fatherland was particularly persuasive in this case. 'You will not ride in a coach to examine your own fields but drive a car inspecting the whole country', they told themselves. 'All we knew was agriculture, nothing else. Our own estates ceased to exist, so we went to work on state farms', they said. Since the gentry found jobs in agriculture and related fields, education, and management, the skills which served them before the war hardly required any adjustment.

After consolidating its power (1948), the strategy of the communist government was to substitute the politically inconvenient and untrustworthy gentry by the new cadres. Imposition of Stalinist order in Poland involved setting up a mechanism of political approval for the incumbents of all strategic positions in politics and economy, later known as a 'nomenklatura system'. While subsequent purges got rid of gentry in one field or another, versatility of their skills and the ability to adapt to the changing political climate, allowed them to move to other domains, domains which were inconsequential to the political system and yet necessary to the functioning of the society. Paradoxically, marginality worked to their advantage. For example, shortly after collectivisation of farm lands had began, those gentry employed in executive management positions in state agriculture were dismissed and shifted to less essential jobs, i.e. jobs not defined by political criteria. It could be the position of a deputy director of a regional seedling station in one case, a research post on an experimental farm in another; in both examples people were placed in situations which allowed them later to pursue scientific careers. The gentry personnel employed in other fields report similar experiences. In the early 1950s, institutions of higher education oriented themselves towards Eastern-block countries with a corresponding privilege granted to Slavic languages, Marxist philosophy, etc. The push to increase the number of specialists in those areas left a niche in the labour market for people with knowledge of western languages. Maria Radziwiłł, for instance, a war widow with three teenage sons to support, established a successful career as a freelance translator of scientific literature in English, specialising in biological and medical texts. In addition to linguistic facilities, the gentry's social skills and cultural literacy made them sought-after employees of international companies and foreign embassies. Such jobs were often found through the mediation of friends and relatives abroad to whom they were connected by the cosmopolitan web which had been at the foundation of their elite status. The cold war did not entirely close borders. Hence a paradoxical situation arose: most people were not able to interact with foreign nationals because it was restricted to the official channels. Nonetheless networks which pre-dated the regime, and had been the prerogative of the elite, continued and even expanded because foreign agencies which were looking for non-governmental contacts relied on the already existing personal connections. These were largely limited to the gentry and the old intelligentsia.

Considering the tremendous status differentiation among the gentry, the value of their historical legacy was unequally distributed. Members of aristo-cratic families were positioned best, but while great names still held their magic, they also placed those who carried them in a precarious nexus of symbolic significance: they could protect as often as they could bring harm.

The careers of Krzysztof Radziwiłł and Jan Zamoyski, illustrate the predicament of personae with notable names. Both men were heirs to immense estates, with ancestors registered in the annals of Polish history. As the first of them aptly put it, there was never a Senate without a Radziwiłł. Yet their post-war lives followed different trajectories.

Krzysztof Radziwiłł (1969: 60) wrote in his memoirs that he 'did not wish to be a former count, a member of an obliterated group; nor a former senator of a non-existent senate; nor a former owner of an estate, the lands of which were given over to peasants, but an active citizen of Poland'. Like others of his class, he took a patriotic stand, but, unlike others, he openly joined the victors so he could actively participate in the nation's future. Immediately after the war Radziwiłł enlisted his services in the new government becom-ing Chief of Protocol in the Ministry of Foreign Affairs. Sarcastic critics claimed that his role was confined to teaching the communists table man-ners, but in fact he was of immense use to the regime. Called 'The Red Count', he was the guide to foreign dignitaries, the bridge to the western diplomatic community, the cultural (or, ideological) broker. Radziwiłł served as the government emissary to the Polish emigrant community in London with a mission to persuade ex-patriates to return. In the tradition of the Radziwiłłs, he subsequently became member of the Parliament (the Senate was abolished). After his term expired, (or alternatively, after he outlived his usefulness to the regime), 'The Red Count' became editor of a major publish-ing company. In addition, he translated German and Russian authors, among them Kafka and Musil.

Jan Zamoyski decided to move as far as possible from his expropriated estate located in the south-east of Poland, so he went to Gdańsk, and first found employment in the UNRWA and later in a shipping agency, the American Transatlantic Line. In 1949, he was arrested, charged with treason and espionage, and sentenced to a 15 year prison term. Released in 1956, he requested a rehabilitation process, which in 1958 proved his innocence. Soon afterwards Zamoyski became the director of Swiss Air for Poland.

The same logic which had an advantageous effect when applied to Krzysztof Radziwiłł, discredited Jan Zamoyski a few years later. The Stalinist years were the darkest period in the gentry's history, with unrelenting propaganda portraying them as class enemies, capitalist exploiters, collaborators with the Nazis, reactionaries, and accusing them of sabotage, espionage, and treason. The trials against members of the gentry were few but — focused on well-known names — strategically chosen and well publicised. Although the charges were manufactured, the public found them easy to believe because they contained a faint echo of the general truth that anchored the interest of the former elite in foreign networks which were hostile to the Polish nation. Jan Zamoyski's case was only a demonstration of the point.

In spite of the current rhetoric of discrimination and persecution which the gentry employs against the communist government, the violence perpetrated on them was inflicted mostly in symbolic forms.[5] After the famous denunciation of Stalin by the 20th Party Congress delivered by Khrushchev in 1956, the gentry quietly disappeared from the official discourse. The policies of the government introduced a new formula of social recruitment which abandoned the class origin criteria and privileged occupational skills. Many of those who had been formerly persecuted were appointed to positions of eminence.[6]

By then most gentry had been officially reclassified as 'working intelligentsia'. This shift in categorical ascription suited both the communist party ideologists and the gentry alike. The term concealed elite standing but also separated them from the working class, the uneducated common folk underscoring the distinction between physical labour and work of mind, or culture. In the absence of material attributes through which the gentry could display their noble status, being a 'cultured' person acquired ever greater symbolic

---

5. Physical violence, including arrests and prosecution, was primarily directed at organised political opposition. When the gentry experienced persecution, it was mainly in such a capacity. An exception was the imprisonment of aristocrats in January, 1945. In an effort to 'drain' the political field and to create a leadership vacuum, 16 members of 4 prominent families were incarcerated in a prison camp in Krasnogorsk near Moscow. They were released in September, 1947 after the communist party established its dominance.

6. One such example is Witold Maringe. Appointed the head of state-run agriculture in 1945, he was arrested, put on trial in the Stalinist period, and sentenced to life imprisonment. Released and rehabilitated in 1956, he was subsequently appointed advisor to the Minister of Agriculture.

effectiveness. The essence of nobility was reinterpreted, the emphasis shifted from 'having' to 'being'.

By becoming intelligentsia, they did not stop being the gentry. Since the only reason for declassation was a permanent subjection to physical labour (a rather hypothetical situation), and possibly a mesalliance, there was hardly ground for plummeting down. Even 'The Red Count', considered a traitor by some of his class, was received in the aristocratic circle without as much as a whisper, his leftist political leanings taken as the 'vagaries of a prince'. However, the activities the gentry engaged in and the roles they assumed doubtlessly broadened the spectrum of their identifications. The skills, which they had already possessed but which largely laid dormant, used sporadically as amusement, hobby, or part of the general elan, became incorporated into identity, transformed themselves into its component, and even created a new identification. They *became* translators, educators, intellectuals. Maria Radziwiłł's pride in the immense medical sciences dictionary which she created for her own use in the absence of appropriate aids on the market exceeded the pride in her origins, although most likely the latter was taken for granted. But women were situated differently in the aristocratic social space. Formerly barred from labour by social convenances, they found it immensely rewarding. One interlocutor, who insisted on remaining anonymous, exclaimed: 'God bless Stalin, the sunshine of my life'. If not for the course history took in this part of the world, she would have been forced to abide by her gender role and could never have become a university professor. Numerous others expressed their joy at being 'productive members of the society', borrowing the phrase from socialist discourse.

Synergetic definition of family, class, and nation

Just as one could not stop being a noble, neither could one join in.[7] The

---

7. Historically, one could acquire nobilitation legally through an Act of Parliament, or illegally, by pretending to be of noble descent. The Commonwealth was a vast land with a lot of minor gentry. If one acted as a noble, assumed an appropriate life style, carried arms, and served in the military forces, it was possible to be taken for one and slip into the nobility without being noticed. Enlisting in the services of a rich nobleman also helped, because in exchange for loyalty he would vouch for his client's noble lineage. During the Partitions, particularly in the periods of severe economic and financial crises, intermarriage with non-gentry, for instance with well-to-do Jewish bourgeoisie, was not uncommon. After the war, however, in the absence of a means to demonstrate one's status, communal knowledge about *who was* and *who was not* of noble descent guarded the group's boundaries, thus making access to it more difficult.

gentry managed to remain a relatively insular group restricting their social contacts to familial (and familiar) networks. Advancing the concept of gentry as a 'family' facilitated, and justified, exclusion of non-members. Since familial organisation comprised the core of sociability circles, it follows that the access of class 'others' was severely limited. The myth of one large kin group — supported by enough heraldic evidence to make it believable, fostered by the depth of vertical as well as horizontal genealogical memory, and compounded by shared cultural heritage and experiences of persecution, made everyone a 'cousin'. The notion of gentry as a 'family' functioned simultaneously on multiple levels binding in yet another fashion persons and generations, with the class and the nation.

Having a 'family' implies a place in the historical chain of ancestors, known predecessors, a succession of persons who long after their death have kept their individuality, and hence corporeality, because their names were registered in the records of memory, a text, a portrait.[8] The society which in the not-so-distant past experienced rigid class distinctions understands this intuitively. It is not that non-gentry in Poland do not have ancestors but that their ancestors have been lost in historical anonymity, their names have vanished from records and memory, and hence they appear as if they had not existed at all. They do not have a 'family' in the sense that the gentry have it because their roots are erased, are not traceable, lost in societal history and memory of their descendants alike. An individual with a 'family', that is with a historically documented existence, stands in a different relationship to the group. As observed by Simmel (1971: 209-13):

it is as though its individual members were, so to speak, nothing but different recastings, nothing but different forms of a constant-value substance that endures throughout the whole succession of inheritances. For the relation of the family and furthermore, of the noble group generally — to the individual, the significance of the 'family tree' is profoundly symbolic: the substance that makes up the individual must have passed through the trunk of the whole, just as the substance of fruit and branch in a tree is the same as that composing the trunk.

The gentry were the producers, the carriers, and the transmitters of memory. Some of them were affecting and talented memoirists, others keepers of rather uninspiring domestic chronicles. Nonetheless all family records, some centuries old — land grants, correspondence, diaries, photographs, and such — have been meticulously collected, salvaged through the ravages of wars

---

8. Zonabend (1984) claims that names are the real tools of groups memory.

and the plunder of peasants, saved for future generations in a desk drawer as tangible proofs of the historicity of being. So are genealogical charts in which every birth is recorded, every person recognised and given a place beyond their death, adding another link and henceforth extending the collective existence. Everyone of them has a face, a life story, an amusing anecdote, a personality with its flaws, virtues, and idiosyncracies. These personae are not only real but also often immortalised in art and literature. They are simultaneously part of a 'family' and a national heritage. Commissioned in a private pursuit of perpetuation of family memory, these objects were often of artistic excellence. As a result, values and achievements of family, status group, and state entity coalesce as if into a reservoir. Family histories are interwoven, if not synonymous, with national history. Although these histories are not the complete history of the nation, nowhere else one finds such a continuity of practices and ideology, nor is the status of a family so clearly defined by what it and others know of its past (Halbwachs 1992: 128).

As Malkki (1992) points out, arborescent tropes configure a genealogical form of imagining nations. The idiom of kinship, shared blood, and botanical metaphors (such as a tree, or roots) naturalise the relationship and provide substantialisation necessary to create convincing and lasting bonds between people who claim some form of unity and separateness from others. As noted before, the gentry went as far as claiming Sarmatian origin.

The myth, discredited since by science, became deeply rooted in the gentry's collective consciousness. Assisted by its continuous social relevance, the gentry argue for their inherent, and inherited, difference, or what they refer to as 'race'. There is only a vague relation between the popular understanding of the term and the gentry use of it. 'Race' connotes physical appearance but in no way does it refer to 'eastern' anthropometric features which Sarmatian origin would suggest. Yet it is conceptualised as genetic endowment in the sense that the outer appearance is a reflection of the inner charisma accumulated through succession, a set of physical and spiritual properties transmitted through inheritance with a capability to enhance personal value of members sharing in the biological pool. Dignity, poise, the total demeanor — all is generated from within and hence inseparable from the body, indeed, inscribed on it. My remark about the relative longevity and good health of many elderly gentry was mockingly commented by one: 'we did not drink peasant blood for generations for nothing!' Indeed, the germane prosperity of the countryside manorial life doubtlessly contributed to gentry's physical appearance.

Historicity

Given the gentry's embedment in the past, it was easier to remove them from their estates than from history. It was imperative for the government — the legitimacy of which was constantly questioned — to demonstrate historical development of the Polish state in a fashion consistent with the communist dogma. The gentry represented connection with the past and were inextricably intertwined with the notion of national identity, a trait which the government wanted to foster in the consciousness of the citizenry. While deploring elites and privileging popular culture, the government propaganda co-opted selected elements of nation-as-class history. Subverting past traditions when necessary, re-presentations of the past produced by the regime largely managed to appropriate the gentry's history. The gentry's formative role in state-building (or, the destruction of it, as some ideologists would have it) was not problematic. Infinitely more troublesome to disqualify were the gentry's claims to historically substantiated patriotic heroism and sacrifice which placed the party demagogues into a dilemma of how to replicate desirable models of behaviour without engaging the gentry's past. Parts that could not be incorporated in the new rendition of history were marginalised, particularised, and denied official presence. However, the degree of persuasiveness of the selected traditions and public acceptance of such a version of representation depends on the degree to which the state controls the means of distribution of social meanings and these, in turn, hinge on relations of the forces in society (Alonso 1994). Forming a counter-elite, or rather, a parallel-elite associated with the old system of differentiation, conservative values, and national tradition, the gentry controlled the unofficial truths. The Katyń report is one such example. The denials of the complicity of the Soviets in the execution of Polish officers in the Byelorussian forest in 1940 were counteracted by the unofficial knowledge of their families, friends, and the deputies of the government-in-exile. The aforementioned social dimorphism operated perfectly here: the official truths were indicted for official purposes, the unofficial truths for the unofficial, hidden, but socially relevant structures. Consistent with the mysticism of the gentry was its continuous connection to the church. It provided the moral and institutional support while the specifically Catholic imagery supplied the model of sacrifice, crucifixion, and resurrection. This paradigm inspired several generations of conspirators and gave resistance historic continuity, cultural tradition, and ultimately social legitimation (Jakubowska 1990).

Concluding remarks

The intrinsic power which the Polish gentry enjoyed through periods of privilege and suppression alike was derived from and located in its historical past and in its ability to fuse conceptual notions of family, class, and nation. While the gentry's legal, political, and finally economic entitlements gradually eroded, the gentry were able to transfigure class traits into national values and heritage, molding the core of the state patriotic tradition in the process. By the same token, privileging culture as enlightened education transformed the class advantage into a lasting benefit to the state. Their accumulated capital made them useful to the incumbent regime. Gentry identity in Poland consists of numerous and interwoven strains which give it strength. The group's vitality derives from the ability to move freely between the various strains and connect them, or lapse, when necessary, while its flexibility allows its members to assimilate apparent contradictions: intensely patriotic yet cosmopolitan, class bound and yet national, occupational and professional and yet defined by social origin, elite that is both egalitarian and status-minded.

Bibliography

Alonso, A.M. 1994. 'The Politics of Space, Time and Substance: State Formation, Nationalism, and Ethnicity'. In: *Annual Review of Anthropology* 23, 379-405.

Bourdieu, P. 1984. *Distinction*. London and New York: Routledge & Kegan.

Halbwachs, M. 1992. *On Collective Memory*. Chicago: University of Chicago Press.

Jakubowska, L. 1990. 'Political Drama in Poland: the Use of National Symbols'. In: *Anthropology Today* 6(4), 10-13.

Malkki, L. 1992. 'National Geographic: the Rooting of Peoples and the Territorialization of National Identity among Scholars and Refugees'. In: *Cultural Anthropology* 7(1), 24-44.

Nagengast, C. 1991. *Reluctant Socialists, Rural Entrepreneurs: Class, Culture, and the Polish State*. Boulder, San Francisco and Oxford: Westview Press.

Narkiewicz, O. 1976. *The Green Flag: Polish Populist Politics, 1867-1970*. London: Croom Helm.

Radziwiłł, K. 1969. Od Feudalizmu do Socjalizmu, unpublished manuscript.

Simmel, G. 1971. *On Individuality and Social Forms*. Chicago: University of Chicago Press.

Tilly, C. 1993. *European Revolutions, 1492-1992*. Oxford and Cambridge: Blackwell.

Zonabend, F. 1984. *The Enduring Memory. Time and History in a French Village*. Manchester: Manchester University Press.

CHAPTER 10

Thinking Together What Falls Apart: Some Reflections on the Concept of Identity

Hans Siebers

The majority of those who knock on Holland's door seeking asylum do not pretend to be in possession of any valid identity papers which might disclose their nationality or origin. It is not farfetched to suppose that any un-equivocal and official anchoring of their identity may obstruct the progress of quite a number of them in gaining access to the promised land, *Fortress Europe*. They prefer to keep their hands free and identity options open for the moment that they are interrogated and have to defend their interests.

At the same time among those who have been born within this fortress it has become quite popular to engage in all kinds of training courses and to read one of the many best-sellers on 'grounding', 'self-expression' and 'working on yourself'. Coming in touch with your deeper self, providing some sort of stability and source of identity construction in the midst of changes and turmoil, seems to have become as indispensable as obtaining your driving license for getting around in contemporary society. One wonders who has become more footloose, or has broken from their moorings more radically, the asylum seeker or the New Age traveller (see Hethering-ton 1996).

Identity construction as handcuffs or as travel guide, these metaphors point to its ambiguous and contradictory character in contemporary culture and society. Is it something to be avoided or desired? Is it still possible or even expedient to pin down its basic traits or are identity constructions melting away, leaving social scientists behind in anxiety and disarray? That much is clear, identity construction is a concept that puzzles and worries many scientists these days, but does it constitute a problem and, if so, for whom? In this chapter I will address basic aspects of these questions and try to redress them into viable perspectives for research. I first intend to sketch the social and cultural context in which these questions have arisen and present some of the basic worries and dilemmas regarding identity con-struction as they emerge from the literature. Second, I will evaluate the relevance and tenability of these dilemmas and worries elaborating on the concept of reflexivity in relation to the fieldwork material I collected among the *Q'eqchi'* Indians of Guatemala. Third, I will work out some methodological suggestions for studying processes of identity construction of contemporary social actors based on the triangle of mind, culture and society.

Fragmentation: as the story goes ...

In the literature of the social sciences, identity construction has not just recently been defined as a *problem*, as such it has already been identified as a consequence of modernity (Bauman 1996: 18-19). It has been proposed that in a pre-modern condition, identity is basically moulded by the immediate social and cultural context of the social actor. The representations and values shared by the community or kinship group determine, to a large degree, the question of who someone is (Lash and Friedman 1992: 4). The gods and spirits are the ones from whom the actors derive their sense and meaning of life. By contrast, in the context of modernity the capacity to offer such a priori meaning or sense to social actors would gradually become lost. Faced with individualisation and the questioning of religious discourses, the actor is called upon to answer the question 'Who am I?', drawing on various sources of meanings. In this way, identity construction becomes a problem.

However, from the cradle of modern society new possibilities for identity construction also emerge. The primordial community may be lost, but is replaced by 'imagined communities' (Anderson 1987) such as the nation or class which provide a new sense of belonging. Institutions of cultural specialists, 'organic intellectuals' (Gramsci 1978) or 'ideological state apparatuses' (Poulantzas 1975) linked to these communities elaborate and distribute ideologies or discourses which guide individual actors in constructing their identity. Modernity has developed the universal claim to be able to identify who the actor is supposed to be, centring on his or her rational capacity to know and change the world. 'Identity construction' is an actor's project for developing his or her 'true self' in the course of his or her life. There is Weber's construction of identity of responsibility, structuring the life and personality of the actor through devotion to a praiseworthy vocation (Weber 1947b: 152). This high modern subjectivity privileges the cognitive and moral capacities of the actor over his or her aesthetic perception (Lash and Friedman 1992: 5).

Nevertheless, according to many contemporary writers these modern structurations of identity have become seriously undermined within the current social and cultural condition marked by fragmentation. What is meant by the latter is not always very clear, but there is much to be said in favour of the supposed fragmentation of the life-worlds of contemporary actors. In their daily lives these actors have to deal with a complex variety of subject positions (Laclau 1985: 28) and roles. He or she becomes involved in a variety of differentiated social spheres such as education, labour and partner markets, consumer and life-style arenas. Each of these positions and roles is linked to a specific perspective from which the actor organises the interpretation of externally carried meanings and his or her meaning-making, whether deliberate or spontaneous. To the extent that people in complex societies have more varying role repertoires, the perspectivation of meaning implies less replication of uniformity, less extensive cultural sharing (Hannerz 1992: 65-66). As individual lives express an increasing and very specific variety of roles and related perspectives from which to organise meanings and discourses, any stable discourse or narrative about the self, as well as any extensive and permanent cultural sharing with others, become highly questionable.

This multiplication of roles and perspectives is not the only argument which undermines the importance of aggregated and rather uniform social and cultural units such as class and the nation. Any strong cultural orientation that may be provided by the class or nation has also become questionable by what is referred to as globalisation. According to several globalisation authors, people, capital, images, goods, meanings, information and symbols increasingly 'flow' across the world without stopping at any border (Appadurai 1996; Hannerz 1992 and 1996) and communication is increasingly disembedded or 'lifted out' of the context of local interaction (Giddens 1990: 21-22). Individual actors can engage in interaction with others many miles away and in their meaning-making process they can increasingly draw on images and meanings stemming from outside of these aggregated social units, from multicultural levels both above and below the nation-state (Hall 1991: 28). The capacity of these social units to guide the meaning-making process of individuals may decrease accordingly.

In addition, it is claimed that cultural and moral unifiers in society have become increasingly hard to find and that ethical systems are pushed to the sidelines. Bauman holds that the state is neither able to produce such unifiers any more, nor do the majority of its citizens expect the state to do so. The present-day contented majority, politically inactive and apathetic, act as independent managers of private destinies and believe that they benefit from the continuous shrinking of the state's interference. Cultural and moral choices have been privatised, i.e. they have become a matter of the individual's decision instead of being determined and imposed by cultural and moral institutions (Bauman 1993: 138-40; Bauman 1995).

Moreover, our image of culture itself radically transforms in character. Culture is no longer seen as an integrated and shared whole oiling the wheels of social life, a system of cultural classification somehow homologous to the differences and divisions between social groups who use culture as relatively fixed markers in social life. In our present view, culture appears as something discordant and pluralistic, characterised by non-sharing and difference and which fails to provide clear recipes for action (Featherstone 1995: 5, 13).

Zygmunt Bauman (1995, 1996) is certainly not the only writer (see Featherstone 1995: 47; Hall 1996: 3-4; Lyotard 1984; and Rorty 1986) who concludes that in the face of such a fragmented life-world, the actor loses the notion of life as a meaningful project which links past, present and future experiences. There is no core of the self, unfolding through history and providing a stable and self-fulfilling sense of cultural belonging. Instead, life becomes a decentred sequence of contingent here-and-now experiences and aesthetised sensations showing no interconnecting essence. Even a positive identification as individual actor, let alone as a group, becomes questionable. Contacts with other people have become fleeting, shallow and one-sided which do not allow for deep attachments, strong commitments or responsibilities towards the other or morality. The individual actor mainly competes with others and uses whatever cultural resources that are available without being interested in any coherence between one symbolic performance and another. He or she keeps all options open, zaps from one cultural repertoire to another and is not interested in any cultural fixation. He or she avoids any permanent cultural sharing with others or identification with a specific cultural repertoire. It is the post-modern *Selbstdarstellung* instead of the modern *Selbstverwirklichung*.

If the reader feels distressed by these statements, he or she may find comfort with Anthony Giddens, who has put himself forward as perhaps the staunchest advocate of the viability of a modern identity construction. Identity constructions remain possible based on the actor's reflexive capacity. 'Self-identity' becomes a reflexively organised project which consists in the sustaining of coherent, yet continuously revised, biographical narratives (Giddens 1991: 5, 32-34). The reflexive monitoring of action is intrinsic to all human activity, but modern reflexivity has the enormous advantage that most aspects of social activity and material relations with nature can be continuously revised in the light of new information and knowledge (Giddens 1990: 36ff; 1991: 20). Drawing on the production of expert knowledge and abstract systems by modern institutions, the actor can work out his or her self-identity and pursue life politics. Giddens points for example to the extensive use that is made by educational institutions and parents of expertise produced by pedagogical experts in the socialisation of children (Giddens 1991: 9, 33).

Evaluation: arguments and objections

These elements of the fragmentation argument have become quite popular recently, but cannot be accepted without any objection. First, many of these elements, as such, present nothing new. Globalisation has its origins in the sixteenth century — or even earlier — and Durkheim already expressed his concern about social cohesion in the light of an increasing division of labour or, if you like, differentiation of roles and subject positions. Processes of individualisation and cultural and moral privatisation are no recent inventions either.

Second, let us look at the image against which the fragmentation argument takes up arms. It is the image of relatively circumscribed and homogeneous social and political units in which identity has become embedded. It is the image of relatively enclosed and coherent cultural systems which correspond with these social and political units and create the conditions for cultural guidance by cultural specialists. However, we may seriously question the assumption that this image has ever come close to historical reality, including that of Western societies. Is it the case that our concepts and understandings have changed more dramatically than social and cultural reality itself?

Of course, as social scientists we are never able to give final answers to this kind of question. Nevertheless, it is plausible to claim that several elements of the fragmentation argument may not be new, as such, but that they tend to increase in intensity and weight. I refer to the fact that not only the primordial, but also imagined communities, such as class and the nation, are trading in their a priori character for an optional one.[1] To an increasing number of people in various parts of the world they become a matter of

---

1. The same holds true regarding ethnicity. Individual members may consider themselves to be part of an ethnic group as an imagined community not knowing all of its members face-to-face (see Anderson 1987). The crucial point here is that this identification as a member of an ethnic group is increasingly coming to the fore as an option, not as an a priori established *fait accompli*. Elsewhere I have discussed ethnic identity as one of several identity options. However, it may adopt an overall, all-encompassing and even violent character precisely in situations marked by fear, instability and uncertainty within the framework of the breakdown of national economic, political and cultural institutions (Siebers 1997b).

choice and switching. This means that the impact of cultural directives on the individual, stemming from participating in a community, is becoming questionable. I refer also to the increasing pluralisation of cultural supply from all corners of the world from which the individual can draw in his or her meaning-making. The power of each single cultural or moral institution to influence or guide this process and to impose their discourses on individual meaning-makers may decrease accordingly.[2]

This decrease may have far-reaching consequences for the life and identity constructions of individual actors in contemporary society, but are we to conclude from this that the very idea of identity construction, as such, is lost and that actors are not able to make some lasting sense any more out of their lives? Or, conversely, are we to resort to the trenches of outright modernity to find stability and comfort regarding identity constructions? The controversy about identity constructions, as epitomised by Bauman and Giddens, is about clear oppositional positions, but these positions may have more in common than expected at first sight. Whether ironically and not without implicit nostalgia commenting on modern identity constructions getting lost in post-modern times, or preaching the blessings and possibility of modernity and modern identity constructions, in both cases there is anxiety about a loss of authenticity, of internal coherence and depth of individual experiences in daily life once modern trenches and grand narratives to hold onto are left behind. This implicit nostalgia is the more remarkable in the case of Bauman since he has convincingly demonstrated the close connections between modern ethical systems and the possibility of the holocaust (Bauman 1989). Nevertheless, it remains an open question whether these anxieties and worries about the loss of coherence and depth reflect the experiences of contemporary actors in their daily lives.

Identity construction: self-narrative and performative

In order to escape from these oppositional stances it may be useful to discuss this controversy about identity construction in more detail. In the end, this controversy comes down to two basic and interrelated questions: one relating to the ways contemporary social actors deal with symbolic repertoires, and another referring to the actor's capacity to make sense of a fragmented life

---

2. It remains to be seen whether the concentration of capital and institutions in the scape of mass media on a global level is able to counteract this pluralisation of cultural supply. Concentration of capital and power in mass media does not necessarily entail homogenization of the cultural supply these institutions deliver.

and life-world. First, do social actors deal with cultural repertoires as something they adopt to identify themselves, or as a resource to optimise their
performance towards and competition with others? On the one hand,
Giddens' social actors adopt knowledge and other symbolic resources in
order to constitute their self-identity and to actualise themselves. On the
other hand, Bauman points to short-term and disconnected sensations
resulting from specific meanings. His social actors avoid any permanent
identification, and in order to optimise their positions towards others,
perform using whatever symbolic repertoire that might benefit them.

Second, are social actors still able to meaningfully interrelate the fragments
of their lives and life-worlds constructing some overarching narrative
referring to themselves and their life? Here we touch the heart of the epistemological controversy between modernists and postmodernists: is knowledge
still possible and is there still any reliable relation between the actor's reality
and his or her account of this reality or self-identity? Are these accounts just
free-floating stories without any intrinsic relation with a presumed reality or
self-identity? In case there is such a relation, knowledge and the construction
of identity are possible, and in case any such relation has been lost, any
effort to establish knowledge and any intention to relate symbols and
meanings on a rather permanent basis to something called one's self-identity,
becomes futile. In the latter case, cultural repertoires cannot be anything else
than floating and temporary stories to impress others. In short, both questions are interrelated: the dealing with symbolic repertoires depends very
much on the possibility of knowledge and of overarching coherent narratives
of self.

Giddens admits that even science cannot produce certainty and that expert
knowledge can never be securely founded. Science depends on the methodological principle of doubt: nothing is certain, nothing can be proved and
knowledge is never unquestionable. Nevertheless, he holds on to the notion
of knowledge in the sense of constructions that are valid 'in principle' and
'until further notice' (Giddens 1990: 39, 48-49; 1991: 21). In addition, he
points to the actor's reflexive capacity to construct and sustain a coherent
and integrated narrative of the self (Giddens 1991: 76). Giddens' pointing to
the actor's reflexivity may be complemented by Weber's emphasis on the
moral capacities of the actor which enable him or her to orient the course of
his or her life through a sense of duty and discipline and a long-term commitment to a praiseworthy vocation (Weber 1947b: 152; see also Featherstone
1995: 35-37).

Bauman's actor can only shrug his or her shoulders for these things. Postmodernists are not very positive about the feasibility of this (high) modern

emphasis on the cognitive and moral faculties of the actor. Consequently, they point to his or her aesthetic capacities. It is the reassertion of perception, sensation and experimentation against their former colonisation by our logical and moral faculties. It is a sensualist paradigm replacing the intellectual one (see Lash and Friedman 1992: 4-8, 18). The experiences, the feeling, the taste or dislikes are dominant. Behaviour becomes a matter of taste instead of moral judgement as expressed in the statement: 'It feels good to act in this way'. It is the aesthetisation of life and the revival of romanticism in New Age cloaks.

Picking up the pieces: rational and associative reflexivity

Within this controversy about identity construction, as epitomised by Giddens and Bauman, the self-narrative and performative elements of identity construction are placed in sharp opposition. But is there anything radically new compared to what we already knew about identity construction? We were already aware that identity construction not only has an inward-looking dimension referring to the ideas the actor has about him or herself, and to the traits the members of the group or community to which the actor belongs may have in common (language, values, symbols, rituals, etc.). Identity construction also has an outward-looking dimension. Simmel (1955) already pointed to the fact that group affiliations and internal cohesion within groups are narrowly related to conflict and competition with others. Following Simmel we may expect that opposition to or competition with 'the other' greatly enhances the construction of a group identity (Barth 1969). However, this outward-looking dimension of identity construction is not the same as identity as performance. In the former case the idea of reflexively constructing a self-image as a group, albeit in opposition towards 'the other', is maintained, whereas in the latter case this very idea is lost even at the individual level.

Finding a way out of the controversy between Giddens and Bauman concerning identity construction depends on whether the actor's reflexivity is feasible and viable. But what kind of reflexivity are they talking about? In this controversy both Giddens and Bauman tend to conflate reflexivity with rationality. Overarching narratives of self would have a rational character or they would not be at all. It does not come as a surprise then that Giddens (1991) again and again emphasises the coherent and integrated character of such narratives. Bauman explicitly writes about identity as a modern life project in orderly, systematic, comprehensive, cohesive, consistent, solid, definite and continuous terms which is built following a premeditated blueprint. In his eyes such a project has become impossible in postmodern unstable, uncertain and disorderly conditions. The self-image splits into a collection of snapshots and identity becomes an unsolved problem with no resources to draw on (Bauman 1997: 88-89, 123).

However, for various reasons this equation of reflexivity and rationality is very questionable. First, the whole modern project of Enlightenment in the West started with the distinction between *ratio* (Descartes) or *Reine Vernunft* (Kant) on the one hand, and culture or more conventional ways of understanding and meaning-making, on the other. Of course, Enlightenment authors privileged the former at the expense of the latter and hoped for the former to advance pushing the latter to the sidelines, but the fact itself that they made such a distinction suggests a differentiation between various modes of reflexivity, a rational mode being just one of them.

Second, the poststructuralist recognition of the distance between language and discourse, on the one hand, and meaning-making on the other, points in the same direction. Meaning-making is expressed in discourse or discursive practices making use of language, but is not the same thing as discourse production or language. Consequently, I would suggest to distinguish two moments within the processes in which our mind works, i.e. two moments of reflexivity. To begin with, our mind processes impulses transmitted by our senses and thoughts by way of activating and extending various associative networks resulting in various activated meanings. After that, our mind structures these activated meanings by way of language in discourse and in other practices.[3]

The human mind principally works through the parallel processing of information, activating multiple networks of association rather than obeying fixed propositions, rules or sentences. Every impulse, such as an observation or a thought, simultaneously activates various complicated and extensive networks of association in the human mind. These networks of association are made up of schemata, i.e. associations which simplify experience and facilitate inference, interpretation and understanding. These connections and associations are inculcated by way of experiences and learning and are potentially invoked by and constitutive of goals (D'Andrade and Strauss

---

3. In elaborating on these two moments of reflexivity, I partially draw on recent contributions of cognitive anthropology and cognitive psychology centred on schema theory and connectionism (see D'Andrade 1995; D'Andrade and Strauss 1992; Holland and Quinn 1987; Ramsey, Stich and Rumelhart 1991). In particular I refer to the distinction made between parallel and serial ways of meaning-making (see Strauss and Quinn 1994 and 1997).

1992; D'Andrade 1995; Dixon Keller 1992: 60). The activation of these schemata or networks by a specific impuls results in various activated meanings, which include identifications, cognitions, expectations, feelings, emotions and motivations (Strauss and Quinn 1997: 6). Next, the moment the human mind structures these activated meanings in order to guide actions or to express them in discourse, other processes are triggered which respond to different characteristics: processes of verbalisation or discursivation. They tend to make these discourses relatively consistent and coherent, i.e. associations become singular and proceed in a unilinear or serial manner.[4]

The associative mental processes which predominate the first moment of reflexivity tend to express various basic characteristics. First, within these associative networks cognitions and emotions are inextricably intertwined. These networks incorporate moral, cognitive, emotional and motivational aspects and connect cultural and psychological processes. Second, the parallel activation of various associative networks can proceed in rather implicit ways and are strongly context-related. The specific context largely determines which meanings become activated. Third, needless to say that the various emotions, ideas and intentions that are activated in a parallel way may easily contradict each other. The human mind is not primarily concerned with such contradictions which especially come to the fore when meanings, emotions and intentions activated in different contexts are confronted with each other. I propose to bring these characteristics together in my concept of an associative mode of reflexivity.

By contrast, a rational mode of reflexivity presents the most extreme and clearest form of discursivation and verbalisation. It is expressed in the requirements which — at least until recently — scientific discourse is supposed to meet. Its rational character is expressed in several fundamental traits. First, it requires the separation, distinction and clear definition of emotions and cognitions. The same requirement is to be met regarding

---

4. Strauss and Quinn develop their theory of mental processes in opposition to language-based theories which claim that our mind stores knowledge as sentences and symbols structured by language (symbolic processing). In doing so Strauss and Quinn tend to downplay the importance of this second moment of reflexivity because apparently in this moment the structuring effects of language are much more operational that in the first moment. As a consequence, they have to admit that their theory is hardly capable of explaining 'deliberate cognitive efforts' or rather explicit or 'conscious' meaning-making which may partially transcend and transform existing schemata (Strauss and Quinn 1997: 57-62, 100, 128). I suggest that the recognition of these two moments of reflexivity, paying due attention to both, allows us to develop a more balanced approach to mental processes than that of Strauss and Quinn.

cognitive, moral and aesthetic aspects of discourse. Second, scientific discourse is supposed to be as explicit as possible and — at least partially — is
required to transcend the research, writing and reading settings. It should
claim a universal validity, relatively independent of the context of the
researched, the researcher and the reader. Third, this decontextualisation of
meanings makes contradictions between them discernible and apparent.
Rationalisation means defining them in concepts with singular meanings
instead of multi-interpretable symbols, relating them in a serial manner and
eradicating contradictions.

Both modes of reflexivity express very different characteristics and dynamics in the way I have just discussed them, but I would like to stress that
they represent two poles on a continuum with many intermediate forms. If
they would only exist in their pure forms we would not be able to get access
to associative-reflexive processes of our mind through discourse analysis.
This is not the case. Although on the one hand discursivation tends towards
rationalisation, it can still express strong associative traits. Brainstorming is
a case in point. On the other hand, although mental processes preceding discursivation tend towards associative reflexivity, they may also express some
rational traits. The (partial and not unconditional) internalisation of rational
ethical discourses propagated by religious institutions presents a good
example. Associative reading and structuring or rational writing may be two
different processes, they do not exclude but rather presuppose each other.
On some occasions mental processes may tend towards rationalisation while
on other occasions the human mind works in a more associative way. Nevertheless, in general the first moment of reflexivity tends towards an associative mode, whereas the second moment tends towards a rational mode.

Associative reflexivity among the Q'eqchi'es of Guatemala

All this may sound rather abstract. Now I will try to render these concepts
operational using my research material on the *Q'eqchi'es* (see Siebers 1996,
1998). The Q'eqchi'es make up a group of about 600,000 people who mainly
live in about 1,600 rural communities in northern Guatemala. Their lives and
life-worlds are fragmented to some extent. For example, they live in a
multicultural context which includes Spanish speaking *Ladinos* and members
of other indigenous groups such as *K'iche'es* and *Poqomchi'es*. They deal with
religious representations and practices stemming from their own traditions
and face religious influences from both the Catholic Church and Pentecostal
churches. They are engaged in subsistence as well as commercial agriculture.
In their agricultural practices they draw on both bodies of indigenous know-

ledge and on scientifically elaborated expertise offered to them by agricultural extension workers. They have both communitarian and individual forms of land control and of labour organisation. They can consult indigenous healers and may make use of modern health facilities such as medical centres and vaccination campaigns. To a certain extent community has become optional to them as in most of the villages there are both Catholic and various Pentecostal communities. Moreover, they face an increasing pluralisation of cultural supply from all corners of the world.

Their reflexive way of dealing with these influences is basically associative. To begin with, this means that meanings have a predominantly contextualised character. For example, their traditional or customary religion is directly related to agricultural activities that belong to the subsistence sphere. At key moments in the cultivation of maize — their basic food crop — they perform customary rituals in which they ask the mountain to provide them with a good harvest. During these rituals they consider their land to be the skin of the mountain which is addressed as a very powerful 'person'. However, concerning the production of their cash crops, or in dealing with government agencies about their land titles, they see no problem at all in paying for their land. They do not consider this to be sacrilege. On some occasions they consider land to be a 'person', whilst on other occasions they deal with land as a 'thing'.

Another example is presented by the symbol of the cross. It refers not only to the death of Christ, but also to the spirit of maize and to the four corners of the universe in which, according to the Q'eqchi'es, there are many 'persons' such as mountains, saints, spirits, and neighbouring villagers. During a Mass served by the priest, the cross refers to the first meaning. While they plant their maize they put a wooden cross on the land symbolising the spirit of maize and they take this cross home at the moment of harvesting. At rituals in which the whole community addresses all those who dwell in the universe and ask for a good harvest, they position four candles in the shape of a cross and relate these candles to the four corners of the universe. At customary rituals there are a lot of 'persons' they address, whereas at religious rituals promoted by churches they only deal with God.

Meanings are occasion-specific and the Q'eqchi'es are hardly interested in decontextualised questions such as whether 'in the end' or 'after all' land is a thing or a person. Contradictions that might arise from such decontextualised questions are hardly relevant to them. They use symbols not as rational concepts which allow for only one (serial) association; to them symbols have various meanings and the occasion determines which one becomes relevant.

Madonna Dressed Up as a Q'eqchi' in the Midst of Agricultural Offerings

Moreover, cognitions and emotions are very much interrelated in their reflexivity. This is clearly expressed in the customary rituals in which they address the mountain. Being present at some of these rituals I could not escape the impression that the awe-struck expression in their eyes and voices on these occasions was intimately related to the fact that in these rituals the Q'eqchi'es try to respond to the basic dependency on nature in all its aspects. These rituals express their need to symbolically 'resolve' their feelings of anxiety and uncertainty in an unpredictable natural setting.

The contextualised character of their meanings does not mean that the Q'eqchi'es are unable to talk about them outside of the specific context related to these meanings. They do have narratives about themselves and the natural and social surroundings, but these narratives are mainly reconstructed at the moment you ask about them. These narratives are flexible and express a highly composite nature in which they hardly care about oppositions such as profane versus religious. Only to a limited extent are they interested in detecting and eradicating internal contradictions or inconsistencies within their narratives and creating some sort of unity of discourse.

For example, meanings that we might categorise as religious play an important role in their world-views. This holds true for both Bible-oriented meanings — promoted by churches and highlighting God — and customary representations — promoted by customary leaders within the local communities and emphasising the role of other 'persons' in the universe, especially the mountain. In some communities Bible-oriented meanings and related practices (the Mass, sacraments, Bible-study meetings and so on) may be characterised as being predominant while in other communities customary representations and related rituals (such as the rituals in which they address the mountain and ask for a good harvest) appear as predominant. In the former communities basic customary meanings are to some extent adapted to Bible-oriented meanings, while in the latter communities the reverse is the case.

A villager from one of the former communities explained the relations between God and the mountain by saying: 'The mountain is alive because he has clouds around and above him. With these clouds he worships God just like a bird who sings in praise of God. Man should do the same.' Thus he puts man, the birds and the mountain on a par: they are alive and have the same obligation to pray to God, to whom all major attention is directed. By contrast, in one of the communities in which customary religion predominates, a villager told me that 'the Word of God is there to enrich our ways of addressing the mountain', thereby emphasising the central role of the mountain. However, in all the communities I studied, both basic customary and Bible-oriented meanings made up vital elements of the world-views of all Q'eqchi'es.

Their associative reflexivity enables the Q'eqchi'es to articulate aspects of all kinds of spheres, sources and categories within their life-world. Regarding almost every aspect of their life-world, their basic attitude is to selectively adopt elements from different sources and spheres and to adapt them to their needs without being worried about the question whether these elements fit into one overall rationality. They adopt influences and elements that stem from outside of their life-world and that are presented to them by 'outsiders' and adapt these elements to a selectively invented tradition, making their own blend of indigenous and exogenous elements. For example in their religion, meanings and practices stemming both from churches and from their traditions play a crucial role. Their harvest of maize, i.e. the fertility of their land, depends on their performance of customary rituals addressing the mountain and asking for such a good harvest, but they do not see any problem in lending the mountain a helping hand by using chemical ferti-lisers. Their basically associative reflexivity very much favours this articu-lation of elements from different sources and spheres.

Associative reflexivity: continuity and change

By contrast, rational or serial processing of impulses and data would leave them a much more limited room to respond to the unknown and to articu-late the various fragments of their life and life-world in a meaningful way. Its claims of decontextualised and rather timeless validity and its dogma of consistency and unambiguity allow only for singular perspectives from which to approach new phenomena and the panorama of fragments. When universal valid or decontextualised discourses are contextualised by specific actors in specific situations, they force a single logic upon the actors' meaning-making and practices. Consequently, they tend to seriously curb the actors' flexibility and creativity in responding and adapting to new situa-tions. They tend to force actors to make a choice between the one and the other, between the known and the new, between continuity and change.

For example, the unconditional and integral acceptance of the rational and systematic religious discourse of especially the Salesian priests, would force the Q'eqchi'es to leave behind their customary religion because the Salesians consider this religion to be incompatible with the Word of God. It would make it impossible for them to pray to God during the Mass while at the same time addressing the mountain when they are concerned about a good harvest. The fact that the Q'eqchi'es deal with these matters in an associative way allows them to be selective in adopting what they like from this official discourse without being concerned about the consequences of other activities on other occasions: consequences that are emphasised in this official discourse.

Associative reflexivity is much more capable of articulating continuity and change, and to selectively interrelate the fragments of the actors' life in a more meaningful way than rational reflexivity. On the one hand, association guarantees an important degree of continuity. Contextualised associative networks, i.e. adapted to specific circumstances, tend to be self-reinforcing (see Strauss and Quinn 1994). This is first of all because the more impulses there are that lead to the activation of these networks, with more or less satisfying results, the stronger the connections of the network become. For example, when the Q'eqchi'es' harvest is abundant after having performed the required customary rituals, existing networks of customary meanings are confirmed and reinforced. Second, existing networks are particularly reinforced when not only cognitions are activated, but also when emotions are aroused. I already referred to the emotional connotations of customary rituals and meanings in the preceding section.

Third, the processing of impulses through associative networks tends to avoid disconfirming evidence arising. If the maize fails to grow well, despite having performed customary rituals, the Q'eqchi'es may feel that they have not performed these rituals with enough dedication or in a sincere enough way, instead of concluding that customary rituals are superfluous. Especially elderly village members put forward such explanations. Moreover, associative networks may be confirmed not only by experience, but also through teaching, such as these elderly village members promoting customary meanings and rituals among youngsters. Finally, associative networks become also strengthened when the activated meanings are shared with others. Customary rituals need to be performed by the community as a whole emphasising the sharing of meanings.

On the other hand, associative ways of meaning-making also allow for an important degree of flexibility and change. Unlike Bourdieu who writes about rather fixed and commanding dispositions regarding his concept of habitus (see Bourdieu 1972), connectionist theory emphasises the loose character of associative networks which enables the actors to react in a flexible way to the particulars of any new event. The combined influence of different networks of meanings activated simultaneously in a given situation can lead to rather different and contradictory perspectives from which to approach a new or different situation or context (Strauss and Quinn 1994: 285-87). The actor can build upon multiple perspectives to construct new ideas and arouse new emotions and intentions when faced with new or different situations, i.e. make a deliberate cognitive effort. Multiple perspectives allow the actor room for manoeuvre in extending existing networks, reworking meanings and reflecting.

My appearance as a researcher — exogenous, unknown, moderately modern — presents a nice example of multiple perspectives from which to approach something or someone new. In several Q'eqchi' villages existing networks of association and interpretation were clearly inadequate to provide the Q'eqchi'es immediately with a satisfying answer as to what to think of me and how to react. I was foreign to them, so belonged to 'the others', but was I to be conceived of as a Ladino? I talked to them about projects and development, but did not belong to those rare species of development workers that visit them on exceptional occasions. I was sent by the Bishop to do my job in their village, as my letter with a nice stamp suggested, but then again, I was not a priest, so what was I? I was doing research that might benefit the policies of the department of social pastoral work of the bishopric and improve its services towards Q'eqchi' communities, but what was their own community going to gain from my work? I was to write a book about them, but what is the use of books anyway and who might read this book? The first few times I came to their community, the Q'eqchi'es in all the villages where I worked had these and similar doubts concerning my work. I do not know what the various reasons were which finally convinced almost all of the villagers to co-operate and to place their trust in me, but I do know that the introduction by the priest turned out to be crucial and the fact that my work could be interpreted as proof that the Bishop was taking an interest in how they live, surely helped a lot.

Based on different perspectives to approaching the new and the unknown, and through various networks of association, different outcomes are possible as this example shows. Associative reflexivity enables the Q'eqchi'es to build upon these multiple perspectives, to construct new meanings and arouse new emotions when faced with new situations, events and experiences. It allows them to selectively deal with meanings and impulses from different sources and to combine a certain level of continuity with some degree of change in a flexible way.

Reflexivity, identity and power

Here we touch upon the heart of what identity constructions are about. Associative reflexivity is viable and capable of interrelating the various fragments of one's life articulating some level of continuity and change in a meaningful and flexible way. As such it allows actors to escape from the dilemmas created in the above mentioned controversy on identity construction. It means that, on the one hand, they do not need to resort to developing rather essentialist, stable and authentic narratives of self, consistently and transparently structurated and valid in all spheres of life. On the other hand, the viability of associative reflexivity enables the actors to be more self-reflexive and meaningful than just presenting one superficial and disconnected performance after another, interested in impressing 'the other', as Bauman would have it.

In the case of the Q'eqchi'es, associative reflexivity enables them to combine identifications as a member of various social groups at various levels such as gender category, local community, kinship line, ethnic group, institutions such as the church community, class and nation. It allows for contextualised meanings which from a decontextualised perspective may be contradictory. In one context a Q'eqchi' woman may define herself as belonging to the Q'eqchi' ethnic group, whereas in another context she may express her contempt for Q'eqchi'es of a neighbouring village with which her fellow villagers are involved in a land conflict. Associative reflexivity allows both positions and identifications to be possible — rational reflexivity would rule one of them out — and is expressed in the stories the Q'eqchi'es tell about them and their lives.

Associative reflexivity opens up the possibility for constructing narratives of self. However, the crucial point here is what kind of narratives are we talking about and how are they structured: in a coherent and rather fixed way leading to unequivocal prescriptions for how to act, or in a rather loose and flexible way including both ideas and emotions and without being bothered about coherence. Such narratives can be expressed in a single line of associating unequivocal concepts, consistently structured in an orderly and sequential telling involving a plot with a beginning, middle and end organised in a teleological way (Gullestad 1996: 6), or they can have a multi-centred character in which the various meanings and emotions are clustered around several symbols without unequivocal interrelations. Rational reflexivity tends to take a single universal and decontextualised discourse as a starting point for constructing an overarching narrative of self. Associative reflexivity, however, will allow the actors to take the various meanings, emotions and intentions associated with each specific fragment of their life and life-world as a starting point from which to look for multiple meaningful interrelations.

Associative reflexivity points to narratives of self with a multi-layered structure and expressing multiple and shifting identifications. It entails that

the actors cherish some basic ideas and emotions about themselves and about
the whole of their lives (see Morée 1992: 47) which interrelate the specific
meanings that they attribute to the various fragments of their lives. Such
narratives are related to, but also transcend each of the specific meanings
related to each fragment. Gullestad distinguishes 'identities' linked to specific
roles, and 'identities' not linked to such roles. The latter express a distance
from specific roles and may serve within the 'continuous and processual
effort to integrate the various experiences of the individual' (Gullestad 1996:
18).

At this point power has to come in. Actors such as the Q'eqchi'es do not
just reflect or construct their identities in social isolation, but in the framework of specific power relations. As has been outlined above, meanings may
be structured in the process of verbalisation and expressed in discourse. As
a second moment of reflexivity this discursivation not only tends towards
rationalisation, the resulting discourses may become the object of explicit
rationalisation by cultural specialists employed by modern institutions. As
such, these explicitly rationalised discourses — coherent, consistent, unequivocal, claiming universal or decontextualised validity — are written
down in texts, rules, laws and regulations and adopt, as such, a rather
solidified character. As these discourses are propagated and 'distributed' by
modern institutions, they may be adopted and internalised by individual
actors, i.e. integrated in mental networks. As a consequence, rationalisation
is an intersubjective process in which both the intrapersonal and the extra-
personal, both the individual actor and his or her social and cultural
structuring context are involved. Moreover, just like in the case of any
process of meaning-making, the exercise of power plays an important role.[5]

In this respect there is a remarkable paradox regarding rationality and
rational reflexivity. On the one hand, within the Enlightenment ideal
knowing and changing social reality in a rational way was part of a progressive and emancipatory narrative supporting the 'freedom' and 'agency'
of individual social actors. On the other hand, rationality and a rational way
of thinking also turned out to be a potent instrument in the hands of those
in power to control other actors in modern institutional frameworks. Political, religious and cultural institutions (see Gellner 1983 on education or

---

5. Of course, not only rationalisation has an intersubjective character, the same holds true
   for discourses with strong associative traits. These discourses may also be expressed
   by individuals, gathered and written down by 'specialists', who propagate them and
   encourage their audience to internalise these discourses. New Age books and lectures
   may be a case in point.

Bourdieu 1971a and 1971b on churches) claimed to develop universally valid and decontextualised discourses — consistent, systematic — in short, rational, and impose them on 'lay' actors in society. This imposition had to lead to prescribed thinking and the inculcation of single and incontestable associations within the reflexive processes of those actors. They were told how to react unequivocally to specifically defined situations along the formula: 'If situation X arises, then you should do Y'. As such, the imposition of these rational discourses was meant to counteract the 'agency' and relative autonomy of these actors constructing meaning.

The resulting mental processes of these actors mirror Bourdieu's concept of habitus or the iron cage of bureaucracy Weber feared so much. Bourdieu writes about dispositions which are inculcated in the habitus of actors resulting from individual experiences within the structural framework of society and which determine subsequent mental processes as well as the practices of these actors (Bourdieu 1972). Weber wrote about institutional frameworks, governed by formal rationality (Weber 1978: 85-86), in which these actors become trapped. These institutions oblige them to execute the rules and regulations ordered by those in power leading to prescribed practices and behaviour, whatever their potential personal desires, deviant and plural associations and particular meaning-making might be (Weber 1947a). In this way consistent, unequivocal and stable identities are preached and promoted by these institutions. These identities can be nicely filled in on forms and standard procedures and express a prescribed destiny; they reflect the rational character of institutional discourses.

For example, the official discourse of the Catholic Church bears clear rational traits and entails clear and consistent images of identities to which individual believers are supposed to adhere. In the Q'eqchi' region, the clergy is responsible for preaching and propagating this discourse and for convincing the Q'eqchi'es to adopt its constructed and prescribed identities. However, within this process of transmission the official discourse loses much of its rational character and the same holds true for its prescribed identities. First, the local clergy do not just function as serving-hatches of official discourse. To a large extent these specialists modify and transform these discourses. They cannot escape from interpreting this discourse in their own cultural frameworks and the practice of pastoral work or preaching leaves considerable room for these specialists to develop their own interpretations, understandings and methods of work provoking many tensions and differences of opinion between various groups and specialists within the same church.

Second, the method of transmitting their interpretations to the Q'eqchi' communities also involves a high level of adaptation and modification. Priests and religious women have only limited direct access to the local communities. They visit them a few times a year, but their main communication with these communities takes place through instructing and training local leaders such as catechists. The latter are supposed to pass on to their communities what they have learned from the religious specialists. However, this way of communication involves interpretative processes on the part of these local leaders which can result in individual meanings and practices being transmitted in a rather isolated way.

Consequently, the Catholic official discourse becomes fragmented and loses a large part of its systematised and rationalised coherence while it is transmitted. By losing a large part of this coherence it becomes much less forceful and compulsory. For example, the acceptance of the moral demands of God does not necessarily oblige the Q'eqchi'es to become worried about monotheistic or polytheistic concerns which official religious discourses may also relate to God. The official Catholic discourse is influencing their meaning-making to a certain extent, but the Q'eqchi'es maintain a circumscribed, but nevertheless real space of manoeuvre to continue their associative and selective way of dealing with both their own invented traditions and the elements offered to them by religious institutions. The same may be concluded regarding the influence of other institutions such as the Ministries of Education and Agriculture and NGO's (Siebers 1996, 1998).

It has been outlined above that perhaps the strongest point of postmodern writers highlighting fragmentation is that they question the guiding influence of these institutions on individual meaning-making and identity constructions. However, it remains to be seen whether this influence has ever been as predominant as claimed and whether the partial withdrawal of these institutions will open up the space for something fundamentally new in terms of reflexivity and identity construction. On the one hand, Giddens does not help us any further in this question because he continues to see individual identity constructions to be fundamentally moulded by expertise and expert knowledge created and distributed by these institutions. Hence, he fails to pay due attention to the consequences of processes of cultural pluralisation in a globalising context.

On the other hand, the fact that scholars such as Bauman question the meaning-making capacity and 'agency' of contemporary actors may be more determined by the fact that they themselves cannot get rid of the standards and viewpoints of the very institutions they claim to be receding, rather than by the relatively open approach of the actors concerned. They share with these institutions the very idea that the reflexive capacity of these actors must not be overestimated. They tend to equate reflexivity with rationality and identity constructions with the ideal images painted and promoted by such high modern institutions. Where they see rationality and this image losing ground, they seal the fate of reflexivity and identity as such. Nevertheless, there may be much more continuity in identity constructions and reflexivity between premodern actors, modern actors partially escaping from the yoke of institutional pressure and presumed postmodern actors than assumed by these writers. Even ambiguity, one of the central concepts of postmodern writers, has its relevance in a basically modern context. Has not the domination of modern official institutions and discourses always entailed the emergence of a semi-secret sphere of deviance, dissent and 'sin' creating an equivocal and contradictory picture of social life and individual identity constructions?

Conclusion

In my view, identity constructions, reflexivity or the actor's 'agency', are not in crisis as such, but a crisis does exist with regard to a particular version of identity constructions driven by rationality and inscribed in encompassing grand narratives which we may classify as 'high modern', preached and promoted by rational bureaucracies. It is exactly this kind of identity construction that Giddens tends to defend in vain. There is no ground for the worries and anxieties that are at the heart of the controversy on identity constructions. Identity constructions as such present no problem, but an open question to be answered regarding specific actors in specific circumstances by way of fieldwork.

However, in studying the ways actors position themselves in the world and the images they create of themselves and others, a much more circumstantial and processual or dynamic approach is needed than the one suggested by the term 'identity' itself. This term may easily create the association of something static and massive that can become diluted or may be crumbling down. Instead, the non-essentialist character of the processes we are dealing with may be stressed by terms like identification processes or identity *constructions*. Moreover, understanding the associative ways in which the human mind may work allows us to understand that there is no need for exclusive choices between the self-narrative and performative aspects of identity constructions. One aspect does not rule out the other. It is far more fruitful to try to demonstrate how specific actors articulate specific performative aspects with self-narrative aspects in their ways of locating themselves in the world.

The study of identification processes or identity constructions calls for the need to bridge the conventional separation within social sciences between (private) individual experience, on the one hand, and (public) collective representation on the other. The former has conventionally drawn the attention of especially psychological approaches often using supposedly universal notions of emotions, attitudes, motivations and personality, whereas especially interpretative anthropology in line with Geertz has pointed to cultural differences underscoring the public and collective nature of culture as socially established structures of meaning (White 1992: 21-22, 30-31, 39-40). However, the recognition that cultural models influence the definition and experience of emotions and personality has pointed to the need for psychologists to include social and cultural contextual factors in their analysis (White 1992: 26, 32-38). Simultaneously, the breakdown of monolithic collective views of culture has encouraged person-centred ethnographic approaches (White and Lutz 1992: 1) and has contributed to the revival of the life story method in anthropology. Moreover, as I have pointed out regarding the Q'eqchi'es, identity constructions and the relevant reflexive processes that guide them cannot be studied in isolation, but need to include attention to power relations within society and discourse. Consequently, in my view, the study of identity constructions has to focus on the interplay between mind, culture and society paying attention to both social and cultural context and reflexive mental processes.

Bibliography

Anderson, B. 1987. *Imagined Communities. Reflections on the Origin and Spread of Nationalism.* London and New York: Verso.

Appadurai, A. 1990. 'Disjuncture and Difference in the Global Cultural Economy'. In: M. Featherstone (ed.), *Global Culture: Nationalism, Globalization and Modernity.* London, Newbury Park and New Delhi: Sage, 295-310.

Appadurai, A. 1996. *Modernity at Large. Cultural Dimensions of Globalization.* Minneapolis and London: University of Minnesota Press.

Barth, F. (ed.), 1969. *Ethnic Groups and Boundaries. The Social Organization of Cultural Difference.* London: Allen & Unwin.

Bauman, Z. 1989. *Modernity and the Holocaust.* Cambridge: Polity Press.

Bauman, Z. 1993. *Postmodern Ethics.* Oxford and Cambridge, Mass.: Blackwell.

Bauman, Z. 1995. *Life in Fragments. Essays in Postmodern Morality.* Oxford: Blackwell.

Bauman, Z. 1996. 'From Pilgrim to Tourist — or a Short History of Identity'. In: St. Hall and P. Du Gay (eds.), *Questions of Cultural Identity*. London, Thousand Oaks, New Delhi: Sage, 18-36.

Bauman, Z. 1997. *Postmodernity and its Discontents*. Cambridge: Polity Press.

Bourdieu, P. 1971a. 'Genèse et structure du champ religieux'. In: *Revue Française de Sociologie*, XII(3), 295-334.

Bourdieu, P. 1971b. 'Une interpretation de la théorie de la religion selon Max Weber'. In: *Archives Européennes de Sociologie*, XII(1), 3-21.

Bourdieu, P. 1972. *Esquisse d'une Théorie de la Pratique*. Genève: Droz.

D'Andrade, R. 1995. *The Development of Cognitive Anthropology*. Cambridge: Cambridge University Press.

D'Andrade, R. and C. Strauss (eds.), 1992. *Human Motives and Cultural Models*. Cambridge: Cambridge University Press.

Dixon Keller, J. 1992. 'Schemes for Schemata'. In: Th. Schwartz, G. White and C. Lutz (eds.), *New Directions in Psychological Anthropology*. Cambridge: Cambridge University Press, 59-67.

Featherstone, M. 1995. *Undoing Culture. Globalization, Postmodernism and Identity*. London, Thousand Oaks, New Delhi: Sage.

Gellner, E. 1983. *Nations and Nationalism*. Oxford: Blackwell.

Giddens, A. 1990. *The Consequences of Modernity*. Cambridge: Polity Press.

Giddens, A. 1991. *Modernity and Self-Identity. Self and Society in the Late Modern Age*. Stanford: Stanford University Press.

Gramsci, A. 1978. *Marxisme als filosofie van de praxis*. Amsterdam: Van Gennep.

Gullestad, M. 1996. *Everyday Life Philosophers. Modernity, Morality, and Autobiography in Norway*. Oslo: Scandinavian University Press.

Hall, St. 1991. 'The Local and the Global: Globalisation and Ethnicity'. In: A.D. King (ed.), *Culture, Globalization and the World-System. Contemporary Conditions for the Representation of Identity*. London: Macmillan, 19-39.

Hall, St. 1996. 'Introduction: Who Needs "Identity"?'. In: St. Hall and P. Du Gay (eds.), *Questions of Cultural Identity*. London, Thousand Oaks, New Delhi: Sage, 1-17.

Hannerz, U. 1992. *Cultural Complexity. Studies in the Social Organization of Meaning*. New York: Columbia University Press.

Hannerz, U. 1996. *Transnational Connections. Culture, People, Places*. London and New York: Routledge.

Hetherington, K. 1996. 'Identity Formation, Space and Social Centrality'. In: *Theory, Culture & Society*, 13(3), 33-52.

Holland, D. and N. Quinn. (eds.), 1987. *Cultural Models in Language and Thought*. Cambridge: Cambridge University Press.

Laclau, E. 1985. 'New Social Movements and the Plurality of the Social'. In: D. Slater (ed.), *New Social Movements and the State in Latin America*. Amsterdam: CEDLA, 27-42.

Lash, S. and J. Friedman 1992. 'Introduction: Subjectivity and Modernity's Other'. In: S. Lash and J. Friedman (eds.), *Modernity and Identity*. Oxford, U.K. and Cambridge, Mass.: Blackwell, 1-30.

Lyotard, J.-F. 1984. *The Postmodern Condition: A Report on Knowledge*. Minneapolis: University of Minnesota Press.

Morée, M. 1992. *'Mijn kinderen hebben er niets van gemerkt'. Buitenshuis werkende moeders tussen 1950 en nu*. Utrecht: Jan van Arkel.

Poulantzas, N. 1975. *Classes in Contemporary Capitalism*. London: New Left Books.

Ramsey, W., S. Stich and D. Rumelhart (eds.), 1991. *Philosophy and Connectionist Theory*, Hillsdale, N.J., Hove and London: Lawrence Erlbaum Associates.

Rorty, R. 1986. 'Freud and Moral Reflection'. In: J.H. Smith and W. Kerrigan (eds.), *Pragmatism's Freud*. Baltimore: John Hopkins University Press.

Siebers, H. 1996. Creolization and Modernization at the Periphery: The Case of the Q'eqchi'es of Guatemala. Ph.D. thesis, Nijmegen: Katholieke Universiteit.

Siebers, H. 1997a. 'Mixing and Mingling in a Globalizing World: Identity Constructions of the Q'eqchi'es of Guatemala'. In: R. Staring, M. Van der Land and H. Tak (eds.), *Cultural Identity: Globalization, Localization, Creolization. Focaal. Tijdschrift voor Antropologie*, 30/31, 179-92.

Siebers, H. 1997b. 'Zwischen Fragmentierung und Reflexivität: Gibt es eine Zukunft für Identität und Ethnizität?'. In: *Peripherie. Zeitschrift für Politik und Ökonomie in der Dritten Welt*, 17(67), 46-66.

Siebers, H. 1998.'We Are Children of the Mountain'. *Creolization and Modernization among the Q'eqchi'es of Guatemala in a Globalizing Perspective*. Amsterdam: CEDLA.

Simmel, G. 1955. *Conflict and The Web of Group-Affiliations, with a foreword by E.C. Hughes*. Glencoe, Ill.: The Free Press.

Strauss, C. and N. Quinn 1994. 'A Cognitive/Cultural Anthropology'. In: R. Borofsky (ed.), *Assessing Cultural Anthropology*. New York: McGraw-Hill, 284-97.

Strauss, C. and N. Quinn 1997. *A Cognitive Theory of Cultural Meaning*. Cambridge: Cambridge University Press.

Weber, M. 1947a. 'Bureaucracy'. In: H.H. Gerth and C. Wright Mills (eds.), *From Max Weber. Essays in Sociology*. London: Kegan Paul, 196-244.

Weber, M. 1947b. 'Science as a Vocation'. In: H.H. Gerth and C. Wright Mills (eds.), *From Max Weber. Essays in Sociology*. London: Kegan Paul, 129-56.

Weber, M. 1978. G. Roth and C. Wittich (eds.), *Economy and Society*. Berkeley: University of California Press.

White, G. 1992. 'Ethnopsychology'. In: Th. Schwartz, G. White and C. Lutz (eds.), New Directions in Psychological Anthropology. Cambridge: Cambridge University Press, 21-46.

White, G. and C. Lutz 1992. 'Introduction'. In: Th. Schwartz, G. White and C. Lutz (eds.), *New Directions in Psychological Anthropology*. Cambridge: Cambridge University Press, 1-17.

About the Authors

Martijn van Beek is Associate Professor in the Department of Ethnography and Social Anthropology at the University of Aarhus. He has been working in the Himalayan region since the early 1980s and has been engaged in fieldwork in Ladakh since 1985. He holds a doctorate in Development Sociology from Cornell University. His research interests and publications focus on questions of development, democracy and social justice, and the politics of identity and representation. He is co-editor, with Kristoffer Brix Bertelsen and Poul Pedersen, of *Ladakh: Culture, History, and Development between Himalaya and Karakoram* (Aarhus University Press 1999).

Anton Blok is Professor of Cultural Anthropology at the University of Amsterdam and also serves on the faculty of the Amsterdam School for Social Science Research. His publications include *The Mafia of a Sicilian Village*, 1860-1960 (Oxford 1974), and *De Bokkerijders. Roversbanden en geheime genootschappen in de Landen van Overmaas, 1730-1774* (Amsterdam 1995).

Ad Borsboom (Ph.D. University of Nijmegen) is Professor at the Centre for Pacific Studies, Department of Anthropology, University of Nijmegen. Since 1972, he has conducted fieldwork in Australia investigating religion and social change in Aboriginal societies, identity and land rights. His writings include *De Clan van de Wilde Honing: Spirituele Rijkdom van de Aborigines*, and he is, together with Ton Otto, editor of *Cultural Dynamics of Religious Change in Oceania* (Leiden 1997).

Glenn Bowman is a social anthropologist working in the Anthropology Department at the University of Kent at Canterbury in the United Kingdom. His primary fieldwork has been with Palestinians in Israel and the Israeli-Occupied Territories where he has researched articulations of sectarian and nationalist identities as well as pilgrimage and tourism. He is currently completing a Wenner-Gren Foundation research project in Beit Sahour in the Israeli-Occupied Territories, and is planning future fieldwork comparing nation formation and deformation in the rump of Yugoslavia.

Henk Driessen is a Senior Lecturer at the Department of Anthropology, University of Nijmegen, The Netherlands. His main interests are Mediterranean ethnography as well as symbolic and political anthropology. His publications include *On the Spanish-Moroccan Frontier* (1992), and the edited volumes *The Politics of Ethnographic Reading and Writing* (1993), and *In het huis van de islam* (1997).

Jonathan Friedman is Professor of Social Anthropology at the University of Lund and Directeur d'Études at the École des Hautes Études en Sciences Sociales in Paris. He has written extensively on structuralism and marxism and carried out work on Southeast Asian history and ethnography. Since the mid-seventies he has been involved in the development of global systemic anthropology. His major publications include *System, Structure, and Contradiction: The Evolution of 'Asiatic' Social Formations* (1998, second edition), *Cultural Identity and Global Process* (1994), and the (co-)edited volumes *Consumption and Identity* (1994), *Melanesian Modernities* (1996), and *World System History: The Science of Long Term Change* (1999).

Janneke Hulsker graduated in Cultural Anthropology from the University of Nijmegen, The Netherlands, in 1993. During various periods between 1992 and 1999 she carried out fieldwork in the inner Sydney suburb of Redfern, where she studied Aboriginal community-based organisations. Currently she is at the University of Nijmegen's Centre for Pacific and Asian Studies, where she is completing her Ph.D. thesis on 'Aboriginal Organisations and their Use of the Concept of Aboriginality in Redfern, Sydney'.

Longina Jakubowska, a native of Poland, received her Ph.D. at the State University of New York in 1985. She subsequently taught at Bryn Mawr College and the University of the Pacific. She researched and published in two ethnographic areas, the Middle East and Eastern Europe. She currently works in the Netherlands.

Ton Otto is Professor of Ethnography and Social Anthropology at the University of Aarhus, Denmark. He has conducted extensive fieldwork in Manus and New Ireland (Papua New Guinea) on issues of social and cultural change. His publications include *The Politics of Tradition in Baluan: Social Change and the Construction of the Past in a Manus Society* (1991) and two co-edited volumes, *Narratives of Nation in the South Pacific* (1997, with Nicholas Thomas) and *Cultural Dynamics of Religious Change in Oceania* (1997, with Ad Borsboom).

Poul Pedersen is Associate Professor at the Department of Ethnography and Social Anthropology, University of Aarhus, Denmark. He conducted field studies in India (Tamil Nadu and Ladakh). He is the author of articles on widow-burning; caste and colonial bureaucracy in India; Christian missionaries in India; religion, ecology, and identity; Tibetan Buddhism; history of anthropology. He is the editor-in-chief of *Folk - Journal of the Danish Ethnographic Society*.

Hans Siebers (1957) read anthropology and development studies at the University of Nijmegen, The Netherlands. He received his Ph.D. in 1996 based on a study of identity constructions, religion and economic strategies of the Q'eqchi' ethnic group in Guatemala. He currently is a researcher and lecturer in the field of anthropology of management and organisations at the University of Utrecht. The topics of his writings include religion, churches, economics, and social change in Latin America; theoretical discussions of concepts such as modernisation, globalisation, reflexivity and identity constructions, and management of diversity and culture in human service organisations.

Louise Thoonen received her M.A. in anthropology from the University of Nijmegen, the Netherlands. Currently she is a Ph.D. research associate at the Centre for Pacific and Asian Studies, Department of Anthropology, University of Nijmegen. Her research which included 13 months of fieldwork in the interior of the Bird's Head area of Irian Jaya, focussed on female initiation within the missionary process.

Name Index

Abel 27, 35
Aggarwal, R. 174-76
Akenson, D.H. 47
Aldridge-Morris, R. 102
Alexander, V.K. 98
Alexander the Great 143
Allison, R.B. 99, 102
Alonso, A.M. 230
Anderson, B. 60, 167, 169, 233, 236
Appadurai, A. 143, 158, 172, 234
Arafat, Y. 66-67
Aronson, G. 66, 73
Arrighi, G. 145
Asad, T. 64
Asher, J. 119
Assies, W.J. 169
Attwood, G.E. 101
Attwood, B. 209
Aviner, Rabbi 70
Aya, R. 27, 38
Bairoch, P. 144
Balibar, E. 167
Bame, P. 134-35
Banks, M. 14
Barnes, J. 114
Barth, F. 14, 239
Baru, M. 22, 125-26, 128-38
Barwick, D.E. 210
Bass, E. 103, 105
Bates, B.L. 99
Bauman, Z. 12, 24, 233-35, 237-40,
  249, 252
Bax, M. 15
Beckett, S. 207
Berndt, R.M. 208
Berndt, C.H. 208
Bertelsen, K.B. 164, 177, 180
Bertrand, L.D. 107

Bewes, T. 167-68
Bey, U.S. 148
Bhasin, M.K. 165
Biddle, E.H. 202
Bildt, C. 156
Billig, M. 168, 170
Black-Michaud, J. 32, 75, 81
Blainey, G. 149
Blair, T. 158
Bliss, B.L. 97
Blok, A. 20-21, 35, 218
Bøe, T. 98
Boehm, C. 32
Boon, S. 98
Boor, M. 98
Borsboom, A. 19, 23, 191, 195, 199
Bourdieu, P. 17, 21, 33-34, 51, 218,
  247, 251
Bowman, G. 21, 56, 60, 64, 69, 71
Braudel, F. 142, 145
Brauen, M. 175
Braun, B. 96,
Bray, J. 164, 180
Briggs, A. 144
Bringa, T. 15
Brookman, A. 202
Brown, J.C. 98
Brown, R. 13
Brügmann, M. 15
Brundage, W.F. 37
Buchanan, W. 13
Burgmann, V. 206, 209
Burgus, P. 96, 104
Burke, P. 27
Butler, J. 98
Cain 27, 35
Carlini, B. 98
Carolusson, S. 98

Carroy, J. 101
Carter, J. 206
Charlesworth, M. 193
Checkley, H.M. 96
Chirot, D. 46
Christophe, F. 109, 111-12
Clastres, P. 149
Cleckley, H.M. 100-1
Clifford, J. 160
Clinton, W.J. 158
Cohen, A. 20, 64, 75, 77-78, 81, 126
Cohn, B.S. 172
Comaroff, J. 171
Connolly, W.E. 166
Courtens, I. 125, 130, 133, 135-37
Crabtree, A. 114
Crawley, A.E. 28, 31
Crews, F. 105
Cunningham, A. 172
Dagmar, H. 191
Dahl, G. 147-48
Daley, M. 35
Darves-Bornoz, J.-M. 99
Davis, L. 103, 105
De Klerk, F.W. 47
De Vos, G. 36-37
Dell, W. 32
Denich, B. 39
Descartes, R. 240
Dingane, Zulu king 35
Dirlik, A. 150, 160
Djareware, (Totem) 194-97, 199-201
Djilas, M. 32
Dollfus, P. 174-75
Douglas, M. 143
Doyle, A.C. 95
Dragma, I. 62
Draijer, N. 98
Drew, F. 172-73
Driessen, H. 12, 16, 119, 184, 218
Drummond, L. 16
Dumont, L. 28, 37, 48-50
Dunning, E. 33

Durkheim, E. 31, 236
Dyck, N. 169
D'Andrade, R. 240-41
Eckermann, A.K. 210
Eidelberg, P.G. 46
El-Aref, A. 75, 77
Elias, N. 19, 34, 38, 50-51
Ellenberger, H. 98
Erikson, E. 13
Esau 35
Evans-Pritchard, E.P. 33
Ewing, K. 126
Featherstone, M. 235, 238
Field, S. 101
Foucault, M. 171
Frankel, G. 61
Freud, S. 13, 21, 28-30, 33, 39, 51
Frevert, U. 38
Freyd, P. 119
Friedman, J. 22, 70, 145, 150, 160, 233, 239
Gale, F. 202
Geertz, C. 20, 49, 76, 92, 194, 198
Gell, A. 201
Gellner, E. 82, 250
Ghanem, E. 59
Giddens, A. 12, 24, 158, 234-39, 252
Gillis, J.R. 167
Ginat, J. 75
Ginzburg, C. 27
Girard, R. 34-35, 42, 46, 51
Gleaves, D.H. 107
Glenny, M. 41-42
Glowczewski, B. 191-92, 213
Goettman, C. 98
Goffman, E. 13, 31, 50
Goodall, H. 207
Goudsblom, J. 27
Gramsci, A. 233
Granqvist, H. 75, 81-82
Gravel, P.B. 46
Greenwillow, J. 113-14
Grist, N. 174

Grohol, J.M. 117
Gullestad, M. 249-50
Gutschow, K. 175
Haaken, J. 108
Hacking, I. 95, 98-99, 101-3, 108, 111,
    115-17
Haddad, E.N. 77, 82
Halbwachs, M. 229
Hall, St. 234-35
Hammel, E.A. 40-41
Hammersley, M. 16
Handler, R. 170
Hannerz, U. 143, 234
Harris, G.G. 20
Harvey, D. 142, 144
Healey, D. 102
Heebing, S. 15
Heilbron, J. 27
Herdt, G. 127, 138
Herzfeld, M. 168, 171
Hetherington, K. 232
Hill-Burnett, J. 206
Hirst, P. 144
Hobbes, T. 28
Holland, D. 240
Hollinsworth, D. 206
Holmes, Sherlock 95, 119
Holmes, L. 118
Holmes, S. 166
Horowitz, D.L. 170
Howie-Willis, I. 189, 203
Hulsker, J. 23
Hunter, F.R. 57, 61
Huntington, S.P. 48
Ignatieff, M. 39, 42
Inden, R. 174
Jackson, H. 47
Jakubowska, L. 23, 27, 230
Jalali, R. 170
Jansen, W. 184
Janson, J. 208
Jenkins, R. 16
Jenkins, R. 16, 96-97, 119, 126-27

Jennett, C. 206
Johnson, N. 101
Johnson, S.P. 99
Jones, K.W. 172
Jones, J. 206
Joseph II, 41
Jospin, L.R. 158
Kafka, F. 225
Kaminer, W. 108
Kant, I. 240
Kapferer, B. 148
Karakasidou, A.N. 15
Karilampi, U. 98
Karpin, M. 70
Keeley, L.H. 32
Keen, I. 200
Keller, D. 241
Kelly, J. 143
Kendall, C. 210
Kenny, M.G. 98
Ketcham, K. 105
Khrushchev, N. 226
Kirk, S.A. 102
Kluckhohn, C. 35
Kluft, R. 99, 102, 107-8
Koch, K.-F. 35
Kooiman, D. 177
Kozul-Wright, R. 144
Kris, E. 46
Kutchins, H. 102
Laclau, E. 68, 70, 169, 234
Lasch, C. 157
Lash, S. 233, 239
Lattas, A. 149
le Fanu, M. 119
Leach, E.R. 31
Lévi-Strauss, C. 31
Lilienfeld, S.O. 119
Lilla, M. 46
Lindsay, D.S. 104-6, 108
Linnekin, J. 189
Lippmann, L. 207
Littlewood, R. 97

Loftus, E.F. 105
Long, D. 15
Lustick, I. 64, 71
Lutkehaus, N. 127
Lynch, M. 105
Lyotard, J.-F. 235
Macdonald, S. 14
Maddock, K.J. 189, 194-95, 207
Maimonides, Rabbi 70
Malkki, L. 229
Mandela, N. 47
Mann, R.S. 170, 173
Mansour, A. 61
Maquet, J.J. 42-44
Maria Theresa, Queen 41
Martinez-Taboas, A. 98
Marx, K. 17, 28
Mauss, M. 31, 61
McAleer, K. 38
Mead, G.H. 13
Meggitt, M. 32
Meir, G. 70
Meredith, M. 47
Merskey, H. 98
Mhlangana, Zulu prince 35
Micale, M. 97, 118-19
Michielsens, M. 15
Miller, D. 142
Milson, M. 73
Mirdal, G. 119
Modestin, J. 99
Mohammad il-Zir 82
Morée, M. 250
Morphy, H. 200
Morris, B. 70, 198
Mouffe, C. 68, 70
Mouffe, C. 169
Moynihan, D.P. 170
Mpande, Zulu prince 35
Mulhern, S. 98, 102, 105, 117, 119
Musil, R. 225
Nagengast, C. 218
Namgyal, P. 180

Nandy, A. 171
Narkiewicz, O. 221
Nevels, L.N. 154
Nietzsche, F.W. 13
North, C.S. 96, 98, 101, 103, 106, 117
Ofshe, R. 96, 98, 105
Okohoro, R. 10
Orne, M.T. 99
Otto, T. 9, 11, 18-20, 119, 184, 194, 218
O'Brien, C.C. 46
Pandey, G. 166, 174
Pappe, I. 70
Paracelsus, T. 97-98
Paul, Apostle 136
Pazder, L. 102
Peacock, J. 12
Pedersen, P. 21, 172
Pena, G. 63
Pendergrast, M. 98-99, 102, 105
Peperkamp, G. 207
Peter, Apostle 136
Peters, E. 75-76, 80, 82
Phylactou, M. 175
Pinault, D. 165
Pinault, D. 174
Piper, A. 96, 99, 104, 118
Pope, H.G. 118
Poulantzas, N. 233
Prodi, R. 158
Proteus 10-11
Prunier, G. 43-45
Putnam, P.W. 96, 98, 100-111
Quinn, N. 240-41, 247
Qumsiyyeh, B. 72-74, 77, 83-85, 89
Qumsiyyeh, F. 66, 71-72, 74, 77, 81, 84-86, 88-89
Qumsiyyeh, S. 66, 72, 74, 77, 81, 83, 85, 89
Rabin, Y. 65-66
Radziwill, M. 224, 227
Radziwill, K. 225-26
Ramsay, H. 173

Ramsey, W. 240
Randolph, J. 184
Rao, N. 164
Rata, E.M. 152-53
Read, J.D. 104-6, 108
Remie, C.H.W. 207
Remus 35
Renan, E. 169
Rishmawi, B. 56-59, 65-66, 71-74, 76, 78, 84-85, 87-91
Robertson, R. 142-43
Robinson, G. 49, 57, 61, 64, 65, 67
Roepstorff, A. 119
Rohde, D. 41
Romulus 35
Rorty, R. 235
Roseberry, W. 167
Rowley, C.D. 202
Rumelhart, D. 240
Said al-Din al Alami, 64
Sar, V. 98
Sassen, S. 145, 153, 156
Sayigh, R. 62
Schacter, D.L. 104, 106
Scheible, H. 51
Schiff, Z. 61
Schlaps, A. 108
Schmitt, C. 46
Schnabel, J. 108
Schnitzler, A. 51
Schopenhauer, A. 28
Schreiber, F.R. 101
Schwab, J. 206, 210
Scotson, J.L. 50
Scott, J.C. 181
Seeberg, J. 119
Seward, R. 99
Shaka, Zulu king 35
Shapira, A. 70
Sharon, A. 65-66
Shorter, E. 119
Showalter, E. 105
Siebers, H. 24, 236, 252

Simmel, G. 30, 38, 49-51, 228, 239
Singh, A.S. 172
Singh, T. 173
Smith, M. 99, 102
Smith, R.S. 171
Smith, H.M. 202
Sökefeld, M. 20
Soros, G. 155-56, 158
Spanos, N.P. 106-7, 119
Spicer, E.H. 14
Spivak, G.C. 167
Srinivas, S. 174
Stajano, C. 36
Stalin, J.
Stanner, W.E.H. 193, 197
Stavenhagen, R. 169
Stephen, M. 127, 138
Stich, S. 240
Stille, A. 36
Stirling, P. 85
Strauss, C. 240-41, 247
Sulloway, F.J. 35-36
Sutton, P. 192
Swann, A. de 17
Takahashi, Y. 99
Tamari, S. 73
Tambiah, S.J. 48
Tatz, C. 189
Taussig, M. 164, 167
Temple, A. 112-15, 119
Thigpen, C.H. 96, 100-1
Thoden van Velzen, H.U.E. 35
Thompson, G. 144
Thoonen, L. 19, 22, 127
Tilly, C. 221
Tocqueville, A. 28
Tonkinson, M.E. 189, 191, 209
Tonkinson, R. 190, 213
Tudjman, F. 40
Tully, J. 166
Tuzin D. 127
Ulrich, G. 119
Usher, G. 68

van Beek, M. 22-23, 164-65, 172, 177, 179-81
Van der Kraan, Pastor 132
Van der Pijl, K. 150
van der Vlist, L. 207
Van Praag, H.M. 97
Varhola, L. 117
Verloop, R. 9, 11
Victor, G. 101
Völgyese, F.A. 97-98
Wacquant, L. 17
Wagatsuma, H. 36-37
Wallerstein, I. 167
Walter, E.V. 35, 38
Ward, F. 208
Warner, W.L. 198
Warwick, M. 98

Watson, J. 197
Watters, E. 96, 98, 105
Weber, M. 16, 233, 238, 251
Weeks, J.R. 107
West, R. 39
Wetering, W. van 35
Wilbur, C. 101
Wilson, M. 35, 102
Wittgenstein, L. 166
Wolf, E.R. 17-18, 38
Woodward, J. 101
Yalman, N. 49
Ya'ari, E. 61
Zamoyski, J. 225-26
Žižek, S. 167-68
Zonabend, F. 228